be applied to high permitting startups and product design as it could one's own life. Customers, colleagues, friends and family all deserve great hospitality."

—SCOTT MARLETTE, Founder of GoodRx

"*The Urgent Recovery of Hospitality* gives us hope for ourselves and for our society while challenging our approach to success and to relationships. In its pages are generous and unflinching stories that illuminate a clear and compelling path from the performative, wounding life of entitlement to a healed, loving and generative world."

—PAUL BOLLES-BEAVEN, Former Managing Director of Union Square Hospitality Group

"Driven by an unwavering passion for hospitality, this book beautifully captures the heart and soul of what it means to create meaningful connections through genuine care and warmth. It's a testament to Steve's transformative power of welcoming others with open arms."

—DAN MCCARROLL, Former President Capitol Records, Warner Bros. Records

THE URGENT

RECOVERY

of HOSPITALITY

HOW REDISCOVERING GENEROSITY

RESTORES A CIVIL WORLD

STEVE FORTUNATO

DESIGN AND MYSTERY MEDIA

COPYRIGHT © 2024 STEVE FORTUNATO
All rights reserved.

THE URGENT RECOVERY OF HOSPITALITY
How Rediscovering Generosity Restores a Civil World
First Edition

ISBN	978-1-962341-53-0	*Hardcover*
	978-1-962341-52-3	*Paperback*
	978-1-962341-54-7	*Ebook*
	978-1-962341-55-4	*Audiobook*

To my younger self. You felt alone and confused for so long.
Even if no one ever reads this book, I wrote this for you.

To Nicole, Sofia, Dario, and Giovanna. You
are, in every way, my people. I love you.

To the epic gang of hosts who work and have
worked with our company over the years.

CONTENTS

CONFESSIONS

"If there is anything that we wish to change, we should first examine it and see whether it is not something that could better be changed in ourselves... We cannot change anything unless we accept it. Condemnation does not liberate; it oppresses."

Carl Jung

Funny how you write the beginning of the book once you are, at long last, finished. So while I'm closing the chapter on writing this book, you're just starting it. We all like to know where we're headed before we decide whether or not to go; so here's the lay of the land.

For those looking for recipes, wine pairings, creative cocktails, suggested playlists, or décor suggestions, great content is readily available through plenty of other sources. It's not that

I'm not interested in ingredients, recipes, or table settings. I totally am. It's not that they're not important. They are. But at this stage, I'm interested in a more esoteric alchemy: the ingredients of a good memory, the recipe for a great conversation, or how to set a table where adversaries can become allies, and impasses become invitations.

The ideas I present in these pages are informed by decades of experience, have proof of concept in competitive markets, validation from experts, apply to any industry or context, and most importantly, have had some time to simmer and get better. In short, the ideas stand on their own. And if this was a "how to" guideline on how to throw a great gathering from a food, beverage, and service perspective, I would be qualified to write it. But that isn't this book.

I wrote a book on how we treat others—whoever the "other" happens to be at the moment you're in. Hospitality, and what that word represented when it was first spoken, has something to teach us about how we treat the people around us, whether we know them or not. I've spent thirty-six years in one profession: nourishing people. Serving people for nearly four decades has exposed me to what encounters with others feel like, and why.

As much as the app developers try to convince us otherwise, life (as it's supposed to be) is not a spectator sport. Everyone is out on the field playing. Most of us playing want to change something, and change it for the better—whether that change is global, like better treatment for the oceans, or local, like better participation from committee members. With as many opinions out there, combined with an understandable rising distrust as to the motive behind the opinion, I suspect that how much I'm influenced by you will be directly related to how much I trust you. And how much I trust you will depend on how open you are about yourself.

And vice versa. I think you may be more influenced by these ideas if I show how they are changing me, and why a change was needed. So I made an intentional decision to be quite vulnerable and transparent in this book. Not because my story is any more fascinating or valid than anyone else's; rather, I opted for setting a vulnerable table for how I presented these concepts because I believe resonance is powerful and I'm hoping something of this work resonates with you. *Resonating* is a sonic word. It happens when something we hear sounds true for us. These ideas have a much greater chance of sounding right for you, sounding true, if you trust that what you're hearing from the person offering them is honest.

Like Jung says, the best thing we can do for our fellow humans is to embody the aspirations we espouse. Offering my ideas without confessing my arena-floor failures that formed the ideas in the first place seemed like a cheap-seat approach. So there are some vulnerable confessions in the pages that follow.

Confessing is like a spoonful of bitter that helps the medicine go down. The front end is miserable, but as the medicine does its work, healing relief sets in. Seeing what needed to be confessed, finding the words, writing them down, picking better words, and now sharing them has been a profound journey. Thrilling, devastating, exciting, boring, clear and foggy, easy, and so hard. My hope is that sharing this journey might lead you to a little more relief where you need it.

Maybe that's why Leonard Cohen's song *Hallelujah* has resonated for so many over the years and been covered by dozens of artists. After you let go and confess, even if it all went wrong, the relief that comes is best expressed by one word: *hallelujah.*

I hope this song resonates.

Steve, Pasadena, October 2024

IT'S URGENT.

Nearly sixty years ago a lovely woman from Pasadena invited cameras into her home kitchen and shared with American homemakers lessons she'd learned about cooking French cuisine. Her revolutionary blend of humility, humor, accessibility, and expertise took off like wildfire, and Julia Child charmed her way into the bellies and hearts of the world. A generation later, Italian American chef Emeril Lagasse took a page out of Julia's book and tried his hand at a similar approach. Today one would be hard pressed to find an American with a heartbeat who has not been exposed to the impact of food media on our society.

The culture of celebrity surrounding and pressurizing chefs, televised competitions for any style or level of cooking, restaurant rating systems that can catapult or decimate a business reputation, innovations in products and presentation, and user-generated reviews that can be viewed globally have forever changed the game. As if mixing media and mealtime wasn't complicated enough, the cultural cannonball of social media infiltrated the oldest form of fellowship: the shared meal.

A collection of services in food, beverage, and lodging came to be known as the hospitality *industry*. So naturally, we look to the trends in that industry for indicators of how we define hospitality as a culture. But what is the unintended impact of allowing a new normal into one of humanity's oldest ways of gathering? What happens to our collective consciousness when competition, self-promotion, empire-building, user-generated reviews that can singularly make or break a host's viability, aggression in the name of excellence, and a constant feedback loop between receiver and provider all become part of what we understand as hospitality?

What are we training ourselves to believe hospitality is and should be?

In its origin, hospitality represented a way of being with others in a generous way. There was a universal understanding that whether among friends or foes, residents or travelers, regardless of the occasion, the table was the place where a host would offer what was theirs to share with others as an act of basic kindness.

Basic.
Kindness.

How desperately do we need basic kindness in our society today? The word "civil" no longer applies to our discourse. Our divisions are no longer relegated to trivial matters of policy. Issues are now foundational to our existence. These existential conversations across the high tables of power aren't the only place it's become hard. Even among us common folk, knowing how to, at a minimum, meaningfully interact and, at best, build lasting connections has become complicated.

The stakes are too high.
I can't fix this.

The layers of interpersonal tensions, stacked underneath the outrage culture, ominous national and international zero-sum conflicts, and global threats to coexistence with each other and our planet simmer on the back burner of my mind.

It's all too much.
I'll just go get some dinner with some friends.

But even there, it's not safe.

Whatever got in the water of society has as well infused the institution of hospitality. We don't recognize it as a foreign tone because it's a tone that has become our new normal in every other environment. There's not some sacred invisible boundary around hospitality where the agreements we've made don't apply.

We've grown accustomed to the rules of the influencer society, or the attention economy, where despite our methods or the content of our contribution, the ability to grab our gaze, get a headline, and leverage our "influence" has replaced basic kindness, civility, and making things better.

There's an all-too-common energy in our interactions. We may keep it at bay on behalf of our closest relationships (and even there it sneaks in), but for everyone else, if this energy is left unchecked, it can disassemble any connection we have with our fellow humans. It's a preoccupation with what we're *owed*, our rights. And what makes it so hard to recognize is that it's nuanced. Because we do have rights. And as humans, there are certain basic rights we deserve. So how do we know when we've moved into the territory of becoming *preoccupied?* That's what entitlement is. It's not about our rights. It's a preoccupation with them that blinds our ability to see the basic rights of others.

Like basic kindness.
Civility.

Hospitality can fix this. At its core, hospitality is the ability to make other people feel valued. It's being generous with our intentions.

There's a role that every single human plays, yet only some of us knowingly enlist. It's the role of the host.

If you are breathing, you're a host.

For many the word "host" has connotations of either web servers on the internet or Martha Stewart throwing garden parties in the Hamptons. But hosting isn't reserved for a profession or even a passion. Hosting is simply the space between someone who has something to offer and the person they're offering it to. When you have a design for your client, a compromise for your adversary, a lesson plan for your students, an agenda for your direct reports, a vision for your team, a route for your passenger, a diagnosis for your patient, a latte for your customer, and yes, a dinner for your family, you're hosting.

Hosting is offering something of ours to others. But hosting doesn't guarantee hospitality. Hospitality is an *intention*. It's the host's intention to make others feel valued by what they're offering. And just like everyone is a host, everyone wants to feel valued.

Our need to feel valued, validated, and seen is as universal as our need for air. But just like breathing, feeling valued by others is a cycle. You have to give it away to get it back. Even though we might get that conceptually, it can be hard for us to see how that plays out in our interactions and in what we offer others in our daily lives. We might believe it, but we don't always see it for ourselves.

It's hard to confess that we might be blind in some areas. That's the conundrum of blindness. You have to have seen at one point to know that you're now blind. But you can't see your blindness if you're blind. As philosopher Alan Watts said, "A pin can feel everything but the prick of its own point."[1] When we become so preoccupied with our rights that we can't see the rights of others, it can tear us apart. And yet we don't think we're preoccupied or entitled.

1 Watts, Alan. *Become What You Are.* Shambhala, 1995.

We're just...us.

That's probably the best litmus test to gauge your own entitlement. Do you feel apart from others? Do you find yourself preoccupied with their *otherness?* Or their wrongness compared to your rightness? Or their irrelevance compared to your relevance? Their ignorance compared to your intelligence? Their manipulative agendas compared to the purity of your intentions? Their mediocrity compared to your excellence? Their blindness compared to your clarity?

Do you feel part of a greater whole?
Greater than just your tribe?

Or is there a filter through which only certain people, certain services, certain ideas, certain ways of being are accepted and worthy of basic kindness?

Do you espouse tolerance as your highest value? That is unless someone seems intolerant, and for them, there can be no tolerance?

Entitlement is in the water of our society. And here's the tragedy: it got into the water of the hospitality industry as well. But that's a misnomer because hospitality isn't an industry.

It's a virtue.

There's no such thing as the kindness industry.

Or the generous industry.

Hospitality isn't a collection of services.

It's the act of making people valued.

It's something literally

every

human

needs.

Hospitality, valuing people, creates a virtuous cycle of generosity. When people receive generosity, they can't help but return it in kind. Like picking what we plant, it's a cosmic pattern. It's what I call *virtuous hospitality*. There's a virtuous cycle of generosity that's created between people when they feel valued.

It's the antidote to another cycle.

The vicious cycle of entitlement.

When people face entitlement, they can't help but return it in kind.

Two cycles.

One unites and builds.

One divides and breaks down.

Virtuous hospitality can be hard to find among all the noise of how we've come to view hospitality. To go forward, we need to pause and look back and recover what this timeless virtue was meant to be. A tone of generosity that started at the table but was carried far beyond, to the community, the marketplace, the public square, the halls of power, the institutions of governance.

In the face of what lies before us personally, and existentially, we have to recover an understanding that in order to create solutions, we need to set a generous table where common ground can be found. We can share a common meal and a common goal.

We *have* to recover the virtue of hospitality, not just for our gatherings or meals, but for how we interact with fellow humans.

It's urgent. Let's find it.

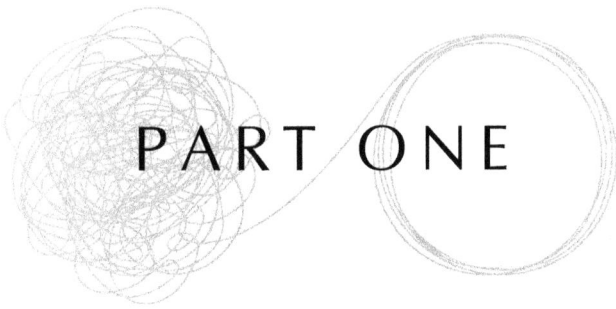

PART ONE

ORIGIN STORIES

I was a ruthlessly bullied kid. Now that I have kids of my own, I see that what children choose to mock is a generationally moving target. As a kid of the eighties, I was granted a double portion of what kids chose to make fun of: I was always the shortest for my age, and I had red hair and glasses. Ours was a house of music educators and I studied piano from the age of six. The cool kids played "Stairway to Heaven" on guitar; I was playing Chopin and Mozart. In seventh grade I got braces (which a lot of kids had), but I had an overbite, which at the time required a horrific contraption called (you know the name) "headgear." The headgear would go around my neck, over my head, and culminate with straps that covered all sides of my head and attached to a metal bracket that stuck out of my mouth.

My mom made me wear it to school so that the orthodontist expenses weren't extended beyond their projected time-line. Usually the mockery was so bad, I would shun her instruction and take it off. I was labeled intellectually "gifted" and moved to small private schools where I naïvely begged to return to the normalcy of public schools and, as a result, went to six different schools throughout elementary and high school. Suffice it to say, school was a place of trauma for me. The crazy thing I've come to see about kids is that they are as susceptible to reputations and branding as adults are. Once you are branded "shrimp, geek, dork, nerd, four eyes," it becomes the lens through which everyone, not just the bullies, sees you, no matter how much you change.

I was the kid who summoned all the courage I could find to ask Brenda to dance with me, only for her to say, "I'm too tired," and then go dance with handsome John. I remember one conversation in the Branciforte Junior High locker room where I asked one of the popular kids, Zach, if he was mad at me. He looked at me like I had three heads and said, "You don't exist to me. I don't even notice you." The bullying carried through to high school.

I remember driving in the parking lot with my first new car, so proud, and Luke throwing a football as hard as he could in my direction and denting my car. I stopped the car, and he looked at me with fire in his eyes and said, "What are you going to do, shrimp?" just hoping I would willingly walk into a beating. The fire of rage in me burned hot during moments like that. I hated Luke. I hated that he'd dented my new car that I was so proud of. But more than that, I hated myself for not being able to do anything about it. And I hated that I was too afraid to try.

I was picked last for the team sports, and grudgingly at that.

"Fine...I guess we'll take Steve."

I never went to a formal or prom, because I knew no girl would accept my invitation. I abandoned my "all night long" high school grad night at ten p.m., because I didn't have any friends to celebrate with and spent grad night walking around not knowing what to do.

The trauma of bullying didn't end at the schoolyard. I grew up in the redwoods of Santa Cruz, close to the ocean. We lived on a private road in the country with three other houses on our street. There were boys in two of the houses, both older than me. The trauma I experienced from the two older boys was endless and some of the wounds, from one of them in particular, have taken a lifetime of therapy to heal from (more on that later). After becoming an adult, and learning about the human need for connection, and how isolation is like dying, I see now why I chose to knock on the neighbors' doors and ask to play, day after day. I didn't have the language for it then, but I preferred being the whipping boy to being alone. So, I showed up to be mistreated and abused, day after day.

Sadly, despite what I know were my parents' best intentions, I didn't find much solace on the home front either. I'll say at the outset, now that I'm a parent myself, I know every parent is just doing their best. We're all trying to do right by our kids, playing the cards we've been dealt. *And,* to understand the origin of my wound, the truth is that I would return home from the bullying at school and from the neighbors to see (through my young eyes) my dad bullied at the house. I know a child's perception of their parents' marriage is going to be incomplete, but other than Bach and Beethoven, the soundtrack I remember in our house was my mom frustrated with my dad, and my dad hanging his head and apologizing.

Bullied at school, bullied in my neighborhood after school, and then when I got home, witnessing my dad's experience felt like looking into my future. I concluded I could expect a lifetime of what I currently felt: inadequacy, shame, anger,

self-hatred, trapped. We don't always know the exact moments we have revelations, but at some point, after receiving
waves of messages about who I was in the world, I had one:

I.
Am.
Worthless.

I could feel the curse. The things that I hated and others
mocked in me, I couldn't change. I couldn't change my
height or my eyesight or hair color or my parents' marriage.
My mom was a classical piano teacher, so in a town of gui-
tar-playing surfers, learning piano and singing in choirs were
the options I was given—and they made me more "other." I
was stuck.

And I don't know when, but at some point a reaction welled
up in me, soul deep and encoded in my operating system.
Here were the basic (subconscious) tenets:

Fuck *that*.
I'm going to prove to myself, and to everyone around me,
that I'm *not* worthless.
I will never be overpowered again.
I will never be dismissed.

Or small.

Or ignored.

Or insignificant.

I set out in my life to prove that I was valuable. That I was influential. That I was significant. That I was cool. That I was strong. And I carried that operating system with me into every environment I occupied.

In fourth grade, my parents could tell I was bored in school and moved me to a "school for the gifted" where we called teachers by their first names and worked at our own pace. Intelligence was the prized commodity. So, I worked hard to prove I was the smartest guy in the room.

Then after begging to go to a "normal" school in junior high, I carried that programming into my new environment and was quickly branded a "nerd." Recognizing that the surfers were at the top of the food chain, I worked hard to shed my nerdy tendencies by surfing every day, changing the way I talked, and trying to prove I was a surfer through and through.

I arrived at Pepperdine for college, thrilled for a fresh start with new people. Malibu is truly one of a kind, wonderful and crazy. When I was there, the top of that food chain were the wealthy, famous, and fit. As a college kid I had no chance at the fame and wealth game. So, I became a gym rat, working out like a maniac and using resentment as my steroid of choice. Studying fitness enabled me to become a personal trainer to Malibu moms, as I went on trying to prove I was the fittest guy in town.

After college I didn't have any more clarity on what I wanted to do than when I'd started. I had grown up in a devout Evangelical Christian home and spent most of my time at college shedding that cloak through the typical college partying. After a post-college spiritual awakening of sorts, I joined a rock and roll church in Malibu, embraced my piano skills, and became a singer for Jesus. The funny term that was used to describe the top of that community's ladder was "anointed," which basically meant God's preferential endorsement of someone. So, naturally, I tried to prove I was the most "anointed."

There's a unique kind of crazy that happens when you mix having a platform, momentum, money, power, unacknowledged brokenness, and *religion*. We've all heard the cautionary tales of various faith movements, churches, cults, or communities where ego caused them to utterly lose the plot and come crashing down. The Malibu rock and roll church suffered the same fate. Luckily, I had the wherewithal to leave the church before the crash, but not without taking on some extra bags of spiritual trauma while having an existential crisis about what I was going to do with my life now that my dream of ushering in a spiritual awakening had been eviscerated.

I obviously couldn't see this at the time, but there was an insidious reward for trying to prove my value:

It worked.
Sort of.

By obsessing about surfing, I became a decent surfer and could paddle out and catch waves like the cool kids. Training like a maniac had its benefits as well, and for the first time in my life, ladies not only wanted to work out with me, they also wanted to make out.

Additionally, channeling my musical skills with my religious fervor opened lots of doors, and I tasted the indescribable rush of playing live music and connecting with a crowd in the intimate way only live music can deliver.

So, like all the professionals, athletes, and artists who use a chip on their shoulder to fuel their fire, I had *just enough* endorsement to feel like my program for life was working.

But it was a trap.

The poisons of following a regimen to prove your value are numerous, but one daunting truth is that no matter how accomplished you get, life has a way of keeping you just in the shadow of people higher up the ladder you're climbing. Which makes you very resentful.

When I was trying to prove I was the smartest guy in the room at the gifted school, other kids would show up and run code for a new computer program they had written in their free time.

Santa Cruz is one of the surfing capitals of the world. Some of the world's greatest and boldest surfers ride there. Trying to prove that I was an accomplished surfer in Santa Cruz was as futile as this shrimp trying to tackle a star linebacker.

As a late bloomer, I grew five inches and gained thirty pounds of mostly lean muscle mass in college and loved that I went from people calling me shrimp in high school to talking about my muscles at Pepperdine. But Rambo lived in Malibu. So did all the *Baywatch* people. And underwear models. And fitness gurus who had infomercials running on TV 24/7. I wasn't going to win at that game either. Yet something in the way I saw myself was deep-seated, and despite the fact that I wasn't small anymore, I remained unsettled and obsessed with my body.

Surely (I figured), since I had given up partying and was now mainlining morality and rocking big crowds for the Lord, I would earn some divine favor and promotion. But I wasn't the only guy at my church leading the chorus. So was my friend Jason Wade. David Geffen, the music mogul, heard what was happening at our church and came to hear Jason. He immediately signed him to a music deal with Dream-Works. A band from our church in Malibu became an international phenomenon known as Lifehouse, and their single "Hanging by a Moment" became the most successful song of 2001, peaking at number two on the Billboard charts. How could I ever compare? I was frustrated at the lack of my "big break." So, I treated my bandmates and the sound guys as either the keys to my break or, alternately, as the ones keeping me from the spotlight.

Why couldn't I just enjoy the fact that I had a decent brain, could ride waves, was relatively fit, and was playing music to supportive crowds of passionate people? Our encoded survival programming is often written by our wounded stories. So, finding contentment and "enjoying the moment" did not factor into my operating system.

If music was one of the legs I stood on, there was another leg I was born with that shaped my stride in life. In addition to growing up in a musical home, it was also a hosting home that paid acute attention to the details of service.

Whether we were having stuffed Dover sole or a barbecue, the details mattered. If we were having a barbecue, we didn't put a bottle of ketchup on the table. We poured the ketchup into a fancy dish called a ramekin, placed it onto a saucer with a demi-spoon, and only *then* put it on the table. We had dishes for each of the four seasons and ironed linens to match.

I was exposed to the details of dining and etiquette of serving others from birth. A gift from my upbringing, championed by my mom, was family dinners every night at the table, even if we weren't hosting others. The same manners and attention to detail deployed on behalf of guests were expected at family dinners. Appropriately navigating the table was instinctual to me. And I knew I could easily leverage the reflexes I'd honed on the home front to pay the bills by working in restaurants. So through all the crazy seasons, from tumultuous teenage years to agonizing adulthood, one thing was consistent: I worked in restaurants.

No matter where I lived, throughout all my schooling and professional pursuits, the money to pay the bills came from working in restaurants.

A lot of them.

My first job was when I was fourteen, as a busboy in a Chinese restaurant in Santa Cruz. Then, I went to work at the most famous French restaurant in town at the time, which was my first experience with a chef that screamed and threw things. Next, I worked at a charming restaurant in a private home owned by a white Southern woman named Donna, whose biscuits and grits are to this day the best I've ever had.

During college I worked at a favorite Malibu local hangout that had plywood floors covered with sawdust and served clam chowder in a bread bowl. The property got a facelift and is now the ground on which the world-famous sushi restaurant Nobu Malibu sits.

After college I worked in a twenty-table restaurant in Los Angeles, owned by a crazy Southern woman named Cynthia. Every movie star in the city (literally) would flock to the restaurant. Daily I would serve famous people a religious experience composed of the best fried chicken and blackberry cobbler in town. Cynthia would walk the floor—stopping to pinch the butts of the A-list men and kiss the cheeks of the A-list women, all while being unabashedly inappropriate with us servers—doling out complimentary extra cobbler with a mountain of Häagen-Dazs vanilla ice cream on top.

After Cynthia's, I worked at an Italian restaurant in Beverly Hills where the mafia dined daily alongside Hollywood hairstylists. As the only American server, I literally had to fight for my tables. One time, after having my tables stolen repeatedly by an older server from Rome named Stefano, I channeled my old "I will not be overpowered energy" and put him against the wall, threatening that if he took another table of mine, we'd meet outside. (Maria, the owner, who was from Naples, looked on with a passive "boys will be boys" casual glance and said nothing of it.)

Restaurants and playing live music were the big themes (or so I thought) in my life. Music was my passion and what I assumed would be the vehicle for my contribution to the world. Restaurant work came easy because of my upbringing and provided a way to pay the bills. I hadn't yet recognized the deeper themes that, when done right, provided the best foundation for both live music and restaurant service. As they often are, time and suffering would be needed to open my eyes, to see what I couldn't see. My real passion, my gift, was hospitality. Hosting others in a way that made them come alive made me come alive.

Before everything came crashing down, rocking for Jesus was picking up momentum at the church in Malibu. But the excitement of the season, and the opportunity to help people with my talents, blinded me to the sinister way the church was exploiting my passion to get leadership from me, for free. I needed money, and restaurant work came easy. So I picked up shifts between church commitments at a Malibu ocean-front restaurant called Geoffrey's that was such a choice destination, couples would get engaged every night. Yet over time, reality started setting in. My music career wasn't translating to money. I didn't want to scrape by financially by waiting tables in the few spare hours not dedicated to music. And without question, the church that had provided an opportunity I was deeply passionate about had gone batshit crazy.

As time passed, my as-of-yet unsuccessful music career, complicated by the church circus baggage, left me in a professional no-man's-land. I'd graduated from a great university yet was unemployed and directionless. The last thing I wanted was to keep working in restaurants. I didn't mind doing it to make some extra money in high school and college, but now that I was out of school, I was dying to be done in restaurants. But, like Al Pacino said in *The Godfather,* "Just when I thought I was out, they pull me back in…" In this directionless season, I met a beautiful woman (on a plane if you can believe it) that I respected, admired, and wanted to marry. I needed a job. I needed money. Devastated, I returned to restaurants.

My return landed me at a white tablecloth restaurant for an iconic national chain, which was my baptism into the world of fine dining. Food knowledge, wine know-how, screaming chefs, restaurant empires, and surprise visits from food critics was mostly a whole new world for me (other than the screaming chef part). Managers would race to read the *LA Times* food section every Wednesday, hoping Irene the food critic had said something nice about us and something mean about the competition.

I'll never forget the first time the general manager asked me about starting the path to management. He might as well have asked me to run in traffic. Service might have come naturally to me, but that was something I took for granted. It might've been my heritage, but it wasn't my dream for the future.

What felt to me like instinctual reflexes, restaurants saw as high-value skills. Every restaurant I worked for rapidly promoted me, gave me the best sections, or asked me to join management. Essentially, I could climb the ladder at whatever restaurant I worked for. But that wasn't a ladder I wanted to climb. At all. I was longing for the day when I would graduate from the restaurant routine. Where was *my* big break?

As irony would have it, someone did come to hear me play music that had the ability to get me a record deal. He was no David Geffen, but it didn't matter. Malcolm could help me, and he wanted to. He didn't sign me on the spot, but he and I became friends, spent a lot of time together, and I held out hope that the closer we got, the sooner a break was coming. We cultivated a friendship but in the back of my mind I was holding out hope that he was going to open the door to a record deal. After about two years of friendship, Malcolm finally presented his long-awaited announcement:

"Have you ever thought about opening a restaurant?"

CHAPTER TWO

CONFESSIONS

To say I was brokenhearted by Malcom's suggestion is an understatement. Restaurants merely represented a means to pay the bills. It felt like I'd been cleaning houses to eat, and he had just suggested that I open a housecleaning business.

He went on to tell me that the "housecleaning" feelings of obligation and dread had more to do with working in environments that missed something. He argued that the actual *practice* of serving others was something he could see I enjoyed. As the lead singer of a band, who loved hosting, my house was a hub for our gang. He told me gatherings at my house weren't like other gatherings he had attended. He told me there was something in the way that I hosted that was unique. Growing up in a hosting home, I took my hospitality instincts for granted. To me, they were just obvious. Thoughtfully preparing food, selecting the right dinner music, lighting the candles, finding affordable wine that went with the food, clipping flowers from whatever was growing outside my bachelor pad was something that came naturally to me.

Something in me knew that details are doorways. Paying attention to the details wasn't so people could froth over the chicken (chicken was all I could afford at the time). I knew when you pay attention to the details and then generously *give* them away, instead of trying to *take* affirmation for the preparation, it opens the door to something greater than the sum of all the details. Sometimes we don't see our instincts as talents because they feel as naturally reflexive as tying our shoes. But the more Malcolm spoke, the more I replayed twenty years of experiences in restaurants, obtaining hard-to-get positions, rapid promotions, and offers of management. The suffering of the directionless season started to open my eyes. I realized I had been running from my life. I had been banging on doors to other paths, and all I had to show for it was bloody knuckles and no direction.

More importantly, I realized Malcolm was right. I absolutely loved serving people I cared about. I loved the way being creative and thoughtfully not just setting the table but setting the tone of an experience brought out the best in humanity. I was naturally good at asking thoughtful questions and getting people to open up. I was passionate about the conversations we had at the table. I loved how evenings with the crew of friends at my place would go from navigating deep topics to hilarious laughter. The strength of the connection even made healthy debate and conflict unthreatening. There was a safe space to see things differently. Especially since with musicians for friends, most nights we'd take turns on instruments, singing songs we all knew. It's hard to hate someone you're singing next to.

None of us had much money, with jobs that barely covered the bills, but the practice of gathering and putting a soulful, generous intention into what I offered provided a break in the monotony of the daily grind. Gathering this way had become the highlight of my and my community's days.

Rent was made by waiting on tables. But memories were made by thoughtfully serving and hosting others. As it has a way of doing, life turned me around. After a lifetime of trying to figure out how to connect my passion with my paycheck, the answer had been standing there all along, waiting for me to see what was always there. I pressed on different doors, and wouldn't you know it, they began to open.

I married the woman I met on the plane, and even though we had our first child on the way, Nicole knew something deep in me was coming alive. Since I was tending bar and waiting tables when we married, Nicole was the primary breadwinner but understandably wanted to take time off to be with the baby girl that was soon to arrive. Even though she had been a successful businesswoman, once Sofia Grace came into the world, Nicole came to me and said there was no way she could leave Sofia and go back to work.

Her support and belief that I could create something out of nothing that would provide for us only added fuel to the fire of my passion for building something special.

The restaurant landscape had changed, and most owners were chefs as opposed to restaurateurs or businesspeople. I was a good cook, but I wasn't a chef. I didn't have a customer base and didn't know anything about marketing. But I knew how to throw an epic dinner party. So, I did the natural thing most guys starting a business would do: I jumped in head-first. I took nine months to build an arsenal of wooden farm tables that could be disassembled and stored. I didn't know business terms like "pro forma" and didn't know anything about financial projections, but I knew my way around a woodshop, and I knew hosting.

While working in restaurants, I had served at several wine-maker dinners, where the winemaker would co-host the dinner with the restaurant. I loved how the food and wine worked together and how guests were taken on a journey through each course of the dinner. I decided I would build a customer base by hosting winemaker dinners in people's backyards and talking up the restaurant I was about to open. I just needed to convince winemakers to come. I drove to wine country and pitched a winemaker on my concept. He said he wouldn't come, but he'd give me a discount on the wine and send his tasting room manager to talk about the bottles. I rallied my friends in the business to help me cook and serve, used a friend's backyard for events, and invited as many people as I could. The tasting room manager put order forms for the wines under people's menus so if they liked the wine they drank, they could order more.

The evening was indeed epic. Everyone was elated. The diners loved the juxtaposition of a fine dining food product with the warmth and comfort of a backyard. At the time, this was a new concept for people. The term "pop up" didn't yet exist, and the lines around what defined the restaurant experience were firmly drawn. The winery went home with a stack of orders and a community of new customers. The crescendo of "when is the next dinner?" culminated in a convincing chorus that I needed to do more dinners.

We did just that and went from persuading winemakers to come to charging winemakers to be there. We were setting the stage for them to meet customers in an organic, intimate way, and they loved it. One piece of feedback we kept hearing over and over: "man, I wish we could have had something like this at the event we just had catered."

I realized that restaurants open and close daily and that the big "blue ocean" opportunity was to start a catering company with incredible food and service. So, the second perspective shift came, and I abandoned the idea of opening a restaurant and started our catering company, "roomforty," instead.

I'd lived in LA and worked in many of its restaurants so I knew a lot of people. Even though I was a good cook, I knew I needed a classically trained chef who was a better cook than me and who would free me up to do what I had been doing at my apartment, bringing all the pieces together: finding clients, setting the tone, overseeing service, and building our new business. Since money was tight I couldn't offer big salaries, but I could offer creative liberty to work together with aspiring chefs to try their own dishes.

After employing a string of temporary sous chefs from other restaurants who would moonlight with us on their off days, I found a tattooed and dreadlocked genius culinary artist named Libry Darusman, whose highest position in a restaurant up to that point had been lead line cook. His food blew me (and more importantly our clients) away, and since I'd never been a CEO and he'd never been an executive chef, we made a great team.

The early days were bootstrappy, but I had confirmation we were on the right track. Lots of doors began to open, and our fledgling catering company was getting business. For the first time in my life, I was being paid (close to nothing, but still something) to do what I loved and was uniquely adept at.

I was fueled by the fire to provide for my family, while also making my mark in the LA hospitality scene. Even though we had minor-league resources, I came with major-league experience and leveraged a lifetime of hospitality instincts on behalf of the business. We approached events the same way we approached our early winemaker dinners—with thoughtful, artistic menus, consciously paired wines, and great service. We weren't the only catering company trying to narrow the gap between great restaurants and the catered format, but we were certainly at the front of the movement.

Catering companies grow primarily through relationships with event planners and event venues. Our commitment to excellence in service and food helped us build relationships with both, and soon we were winning jobs over much larger companies. Our first kitchen (that wasn't in my apartment) was a taco stand that we took over and remodeled. It was ten feet by ten feet, had one oven, a two-door fridge, and two little prep tables. I didn't care. My company was growing, and I was spilling blood, sweat, and tears while earning amazing opportunities.

One of those opportunities was our first job for an American president. We cooked for Bill Clinton out of that hundred-square-foot kitchen, located in the heart of gang territory. Going from prepping food in our tiny commissary kitchen in pre-gentrified Glassell Park to serving it in Bob Hope's house in Palm Springs to a president and his friends was some crazy whiplash. But I was good at what I was doing. And I was happy.

Sort of.

Remember how I said that when you're trying to prove yourself, life has a way of keeping you in the shadows of those higher on whatever ladder you're trying to climb? Now I was trying to climb the hospitality industry ladder.

In Los freaking Angeles.
A city that owns the culture of celebrity and is a media-driven machine.

A city that had thrown the doors wide open to the odd concept of "celebrity chef" and created a phenomenon like the Food Network where millions of people were watching cooks demonstrate recipes and compete in cooking contests, while glorifying chefs making kitchens feel like hell.

It felt like the hospitality scene was becoming confused with entertainers looking for fans, and I was not impressed by the performance.

Regardless, I was on like rung two of a
Very
Tall
Ladder.

I didn't necessarily want to be on *that* ladder, but the subconscious oath of "I will not be insignificant" kept me pushing for influence, while simultaneously feeling defeated by our lack of platform and momentum. Every time we were contacted by the press, they would ask me questions like "who's your chef?" or "what farm did your carrots come from?" Their responses to our answers had a familiar ring to them: "yeah, we're gonna dance with someone else." Thanks, Brenda.

A big shift in momentum came when I opened our first event venue, the Fig House. A mentor in catering loaned me the money to buy a property that housed an abandoned bike shop and a tired Chinese restaurant. As aesthetically conscious as I was (I was a dude that surfed, after all), I knew I needed a designer to create an interior that would appeal to brides. I contacted a quickly rising star in the interior design community named Emily Henderson. She already had a TV show on HGTV and was wildly popular among design-loving women, but she had never designed an event venue. She was concerned I was opening a nightclub. I convinced her that it was more of a modern reception hall, an event space with a design aesthetic. A gathering space for all types of events that wasn't a restaurant, but a place only for celebrations. She named a very fair price and agreed to do the job. Thanks to her involvement and her Instagram, brides were booking the Fig House while there were still tractors digging trenches. They knew if a new event venue was opening in LA, with her interior design, it was going to be good.

Getting to opening day wasn't exactly easy. Between a vertical learning curve on running a construction project, dealing with Los Angeles building inspectors, city issues, and money issues, while still trying to work our catering jobs, I was a wreck.

The stress was straining my marriage. My growing family now had two young kids, as our son Dario had arrived. I was working between eighty-five and one hundred hours a week, all while feeling unjustly unseen. My wife Nicole had been supportive of the business from day one but adding the stress of the business and the new venue to the stress of a young family felt like an anvil on my chest. There were unsealed cracks in me from my childhood trauma and the weight of it all was breaking the bridge between Nicole and me. The joy of building a new business was leaving, and everything was just…hard. I had servers complaining about meal breaks, cooks complaining about pay, and subcontractors complaining about inspectors.

Watching the explosion of the "pop-up" movement while we were busy building our catering company just made it worse. We had been doing pop-up dinners before that was even a term, and classically trained chefs would laugh at us for attempting to serve fine dining in a backyard.

Now chefs were taking over diners, warehouses, and homes, and the press was going wild. I seethed. Pop-ups were fun, but they made very little money and we had long since abandoned them for paying catering jobs. When the press was drooling over a Michelin-starred celebrity chef cooking in a pizza joint and then asked us which farms we sourced our produce from, "we used to do pop-ups" wasn't really a compelling answer.

I was bitter.
More than bitter, I was tortured.
I was in a business that is all about being gracious.
And hosting others.
Celebrating others.
Making people feel valued.
And when I took an honest inventory of my internal ecosystem, mostly, I was ashamed.
Because as much as I wanted to make my clients feel valued, *I* wanted to feel valued.
Something didn't feel right.

Most of the influential leaders in my industry were demonstrating how talented they were and seemed to care more about building their empires and portfolios on the backs of other people's special occasions than actually making the people they served with their craft feel special. It felt tragically ironic to me that somehow, in an industry that was supposed to be an invitation to celebrate others, we had accepted that it was about a demonstration to be celebrated.

But I felt the same urge for impact, influence, and accolades. The same drive to show the playground that I could play too. The ladder was a mystery to me.
I'd have experiences that felt like I was finally climbing.
Like Jay-Z launching his streaming music site Tidal at our venue, the Fig House.

I sat open-mouthed as Jay-Z, Madonna, Rhianna, Kanye, Chris Martin, Jack White, Daft Punk, and Beyoncé walked into *my* venue. *This* was the big break. Beyoncé loved our short ribs so much that she took some to go.

Shocker, Jay-Z didn't post on his Instagram that he was at the Fig House and Beyoncé didn't mention the roomforty short ribs.

The breaks never came.

The quest for influence in our industry continued to feel elusive. The truth was, I longed to disrupt our industry. I wanted to show how we did it "differently." Like Volcom or Trader Joe's or Southwest Airlines, I wanted to buck the system.

I saw the energy of performance that was dominating our industry and I wanted to show how we were different. I despised the way that energy was allowed in the hospitality space. Like moths drawn to the flame, I could see how susceptible people were to being served by whoever seemed "hot" at the time. But more times than not, the intention to become (or stay) "hot" drowned out the intention to make customers or clients feel valued. Many of those who were known as influential hosts in the hospitality industry seemed more driven by demonstrating their skills. It wasn't hospitality. It was a performance. It wasn't about the guest; it wasn't even about their team; it was about them. But the honest reality was that the drive for validation and influence had *me* performing, and the energy I despised in others was alive and well inside me.

Like so many well-intended entrepreneurs with a dream, as I kept going, the love for what started it all was leaving me.

All I could find was conflict.
In my homelife.

In my business.

In my team.

In my plans.

But mostly in myself.

Internal conflict has a maddening effect, because as Jon Kabat-Zinn has so insightfully taught us in his book *Wherever You Go, There You Are,* wherever you go, and whatever you do, you take yourself and your problems with you.

Moments of progress teased that the oasis was just a little bit further away.

But if I was honest with myself, there was a canyon between what I wanted our company to be, what type of leader I wanted to be, what type of husband and father I wanted to be, what type of person I wanted to be...

And what I was.

I was desperate for clarity. I headed to the ocean to try to clear my head and desperately look for some peace. But even there, the rumble seemed to come along. Fighting other surfers for waves, jockeying to be in the right position, and exuding a dominating energy so I could get the surf session I deserved kept clarity and peace at bay. Even in my happy place, the madness overshadowed the joy. There was a large swell at the time, and the biggest wave of the day appeared massive on the horizon.

The pack of us paddled frantically to be in perfect position. It looked like I was in the right spot. I paddled with all my might and stood up.

I hardly ever fall taking off on a wave, but the wave was already breaking as I stood up. The power and size of the wave curling shot me out like a rocket, and then what felt like a mountain dropped on my back, slamming me to the ocean floor. I tumbled in blackness feeling like I was in the spin cycle of a washing machine.

Losing air and panicking, I figured out the direction of the surface and swam to find air. I came to the surface and gasped in a breath.

But that wasn't the only wave. Waves come in sets. An even bigger wave was cresting where I had popped up for my life-saving breath. And now I was in the impact zone, that spot where all the designated force of the wave's arc, called "the lip," pounds onto the ocean's surface—and my head.

Once again, I was slammed to the bottom, but this time, with only one panicked breath of air inside my lungs.

A needed break from the daily treadmill had suddenly become a fight for my life. I fought for the surface with a primal instinct to live. And after what seemed like a doomed eternity, I cracked the foamy whitewater surface.

Broken.
Alive, but broken.

I washed up on the shore, defeated and done. I was too exhausted to feel rage. Overcome with despair, I sat looking at the ocean. She was so beautiful. How could something so beautiful be so…harsh?

Why was absolutely everything in my life
So.
Damn.
Hard?

And in that utterly broken place, I began to see something new.

It was one of those moments when the fight has been knocked

out of us, and we hear and see what we couldn't, or wouldn't, hear and see before.

You're fighting reality, Steve.
And reality.
Doesn't.
Lose.

I saw that, like waves, I was in a cycle. A vicious one. And it started with me. I saw that the little boy who was trying to show the world he wasn't worthless, that he had value, was creating a vicious cycle.

Sometimes the deepest truths are the simplest. I realized that my deep pain, and wounds that still bled, had turned me into a simple word that the world resists:

A show-off.

I was showing up in the world, holding out my trophies. My conversations and agendas were fueled by both subtle and overt attempts to display my badges of validation. And any contentment I felt from applause I received was quickly evaporated by someone else with a bigger trophy. While I liked being among others who had the same sized trophies as mine,

I *loved* settings where my trophies were the biggest. And I hated the rooms where my trophies looked insignificant by comparison.

I saw that in every place I occupied—every relationship, every conversation, every contribution—this urge to show that I mattered, that I wasn't worthless, that I had value, my clawing need for influence was creating a perpetuating cycle of conflict.

It was a cycle of taking that placed me at the center.
And left me feeling like everyone owed me more.
And left everyone around me feeling like I owed them more.
I was entitled.

By being preoccupied with what I deserved and what I was owed, the people I worked with felt used like a commodity and consequently started looking out for themselves. The people I served might not have been able to name it, but something in them could sense my offering was as much about me as it was about them. Which left them asking if they were impressed with what was being offered. I realized that when people feel really cared for on a soul-level, when they *feel* generosity, asking if what was given was impressive is a totally foreign question.

"What's in it for me?" and "Am I impressed?" are questions that lead to entitlement. By being entitled myself, I was literally evoking entitlement in others. It was a cycle, and it was vicious.

The right questions often lead to the best answers.

In his book *Reboot* author Jerry Colonna asks: "How are you culpable in the circumstances you find unfavorable?"

I felt culpability in my bones.

The clenched fists I had misinterpreted as grit, I came to see as resistance. I had prized my determination to keep climbing the rungs no matter what, viewing it as the tenacity it takes to succeed.

But in the grace of that reflective moment on the beach, I saw that my ladder was leaning against the wrong wall.

I had preached a message of contributing something good. But I was living a life that craved credit. And sitting on the beach, breathless and exhausted, I surrendered a confession that I had been blind.

I had been blind to the self-centeredness of my mission.

I had been blind to the ways my approach left people feeling used by me.

I had been blind to how much I was driven by the fear of being average.

I had been blind to how behaving like a performer instead of a giver changed those I meant to serve from gracious recipients to judgmental critics.

I had been blind to my own entitlement.
That's what entitlement does.
It blinds us.
All we see is what we're owed, what we deserve.

It's so blinding that we can no longer see what others deserve or what they're owed.

I had been blind to the reality that it is literally impossible to make others feel valued while trying to feel valued yourself.

And in the exhale of those hard confessions, I saw another way.
An alternative.
I saw a beautiful cycle.

A virtuous one.

One that gives life, instead of takes it.

That creates an energy that is the opposite of entitlement:
Generosity.

I realized that the people I was drawn to, the relationships that fed me, the companies that inspired me, the artists that motivated me, the entrepreneurs that truly *created* something that left the world better than they had found it had something in their DNA that I longed for: they were generous.

Sure, show-offs could make a splash and even mask their self-promotion in culturally acceptable ways, but real *beauty* was born from those who existed for more than just themselves.

They existed to make *others* feel valued.

I saw two cycles.

Two different ways of showing up in the world.

One that I embodied,

and one that I longed to embody.

And then I saw it not just in me; I saw it...

Everywhere.

SEEING THE CYCLES

Sitting on the beach, the vision of the two cycles came to me like a download. I saw with clarity that what separated my experiences as a giver and a receiver all came down to an invisible but palpable energy that pervaded everyone involved. The driving motivation of the host had a way of setting the tone that became the aroma of the experience.

I walked up the beach back to my car, grabbed a piece of scratch paper, and sketched a crude version of this:

THE VICIOUS CYCLE OF ENTITLEMENT

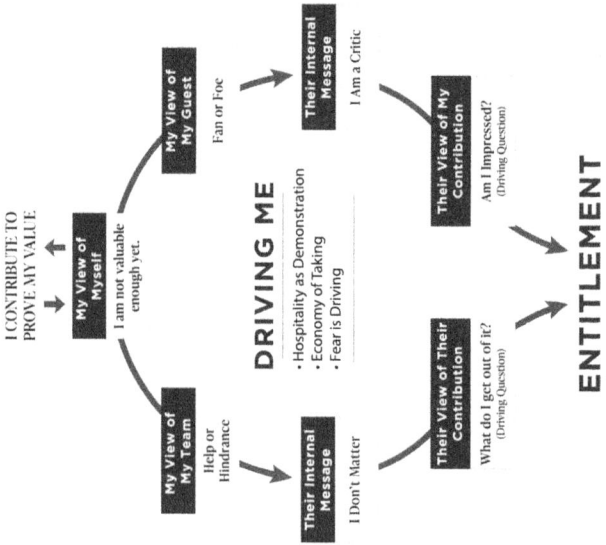

I CONTRIBUTE TO PROVE MY VALUE

My View of Myself
I am not valuable enough yet.

My View of My Guest
Fan or Foe

My View of My Team
Help or Hindrance

DRIVING ME
- Hospitality as Demonstration
- Economy of Taking
- Fear is Driving

Their Internal Message
I Am a Critic

Their Internal Message
I Don't Matter

Their View of My Contribution
Am I Impressed?
(Driving Question)

Their View of Their Contribution
What do I get out of it?
(Driving Question)

ENTITLEMENT

THE VIRTUOUS CYCLE OF GENEROSITY

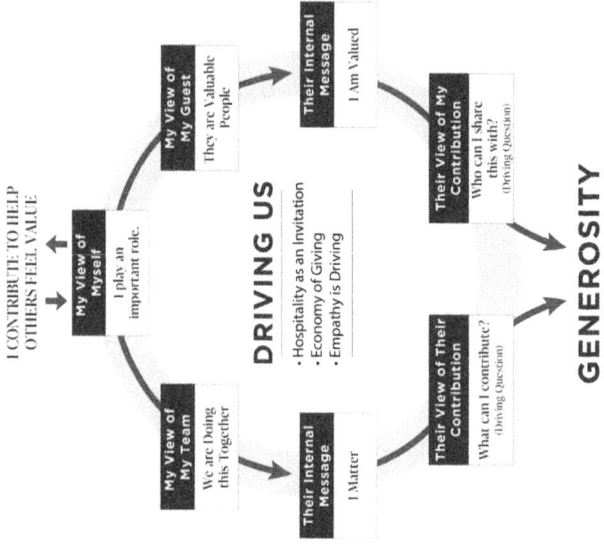

I CONTRIBUTE TO HELP OTHERS FEEL VALUE

My View of Myself
I play an important role.

My View of My Guest
They are Valuable People

My View of My Team
We are Doing this Together

DRIVING US
- Hospitality as an Invitation
- Economy of Giving
- Empathy is Driving

Their Internal Message
I Am Valued

Their Internal Message
I Matter

Their View of My Contribution
Who can I share this with?
(Driving Question)

Their View of Their Contribution
What can I contribute?
(Driving Question)

GENEROSITY

52

I saw how these cycles weren't just represented in hospitality experiences; they were represented in relationships and interactions. Whether innocuous or important, they shaped how an interaction felt. Like the lasting finish of a great wine, they were the flavor that stuck with you.

I realized that hosting had nothing to do with throwing parties or serving people. It was bigger than that. Much bigger.

It was universal.

I realized everyone, *literally everyone*, is a host.

We all play the roles of givers and receivers. Multiple times a day.

Hosting is just the space someone stands in when they give something of themselves.

Yes, the couple having friends over for dinner are hosts.

But the barista making my coffee is also a host.

The Uber driver giving me a ride is a host.

The teacher teaching my kids is a host.

The executive leading a meeting is a host.

The parent leading a PTA meeting is a host.

The child inviting a friend over to their house to play is a host.

The parent making dinner for their family is a host.

The coach leading a practice is a host.

The speaker delivering a keynote is a host.

And like hosting, hospitality is a much bigger concept than food or craft cocktails or hotel stays.

Hospitality is and has always been a *virtue*.

An industry of similar services had co-opted this virtue as its namesake. But hospitality wasn't limited to a set of services.

Hospitality was an intention to make other people feel valued.

And when a host stood in the space of offering their contribution with the intention of making the recipient feel valued, they had extended hospitality.

I realized the power of this virtue when it was felt.

It *moved* people. It was an animating energy.

It brought out the best in everyone.

When the recipient experienced this virtue, when they felt valued, the natural reflex was to respond with a similar energy.

When people feel valued, they value others.

It's a cycle.

A beautiful, virtuous cycle.

It was a life force.
It created beauty.
It built bonds.
It made memories.

It made people feel generous. That giving energy took on a life of its own and *generated* something new. Generativity means the ability to create.

This virtue literally had the power to create something that didn't exist before. It leads to emergence, where something beautiful emerges from the collective energy of a shared space.

I felt both inspired by the possibility and grieved by the tragedy of how many experiences fell short of what they could be. How much could change if we paused and reset to align with the power of this virtue.

How much could change if *I* paused, cleared out all the noise of what success had come to mean to me, and realigned myself with the north star of making people feel valued.

I realized that the mixed bag of my experiences with people came down to what the interaction *felt* like in the space between givers and receivers.

How did I feel after the encounter?

What questions did I ask myself?

Was I asking what I could contribute?

Or was I asking what was in it for me?

Was I asking if I was impressed?

Or was I asking who I could share this experience with?

Did I feel like I deserved better?

Or did I feel grateful and wanting to give something back?

Was I thinking about myself?

Or had my lens widened to incorporate others?

Did I feel an urge for affirmation and to be seen?

Or did I feel seen enough to move into a place to see and notice others?

I realized thirty-five years in this industry called "hospitality" was presenting a lesson about life, interactions, and relationships.

I've found that typically I need to see something outside of me before I can recognize the same thing operating *inside* of me.

As the vision of the two cycles started to crystalize that day on the beach, I recalled two vivid dining experiences I'd had years before that were emblematic of these opposite cycles.

The first was a dinner at a restaurant in the arts district of Los Angeles.

It was memorable, but not in a good way, because it was an awakening—of the rude variety.

It's not that what happened in the restaurant (I'll call it "Luna") was unique among the thousands of other dining experiences I've had. What transpired was at once shocking and, sadly, typical. In hindsight, I realize that until that night, over the years I had become comfortably numb to occasional experiences with these feelings. But this time, something shifted.

I had been hosting a band in town from Nashville and was excited to showcase what was (at the time) a shiny new star on the city's robust dining scene. I knew the restaurant was in a season of buzz, and normally a reservation would be essential. But it was a weeknight, and it was late—not right before closing, but well after the evening rush. The hostess who greeted us employed little subtlety in conveying her indignant displeasure that we were either naïve or arrogant enough to believe we could "get in" without a reservation. I gamely absorbed the standard back-and-forth and posturing that usually accompanies such situations—a tango of micro-power moves that usually concludes with "All I have available is a table over *there*" (insert look of disdain). I've learned that most of the time the tables over "there" are usually just fine, and this night was no different. The hostess could have spared us the condescending dressing-down, but she, like so many of us stuck in ego's grip, did a lightning-fast assessment of where we stood on her hierarchy of human value and determined that, for our lack of both instantaneous name recognition *and* a reservation, we would receive the greeting (and seating) we deserved.

Nevertheless, soon after we were seated and settled into our table, my guests were excited to spot the lead singer and guitarist from the band The Killers having a late dinner at the table next to us (even though, if the snotty hostess was to be believed, our table was in an undesirable section of the restaurant).

After a few minutes, a server appeared and greeted our party with "Hey guys, what do you want to drink?" We might have forgiven the less than welcoming words, but the blatant dismissive and judgmental body language we've all witnessed as kids on the playground communicated the real, unspoken message that went something like:

Hey wannabes, I'm not sure if you're aware, but this restaurant is a big deal, and actually I'm a big deal, too. I just do this on the side for fun and extra cash. I'll be spending the next couple of hours silently judging you and whether you deserve to be here. (You probably don't.) This is how we roll, and there's a line out the door, so deal with it.

My gracious Southern guests were characteristically deferential. I was annoyed, but after living in LA for almost thirty years, I had grown accustomed to the catwalk strut of attitude that often accompanies people and places at the height of their fifteen minutes of fame, so I tried to ignore it.

After returning with our drinks, the server asked if we had been to the restaurant before.

"Yes," I answered.

"Great. Then you'll know how the chef likes you to order. We *require* you order all your dishes at once. Plates are meant to be shared. We recommend you order two-to-three plates per person."

Receiving instructions about the chef's preferences and requisite process of ordering was something that never sat right with me, but I had become inured to the pinprick of such petty power moves and knew the drill.

Between my co-host Matt and me, the band, and its management, we were a big group. I decided to order basically the entire menu. Considering everyone has different opinions (and tastes) about the proper temperature for steak, I made a single request: that the kitchen please cook the rib eye medium, as opposed to medium rare.

Despite what the opening twenty minutes had felt like, I still was shocked by the server's response:

"No."

Flat out. No commentary or equivocation. Just…no.

As a hospitality professional, knowing that chefs prefer to serve steak medium rare, I had steeled myself for some dialogue about the request and perhaps even more condescension about the chef's staunch opinion regarding steak preparation. But I wasn't prepared for such a brazen, and curt, response.

The tension between the server and me moved from subtle to obvious. Conversation at the table stopped, and I found myself at an uncomfortable crossroads: either acquiesce to the server and chef's thuggish culinary coercion or stand my ground.

In spite of ordering nearly every item on the menu and spending literally thousands of dollars, by asking for a single steak to be cooked to 155 degrees instead of 140, I was put in the position of squaring off publicly with a bully in front of the new friends I was hosting and trying to appease. Irritated but resolved, I repeated my request.

"I can ask the chef if you *want*, but I *know* what he's going to say."

"Yes, please, go ask the chef."

The server returned, triumphantly smug, emboldened by the imprimatur of the chef, who, he took obvious pleasure in telling me, definitely would *not* be cooking the steak *medium*.

And at this point, decades of industry-induced languor had begun to wear off.

I ordered the steak as required and conversation resumed at our table, but mentally, I was no longer present.

Triggered by what was meant to be, at best, a delightfully warm or, at worst, innocuous encounter, I found myself navigating a range of big emotions and even bigger questions about hospitality, service, and our culture at large.

To be sure, I have had incredible, gracious, and hospitable interactions with countless staff in restaurants, hotels, bars, and even on airlines. But there have been just as many, if not more, encounters I have either experienced firsthand or heard about from others where it felt as if a pernicious tension—dare I say even an *animosity*—boiled just beneath the surface between those providing service and those receiving it.

Why is this so common?

Why is reciprocal exasperation between service providers and consumers so frequently present?

Why do these interactions often leave so many people feeling disgruntled?

Is there an identifiable dynamic at play that has eroded decency, manners, and basic kindness in much of the marketplace? Or even in our seemingly innocuous encounters with others?

Where did it start? With the customer? With the business?

How can an encounter with a total stranger have the power to make us feel either connected or alienated?

What is the secret sauce present in the enviable operations that legitimately create both happy employees and happy customers?

Why do some interactions feel like we're in the presence of an advocate, while others feel like we're in the presence of an adversary?

What is the architecture of a wonderfully memorable experience? Can it be engineered?

My experience that night at "Luna" was not egregiously bad; believe it or not, I've had worse dining misadventures and I bet you have, too. But it was emblematic. And that's the real problem.

Prior to that night, I had surrendered to the sad reality that many interactions mirror those on the playground. Based on where you rank within whatever is considered the highest value in the moment—be it medallion status, name recognition, public profile, style, gender, the color of your skin, the color of your hair, or your preference of steak temperature, whatever arbitrary category has been prioritized—determined the tone of the interaction.

Belonging is conditional, right?
Possess enough of whatever currency is arbitrarily valued and you'll *feel* included, worthy, and connected.
Come up short, and you'll feel excluded and isolated.

As I ate the "Luna" chef's interpretation of "modern Mediterranean fare," which apparently was the justification for this awful experience, I bounced back and forth between resignation and indignation, no longer present for the people at my table or the conversation happening around me. Other than asking for the check, I was too preoccupied with my emotions to function as a proper host.

I paid the bill. We got up to leave. And then…it happened.

As I passed by him on my way out of the restaurant, without so much as a hint of grace or gratitude—neither for our patronage, nor the large gratuity the server had added automatically because of the size of our party—the server snarked a condescending "Bye, *buddy*" at me.

Something snapped.

I no longer felt surrendered to the idea that this is just the way it is at LA hot spots. I felt outrage. But under the outrage, I felt motivated. I knew on some cellular level that this enraged version of Steve was not who I was meant to be. This is not who *we* are meant to be. The server, the chef, me, the hostess who greeted us—something about these types of encounters had managed to conjure our lowest selves, and that needed to change.

Years later, as I reflected on the model of these two cycles I had created, I realized that this memory was one of many allowing me to see how these cycles operate in everyday experiences.

The surge of motivation that erupted in me as I left "Luna" wasn't just to course correct something that existed in my industry apart from me. I knew full well that, given the right conditions, I could be as brazen and dismissive as "Luna's" chef and his staff had been.

I wasn't pouting as I sat preoccupied at the table that night, nor was I lost in thought with fantasies dancing in my head of exacting vengeance against a bully in a chef's coat. Rather, I had recognized an endemic cultural condition in which I was both victim and perpetrator, and I was desperate to find a way to remedy it.

As a student of hospitality, I had studied and repeated the maxims of my heroes in our field, like Danny Meyer, the founder of Union Square Hospitality, who teaches that hospitality is a dialogue, not a monologue. Or Horst Schulze, the founder of Ritz-Carlton, whose "ladies and gentlemen serving ladies and gentlemen" mission statement had permeated every level of hotel staff and led to them becoming a beacon in service. But I knew the answer to the questions I was now asking would not only shape how I defined hospitality in my own words but the direction of how we operated as a company as well.

If I was going to contribute something helpful to the space between providers and consumers, I would need to abide by two convictions:

First, that I would speak to a solution, not just a problem. Someone once said if you aim at nothing, you'll hit it every time. I've learned that when we build in reaction to a problem, we just create different problems. If you need directions to get to Oregon, and I shout about how dangerous the road outside of Denver is, that doesn't really help you get to Oregon, does it? I will identify the problem, but I also will propose an alternative solution.

Secondly, I would commit to my ideas being rooted in data. For me, data is more than just numbers—it's connecting the dots. Data meant aligning with the wisdom, science, and guidance that has already been made available to us, so that my contribution to this timeless act of hospitality would be rooted in experience (personal and historical), data and scientific research, and resonate deeply on multiple levels.

It begins with story. As humans, we're finders and makers of meaning. And stories are usually the primary way we find and make meaning for ourselves. I need to share stories that are emblematic of both the problem and the alternative solution.

Scanning my memory for a beautiful contrast to the seed planted at "Luna," I arrived in a place where most things are *bellissima*: Italy.

This was several years ago and marked our first trip after our daughter Sofia, our eldest, had been born. As first-time parents, Nicole and I had spent two and a half years on the vertical, all-consuming learning curve that is new parenthood. We co-opted our moms to share the childcare during our first long break from parenting. Tentative about leaving Sofia, but thirsty for adventure, we booked a room for the night we arrived in Italy and a room for the night before we left, but we decided that everything in between would be spontaneous.

As a food and wine professional, I knew the Chianti region of Tuscany had seven subregions, but the majority of my experience was with the most famous Classico subregion. We set out on the back roads of Tuscany, armed with little more than a map and our road trip playlist. For no reason other than curiosity, we followed a roadside sign in Greve in Chianti that pointed to a winery and stumbled upon a cobblestoned vision of old-world wine history, the Montagliari Winery.

A man who turned out to be the owner and winemaker, David Migliorini, greeted us warmly. I asked him in my best Italian if they were open for a tasting, and he enthusiastically escorted us to a stone building that housed the tasting room. He invited us to sit and began walking us through his flight of wines. Time always moves slower in wine country, no matter where you are, but for us, sitting on David's land, drinking incredible wine, listening to him describe his winemaking style and feeling the place with all of our senses, it felt like time *literally* stood still.

This wasn't a famed producer of the region's better-known Barolos or Barbarescos, and that was totally fine with us. We were giddy for having been embraced in our spontaneous wandering by a benevolent conspiracy that led us to this hidden gem.

Throughout the wine tasting, David kept interrupting the order of wines with a little something we "had to try." From a balsamic vinegar he'd made and bottled that you could spread with a knife but wanted to drink with a straw to a grappa that was as smooth as silk and didn't singe your esophagus like so many I'd had before, the tasting was more a tour of things David had grown and made on his land. Nicole and I were transported in every way. I don't remember whether David suggested it or if we asked (because we were hungry), but he told us the winery had a restaurant and showed us to a table on a patio overlooking the hills.

"Do you see that pink house off in the distance? That's where the *Mona Lisa* was painted."

Because, of course it was. Nicole and I chuckled that the *Mona Lisa* could be spoken of in anything other than reverential tones, but the first hour of our visit to the winery had been a refreshing blend of excellence and ease, so somehow the casual reference to the local roots of one of the world's most renowned works of art made perfect sense.

David handed us menus and invited us to share any specific requests for food. We gladly handed him back the menus and told him we would follow his lead.

And lead he did.

As often happens with turning points in our lives, we don't recognize them as such in the moment. We're just fully present to what is happening. It's only after the moment has passed and we reflect back on it that we realize something transformative took place and we crossed a threshold into a kind of new reality.

I don't know if it's my Italian-Irish blood or that I'm just hard-wired to be emotional, but I'm an easy weeper. And for the record, I am wholeheartedly unashamed of my willingness to cry. Whether tears of joy or sadness, I don't try to stop them when I feel them coming. By the time I was mid-course of the prima pasta that late afternoon in Tuscany, I was crying. Not sobbing, but definitely wiping away tears. From the perfectly prepared pappardelle with asparagus tips and morel mushrooms to the way the main course of *stinco* (slow-braised local boar) fell off the bone, the flavor, the preparation, the seasoning, the texture, the aroma, the decadent simplicity, in short, *the food, was flawless.*

I'd eaten flawlessly executed food before and certainly had never needed to wipe away tears before I finished my meal. What was it about the meal at Montagliari that affected me so powerfully? I knew a fair amount of effort had gone into preparing the dishes, but they still seemed so *effortless*. Surely what moved me on an emotional and perhaps even spiritual level about the meal was something more profound than virtuosity and ease.

In the food industry, as in many industries, trends become labels, labels become causes, causes become liberally applied clichés, and once the cliché becomes diluted, desperate for distinction, a new trend emerges with a new label. And the cycle repeats.

The "all natural" movement of the 1980s gave way to the term *gourmet*. Then once "gourmet" dog food could be found on the shelves of every grocery store in America, "organic" arrived as the distinctive term of the year, and so the pattern goes. Whether describing ingredients and their sources ("farm-to-table," "local," "sustainable") or the processes around preparation ("ingredient-driven," "farmer's market fare," "slow food," "molecular," etc.), movements around terms become inextricably linked with how many in the profession define, differentiate, and ultimately identify themselves.

Our meal at Montagliari had none of the undertones (or overtones) of any clichés, causes, or agendas. We had come to the *source* of many of those trends, where soil is cultivated, seeds are planted, ingredients are harvested, and timeless recipes are followed. David and his colleagues at the winery weren't attempting to espouse some new dining trend. They didn't call it "farm-to-table" or "ingredient-driven."

They just called it lunch.

That meal in Tuscany was like none I'd had before, and I was desperate to speak to the chef. The food was sublime and I wanted to express my gratitude personally. David looked a little confused by my inquiry but was nonetheless happy to oblige.

In the early 1990s, I worked in an Italian restaurant off Rodeo Drive in Beverly Hills that was owned and operated by a couple from Naples. The chef's name was Alfreddo and, no joke, he cooked with a lit cigarette in his mouth, drinking several sixteen-ounce rounds of white wine from a plastic to-go cup each shift while miraculously managing not to drop ash in the pomodoro sauce. Like many Italians I knew, he was loud and lovely. I'm not sure what I expected the chef at Montagliari to look like, but when David emerged from the kitchen with a quiet woman who looked to be in her late seventies, wearing an apron and wire-framed glasses, it wasn't her.

"This is my mom," David said proudly.

I could tell right away she was uncomfortable with me making a fuss over her. Like so many Italian grandmothers (my Grandma Fortunato included) who embody the ethos of their *mangia, mangia* mantra, her fulfillment came not from accolades but from nourishing others with her craft. As a consummate host, this chef's singular pursuit was not for praise but for the contentment of those she served.

I hugged her tightly and thanked her for what she and David had given us: a beautiful, precious memory we would never forget.

Back in the States, as I returned to the groove of catering events day after day, always aspiring for improvement, I often recalled my dinner at "Luna" and my lunch at Montagliari and what had made the meals so diametrically different. It took the full vision of the cycles before I could name what it was.

I knew there were stark differences in these two occasions, but beyond the blatantly obvious or superficial, something about the *spirit* of the experiences was viscerally opposite. One boasted of its "modern Mediterranean fare," while the other actually was in the Mediterranean. Both served fresh pasta, using the correct flour and the ideal cooking time for al dente doneness. Yes, we often hear the secret ingredient to the best pasta is the Italian water, but it was something else. In each restaurant, one generation of cooks had mentored the other. At "Luna," the older generation had passed down product and process to the younger one. But had something been lost—or perhaps ignored—in translation?

Years later, sitting on the beach that day, seeing the extent of these two cycles, the words I'd been searching for to describe the difference between "Luna" and Montagliari came to me:

Entitlement and Generosity.

One of those experiences felt *entitled*. The other felt *generous*.

Those weren't judgments I was making about individual people—the servers, the hosts, the chefs—rather they were atmospheres that permeated *all* the interactions contained in each experience. They were cycles that created chain reactions, looping in participants, fed by the cause and effect of interactions.

One of those cycles was virtuous. And one of them was vicious.

At "Luna," the hostess felt entitled to communicate her disdain for our lack of a reservation, and upon encountering her cold welcome, I felt entitled to a much warmer greeting. The server felt entitled to our collective submission to the rules of engagement. The chef felt entitled to our respect by requiring us to order a certain way and determining how our steak should be cooked. As a result, I felt entitled to be reciprocally respected and treated like a paying customer instead of a sycophantic diner just happy to be there. It was a vicious cycle where everyone, including me, operated from a place of entitlement.

At Montagliari, David and his mother were generous from the moment we stepped onto their property. I lost count of how many times during our tasting David brought out something extra that we "just had to try." But his generosity was more than serving things *gratuito*. He was generous with his time, showing us the winery and the barrel room. He demonstrated a genuine interest in our story, and he generously shared his. He offered guidance and tips on other things in Italy he thought we might enjoy, and his mother, the chef, wanted only one thing from us: that we eat and be satisfied.

David was a host in the truest sense of the word. He had mined the part of his life that was his to share with others and gave of it generously, so my wife and I could find a space to enjoy our own. As a result, all we wanted was to stay in that space and tell everyone we knew about it. (And we have.)

What was meant to be a two-hour wine tasting turned into a two-day stay on the property, where we rented an available room at the vineyard. I found an open-air market nearby and purchased two duffle bags and a stack of beach towels in which to pack and protect the three cases of wine I purchased to memorialize our visit. Were it not for our two-year-old Sofia back home in California, we might have asked to stay at the winery forever.

It was a virtuous cycle where everyone operated with generosity. That made it memorable. That made it magical.

Both the proprietors and craftspeople at "Luna" and Montagliari were committed to excellence. Both had clear intentionality in their approach to products and process. Both were experts in their field. Both worked hard, putting in long hours, and both were committed. Both used their artistry and skill to provide for themselves and their employees. Both knew their way around a braise and a beverage and could serve a drink and a dish that could pass any food critic's criteria for noteworthiness.

Other than the physical and geographic milieu, much about the two restaurants, in terms of product, was similar. But the tone of the experiences, and the impressions left long after the tables were cleared and dishes washed, could not have been more disparate.

It became clear to me that the dramatically different outcomes were a matter of drive. Core motivation was the engine behind all the effort, and it determined which cycle, virtuous or vicious, was operating. As Simon Sinek, the author of *Start With Why*, puts it, the motivation is the "why" that informed the what and the how.

Talent was never in question in either experience. It was the drive *behind* the talent that made all the difference. While I've told these two stories from my context as someone who serves (and consumes) food and beverage, the space I've just described transcends my industry; *it's a universally occupied space.* As I said, hosting is the place we stand in when someone comes to us for something, anything! A meal, or a coffee, or a seat assignment, or an oil change. And when we stand in that space with generous intentions, we've extended hospitality.

Here is the essence: When we are motivated by a drive to *prove* our value to others through our talents and work, it creates a vicious cycle of entitlement. It's a motive that leverages other people's experiences as an occasion for *us* to be celebrated for *our* skills or validated for what we've offered. It's an economy of taking and it leaves us, those around us, and those we serve preoccupied with what they're *owed*, their rights and what they *deserve*. It's an economy (and social ecosystem) of entitlement.

The drive to prove our value to others is understandable and perhaps even ubiquitous these days. But that kind of drive is meant to be seasonal—something we engage in during the early season of our lives but ideally outgrow as we mature.

The drive to offer our contributions to help others feel *their* inherent value creates a virtuous cycle of generosity. It's a motive that leverages our skills, ideas, creations, or expertise as an opportunity to celebrate others. It's an economy of giving and it leaves us, those around us, and those we serve feeling generous and connected to the rest of the world in a more vital way. When we feel generous, we become *generative*—meaning life-giving.

Simply put, when we land in entitlement, we diminish life and create isolation. When we land in generosity, we expand life and create connection. And where we land has everything to do with why we started doing what we're doing in the first place. Motives and intentions are dicey little things. But even though they vacillate, they can be set and reset. The Italian mom who cooked for us at Montagliari wasn't motivated by being celebrated. She wanted us to feel nourished. And we left her presence with full bellies and full hearts. Even though I ordered the whole menu at "Luna," our bellies were full, but our hearts were empty. The entire staff seemed to be motivated by an intention other than nourishment. And equally, we all felt it.

The vicious cycle of entitlement and the virtuous cycle of generosity are opposite energies that create powerful and polar forces. I believe the more we recognize the vicious cycle of entitlement among our interactions, the more prevalent the virtuous cycle of generosity will become a substantially more appealing alternative. Let's dig into the model.

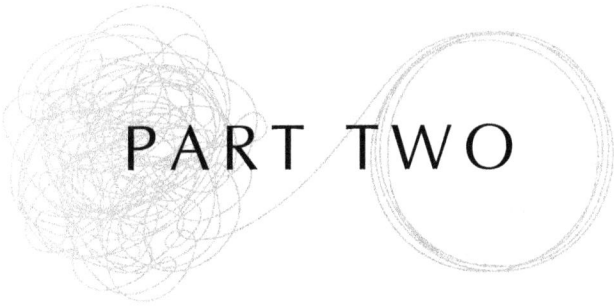

PART TWO

THE VICIOUS CYCLE BEGINS

Recognizing that I had been operating in the vicious cycle named so many experiences for me like nothing else had. I saw where I had been the perpetrator of the cycle. I also saw how I had been sucked in and become an unintended victim of the cycle. I recognized that there is a community of relationships at play in almost every encounter we have. We engage others in literally every human transaction we have. Try as we might to deny it, no man is an island.

From the CEO with numerous departments and thousands of individuals between herself and her end user to the architect meeting directly with his client to draft the perfect dream house, the relational space determines how the experience feels. You could be a twentysomething single throwing a cocktail party for your friends or a married couple collaborating on how to offer guidance to your children. Whether we are a paid employee, creating something to offer others, or a paying customer consuming what has been created, we take a turn at every role in the cycle multiple times a day.

Again, hosting is universal. We are all hosts. Hosting isn't a medium reserved for those who serve mint juleps and use "summer" as a verb. Hosting is just the space between someone who creates something and someone who receives it.

And the opposite side of hosting isn't solely consuming. Yes, there are times we are consumers. But when we teach our classes, or cook for our friends, or lead our meetings, or guide our children, the people we are serving aren't "consumers." They're *receiving* what we're offering them as hosts.

Hosts and receivers.

In nearly every interaction we have, from the significant to the mundane, we are standing on either side of that space.

And switching sides hundreds of times a day.
As a creating host, you might create a product line.
Or a service.

Or a design.

Or a curriculum.

Or a song.

Or a system.

Or a meeting agenda.

Or an idea.

Or a burrito.

It doesn't matter.

The moment you present what you've created to someone else, you're a creator; you're hosting them.

And as others are presented with that product, service, design, song, guidance, or burrito, they become receivers. They're being hosted.

The energy that motivates us as creators comes through in that hosting space. As author and podcast host Rob Bell says: "*you* are the medium" through which your offering is presented. We might think our words are heard but our energy is hidden. But for better or worse, what is inside is being conveyed on the outside.

Let's look at the top of the vicious cycle.

THE VICIOUS CYCLE OF ENTITLEMENT

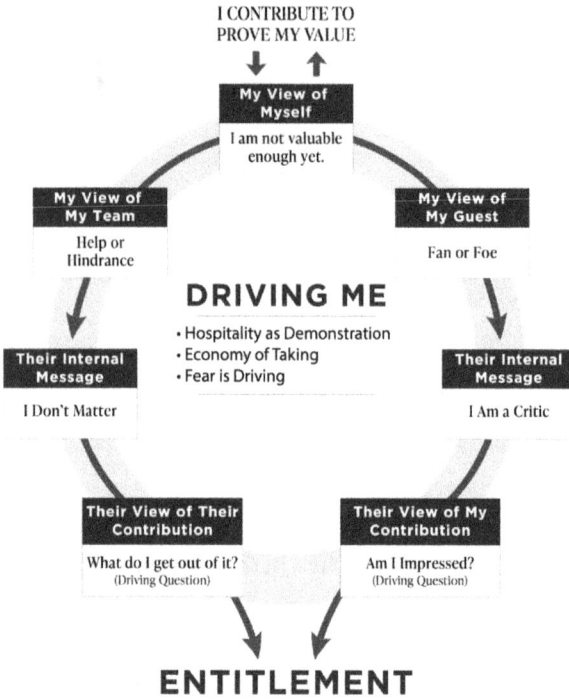

I CONTRIBUTE TO
PROVE MY VALUE

My View of Myself

I am not valuable enough yet.

My View of My Team

Help or Hindrance

My View of My Guest

Fan or Foe

DRIVING ME

- Hospitality as Demonstration
- Economy of Taking
- Fear is Driving

Their Internal Message

I Don't Matter

Their Internal Message

I Am a Critic

Their View of Their Contribution

What do I get out of it?
(Driving Question)

Their View of My Contribution

Am I Impressed?
(Driving Question)

ENTITLEMENT

MY DRIVE: I CONTRIBUTE TO PROVE MY VALUE TO OTHERS

When we're driven by a desire for others to feel valued by

whatever it is that we've created, we've extended one of the oldest virtues in humanity: hospitality.

But when as creators and hosts, we enter that hosting space, trophies held high, seeking to show others that we're valuable, or creative, or important, or powerful, or insightful, or in charge, or influential...

Entitlement rules the encounter.

Starting at the top of the model, our view of ourselves is where it all begins.

THE VICIOUS CYCLE OF ENTITLEMENT

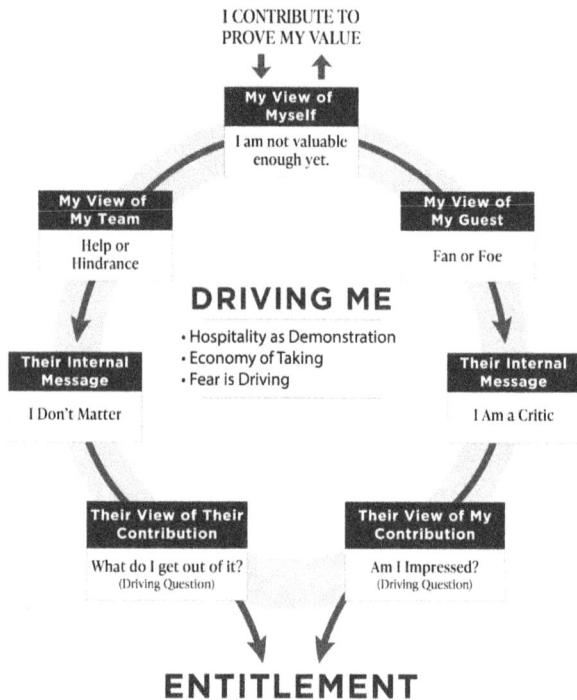

I CONTRIBUTE TO
PROVE MY VALUE

My View of Myself

I am not valuable enough yet.

My View of My Team

Help or Hindrance

My View of My Guest

Fan or Foe

DRIVING ME

- Hospitality as Demonstration
- Economy of Taking
- Fear is Driving

Their Internal Message

I Don't Matter

Their Internal Message

I Am a Critic

Their View of Their Contribution

What do I get out of it?
(Driving Question)

Their View of My Contribution

Am I Impressed?
(Driving Question)

ENTITLEMENT

VIEW OF MYSELF: I'M NOT VALUABLE ENOUGH YET

When I'm driven by a desire to prove my value, my view of

myself is that I am not valuable *enough*.

Yet.

Something deep is unsettled in me.

Questions of our worth, or as author and research professor Brené Brown says, "hustling for worthiness," is a soul-level hustle. And those rumblings aren't occasional; they're constant. When I see myself as not valuable enough, that lens shapes how I see the world. Franciscan monk and mystic author Richard Rohr likes to say:[2]

"We don't see things as they are. We see things as *we* are."

When I see myself as not valuable enough, I see the world, every circumstance, and every encounter as a proving ground for my worth, or lack thereof.

I began to see this not only as a business owner and entrepreneur but as a husband and a father.

Picture me, the bullied kid, determined to prove his value, who made a subconscious oath to never be overpowered or ignored again. How can there be any hope for resolving a

2 Rohr, Richard. *Yes, And...: Daily Meditations.* Franciscan Media, 2013.

routine conflict with my wife, when there is a conflict within myself between hearing her point and a lifelong determination to never have my points dismissed?

Imagine how those conflicts metastasize when our precious kids explore the boundaries of *their* power. Any parent knows the fire of will burns hot during the proverbial f*@k-you fours. When I'm "not valuable enough," I need to prove my value, my authority, *my power* in those parenting situations. But I'm not actually parenting.

I'm dominating.
And I'm damaging something precious, innocent, and fragile.

We don't have to look far to identify others that constantly need to prove their value, due to seeing themselves as not valuable enough. The real transformation comes, however, when we see that energy *in ourselves*.

Spotting the show-offs among us is easy. We made fun of people on the playground who showed off, but our society is chock-full of those that never outgrew the playground urges and at every opportunity need us to see how valuable *or influential* they are. It's become so normative that we now give them a title and a role in our society: *influencers.*

And yet, someone once said: "The more we think the problem is 'out there,' the more *that thought* becomes the problem." I have a choice of what to look at. I can focus on how embarrassingly self-aggrandizing influencers, or our politicians on both sides, can be. Or, I can, as actor Robert Downey Jr. said, "hug the cactus" and explore the ways I too can be self-aggrandizing.

The nuance is that we also see how people who view themselves as "incomplete" in the worthiness category have used that energy to achieve the highest accomplishments. Those messages of "not enough" become the chips on the shoulders of those who became what many of us would call great. As I watched the documentary *The Last Dance,* telling the story of Michael Jordan and the Chicago Bulls, I was amazed how Jordan could use the smallest slight or subtlest diss as fuel for his competitive fire.

So, is seeing yourself as not valuable enough a key to success? Like Jordan, doesn't the drive that comes from proving ourselves help fuel us toward our goals?

I think the question is not one of fuel but one of goals.

What wall is your ladder leaning against?

The wall you choose to climb may very well be scaled by the energy that comes from seeing yourself as not valuable enough yet and wanting to silence the critics.

As I shared, proving myself delivered results. I grew, I changed, I expanded, I accomplished.

It worked.
For a while.
Until it didn't.

Remember the cycles aren't about what we accomplish. I am not proposing some snake-oil formula that the virtuous cycle is a path to greatness, and we achieve it by avoiding the vicious cycle. These cycles are energies that are created among the community of people around us as we *seek to accomplish* whatever we are pursuing. They're more about feelings we evoke than results we achieve. I would argue though, that when we see beyond the immediate and start playing the long game, how we make people feel effects the outcomes we discover.

Let's move to the next phase on the left side of the cycle.

THE VICIOUS CYCLE OF ENTITLEMENT

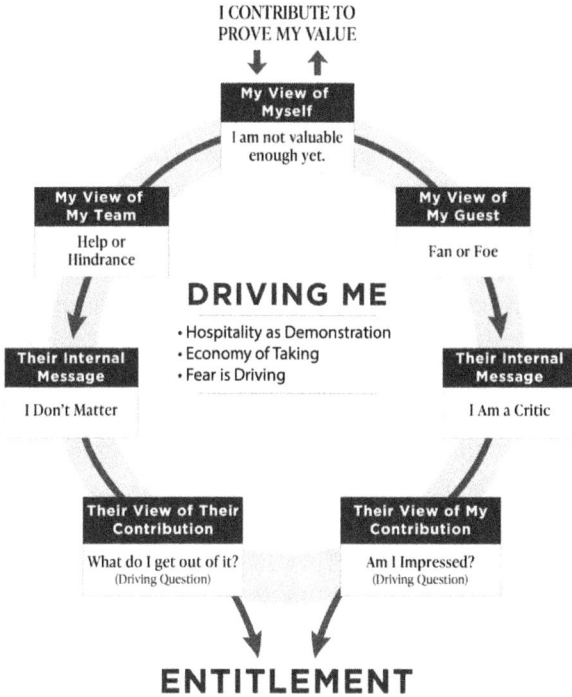

I CONTRIBUTE TO
PROVE MY VALUE

My View of Myself

I am not valuable enough yet.

My View of My Team

Help or Hindrance

My View of My Guest

Fan or Foe

DRIVING ME

- Hospitality as Demonstration
- Economy of Taking
- Fear is Driving

Their Internal Message

I Don't Matter

Their Internal Message

I Am a Critic

Their View of Their Contribution

What do I get out of it?
(Driving Question)

Their View of My Contribution

Am I Impressed?
(Driving Question)

ENTITLEMENT

VIEW OF MY TEAM: ARE THEY A HELP OR A HINDRANCE?

When I'm driven by a desire to prove my value, my view of

myself is that I'm not valuable enough, and my view of the people around me (whoever I've enlisted as "my team" for the moment) is that they are either a help or a hindrance.

I'm on a mission.

I am trying to accomplish something that is urgent. It's urgent because the question of my worth is still unsettled, so every moment is calibrated to fill the bottomless pit of my need to be validated. Remember my season of trying to launch a music career? Carrying that need to prove my value had me viewing my bandmates and soundmen as people that were either going to help me look great, or if they played a wrong chord, or couldn't dial in the reverb on my mic, make me look bad. I can still remember those times, in the humiliation of that moment of someone playing the wrong chord or the sound not being perfect, I'd get pissed. You could feel the impact on my band. Who wants to do something as emotional as playing music with someone who's pissed?

Juxtapose that with the professionals settled enough in themselves to feel comfortable in their skin. They show up, regardless of the circumstances, adapt to variables, and offer what they have. I'm reminded of Foo Fighters lead singer Dave Grohl breaking his leg onstage in front of 52,000 fans. I'm sure he was embarrassed. When divas get embarrassed, they externalize the pressure and look around them to determine who's to blame or who hindered their agenda of proving their value. Dave Grohl could have looked to blame the stage-hands or the production guys who positioned the monitors or some fan for not anticipating his moves in the crowd. But as one of the most anti-diva rock stars around, Dave Grohl left for a few moments, set his leg with a temporary cast, and was carried back onstage. With a broken leg, a doctor by his side, and using a stroke of comedic genius, he played Queen's "Under Pressure." Our bandmates, our crews, and our crowds are *drawn* by that kind of energy. As consumers, we feel the generosity of those moments and lose our minds when we see how compelling that is.

Think of the times your participation has been needed for a project or a presentation but you're not the one delivering it. You could be a line cook making a puree, a designer making a slide for a PowerPoint, an analyst preparing a report, or a teacher's aide helping quiet the class. You can tell when those who have enlisted your involvement see you as a help or a hindrance to *their* agenda. You can feel how you are a means to *their* ends. You're not what's important. They are what's important.

"I'm counting on you."

"Don't make me look bad."

"How could you do this to me? It's *my* reputation on the line."

Let's keep moving through and look at the next phase in the middle left of the cycle.

THE VICIOUS CYCLE OF ENTITLEMENT

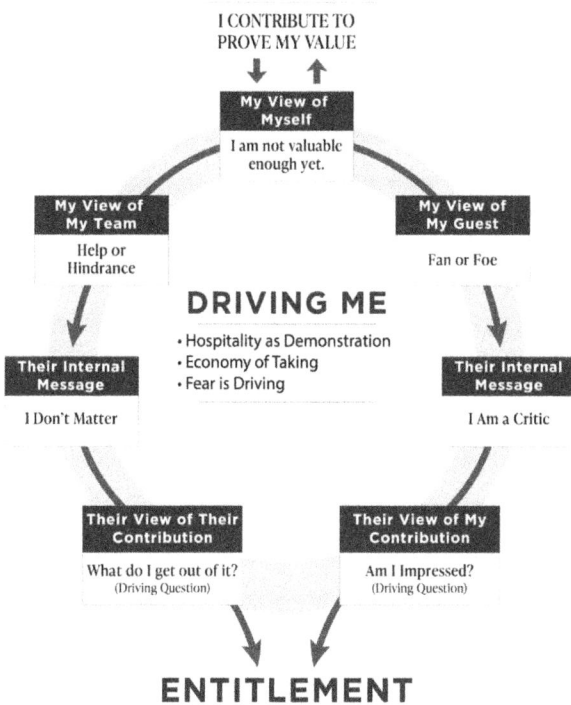

I CONTRIBUTE TO
PROVE MY VALUE

**My View of
Myself**

I am not valuable
enough yet.

**My View of
My Team**

Help or
Hindrance

**My View of
My Guest**

Fan or Foe

DRIVING ME

- Hospitality as Demonstration
- Economy of Taking
- Fear is Driving

**Their Internal
Message**

I Don't Matter

**Their Internal
Message**

I Am a Critic

**Their View of Their
Contribution**

What do I get out of it?
(Driving Question)

**Their View of My
Contribution**

Am I Impressed?
(Driving Question)

ENTITLEMENT

MY TEAM'S INTERNAL MESSAGE: I DON'T MATTER.

When we see and treat people that way, they adopt an internal message that nearly guarantees we will get the worst of what they have to offer: "I don't matter." All messages that they're a cog in our wheel.

When we view our collaborators as a help or a hindrance, it doesn't motivate them to bring their best. It's deflating. If we raise our trophy, they dismiss our victory as built on the backs of their efforts. And if we fail, they brace for our ire as the reason for failure. And when our collaborators aren't motivated to bring their best, the burdens on our shoulders only get heavier.

Years ago, when author Jim Collins published his work *Good to Great,* it had a great impact on many of us in business. Collins talks in depth about the charismatic leader of Chrysler in the 1980s, Lee Iacocca. While Chrysler's success was growing in the automotive industry, Iacocca had the trophy of success to prove his value to the organization. He took credit for the company's success as evidence of his value and channeled his victory lap into a book entitled *Where Have All the Leaders Gone?* The book cover is a picture of himself holding a cigar, looking less like a leader of a team and more like a king on his throne. But as Collins showed us, when looked through the long lens of Iacocca's impact, a less than flattering story is told. A leadership dominated by ego produced a team that knew they were seen as a help or a hindrance to Iacocca's agenda to prove how dynamic he was. The result was a team unmotivated to bring their best of their own volition. When he left the building, so did the motivation. And the company profits plummeted.

The Generation Y and Z teams of today might not know of Lee Iacocca. But they can still identify with the timeless feeling of being seen as a means to someone else's ends. There's a way people see us and subsequently treat us that draws our loyalty, our involvement, our contribution, our investment, and our love. And there's a way people see us and treat us, as a help or a hindrance to their agenda, that might render our submission or acquiescence in the immediate, but whatever we offer is resented and short-lived.

Let's move to the next phase of the left side of the cycle.

THE VICIOUS CYCLE OF ENTITLEMENT

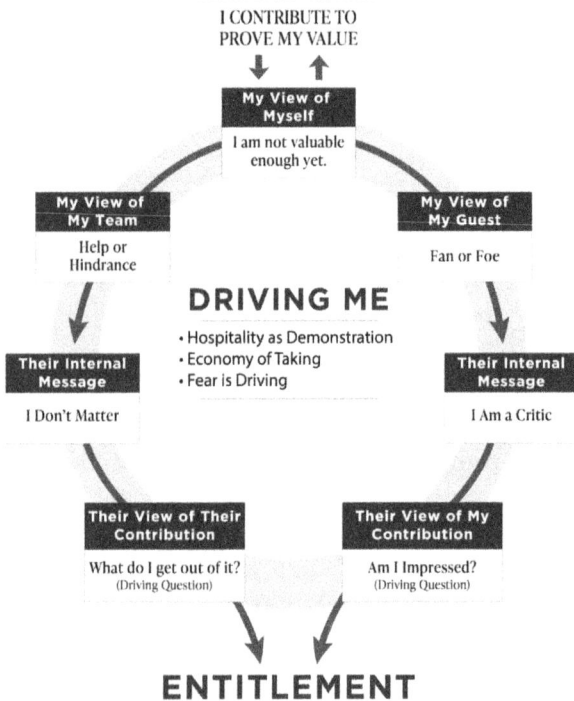

I CONTRIBUTE TO
PROVE MY VALUE

My View of Myself

I am not valuable
enough yet.

My View of My Team

Help or
Hindrance

My View of My Guest

Fan or Foe

DRIVING ME

• Hospitality as Demonstration
• Economy of Taking
• Fear is Driving

Their Internal Message

I Don't Matter

Their Internal Message

I Am a Critic

Their View of Their Contribution

What do I get out of it?
(Driving Question)

Their View of My Contribution

Am I Impressed?
(Driving Question)

ENTITLEMENT

MY TEAM'S VIEW OF THEIR CONTRIBUTION: WHAT DO I GET OUT OF THIS?

When people feel like they don't matter to us, like they're

just being used, it shapes how they view their contribution. However they contribute, their driving question becomes: What do I get out of this?

Here's what happens when driven by a desire to prove our value: we see ourselves as not valuable enough, and we see our collaborators as a help or a hindrance. They can *feel* the expendability and exploitation of their involvement. Despite our words, our handbooks, and the motivational slogans on the wall, they see through our bullshit.

They might do the work, but their view of the work is that it doesn't matter. Because *they* don't matter. *We* matter. The output matters. Not them. They know no one is looking out for them. And here's where the viciousness turns up a notch. They start looking out for themselves. Because no one else is. And their driving question becomes: What do I get out of this?

You would think as a lifelong server turned catering company owner, I would empathize with the plight and perspective of a server more than anyone. Like I was, many of the servers describing the nightly specials or pouring wine are bright, college-educated individuals with creative aspirations of their own. And they're bringing their best to make our occasions special…and maybe motivate a slightly more generous tip in a world where we're led to believe the customer is always right. They're holding on to their dignity in many situations where customers behave in less than dignified ways. I should know, it was my world for two decades.

But when I started my company, I was so consumed by the mission of building a company of influence that I missed the forest for the trees. I didn't mean to be a hypocrite. As I said, I was blind. I would lead meetings with servers before events, talking about our mission of service and making our customers feel valued. And when the event started and the pressure of game time was upon us, despite my good intentions, I would trample over the very people I needed most.

I'll never forget the horror when I discovered one of our company's servers—one that I admired—had gone from a key contributing player to feeling offended and trying to rally a collective complaint from the rest of our servers to the California Labor Board in the span of months. Residing in one of the most business-unfriendly states in the country, typically ruling on the side of the employee no matter the validity, I panicked that our fledgling company would be taken out by onerous government fines we could never pay. Thankfully, other servers didn't bother rallying to his cause. And by some mysterious grace, for California standards, the board representative who heard our sides could see the server was more offended and bitter than presenting any substantive complaints. But what stuck with me more than anything was his transformation from being on our side to looking out for himself. Somehow, the way he was treated started him asking "What am I getting out of this?" and as that question festered, it changed how he showed up for us.

How had a server that was a dynamic asset at our events go from being our first call to calling the labor board? I respected his experience and thought I showed how much I valued him. Yet somehow the way I was operating completely transformed his view of us and changed his mindset. What happened?

Let's keep moving down the left side of the cycle to the bottom center.

THE VICIOUS CYCLE OF ENTITLEMENT

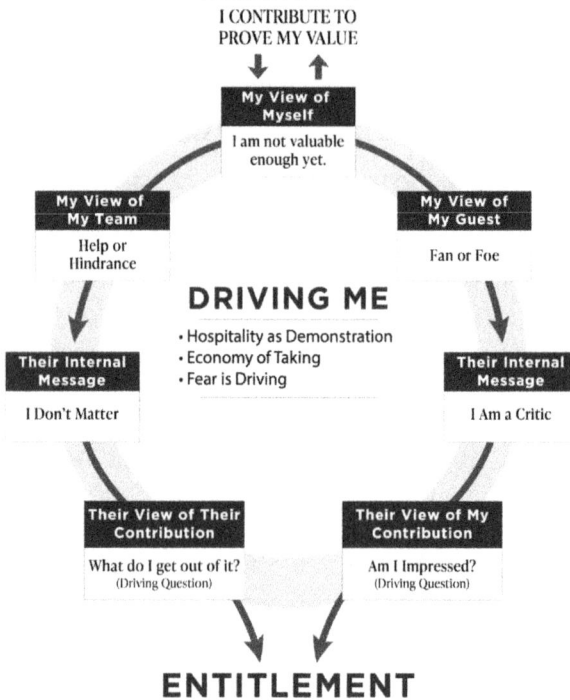

I CONTRIBUTE TO
PROVE MY VALUE

My View of Myself

I am not valuable enough yet.

My View of My Team

Help or Hindrance

My View of My Guest

Fan or Foe

DRIVING ME

- Hospitality as Demonstration
- Economy of Taking
- Fear is Driving

Their Internal Message

I Don't Matter

Their Internal Message

I Am a Critic

Their View of Their Contribution

What do I get out of it?
(Driving Question)

Their View of My Contribution

Am I Impressed?
(Driving Question)

ENTITLEMENT

THE RESULT: ENTITLEMENT

Here's what happens when, as a result of feeling like a cog in a wheel, people start asking what's in it for them. They become entitled. They become obsessed with what they're owed. They become preoccupied with what they deserve. They start demanding that they deserve better. And as they do, we become enraged and reciprocally preoccupied with what we're owed back ("How dare they? After how well we've treated them!"). And we become bitter and start demanding that we deserve better from them. And it becomes, in every way, vicious.

As the vicious cycle model became clear to me, I saw that not only had I been a leader driven by proving my value, but like the server that worked for us in the early days, I too had been an employee looking out for number one, determined that I deserved better.

In a brief break between restaurant jobs, my first job out of college was working for a production company in Hollywood. I had graduated from Pepperdine University, with a degree in public relations, and day one on the job was a lengthy and impassioned training on how to stock the producer's fridge. I was warned to pay attention and commit the order of the things to memory because sometimes the producers grabbed a drink without looking. And if they grabbed the wrong drink due to my mis-organization, I'd be fired.

It wasn't just the producers who needed to benefit from my

college-earned acute attention to stocking details; it was also the talent. The star's breakfast lox needed to come from Canter's Deli, but not their bagels. Their bagels were to come only from Manhattan Bagel, but the onion bagels needed to be bagged separately so the rest of the bagels didn't smell like onion. (Fair enough.) An exacting list of dressing room munchies (including removing certain colors of M&M's) was to be placed in the star's dressing room every week.

In the duration of my time there, the dressing room munchies were never touched.

Not.
Once.

You might say that's show business and they've earned their preferences. Sure, but in addition to running the gauntlet of satisfying a long list of power people's preferences, what was more difficult was that, as production assistants, we worked twenty-hour days every tape day.

Then the morning after taping, on two hours' sleep, we had to shuttle out-of-town guest stars from their hotel to the airport. I wouldn't have ridden in a car I was driving if you paid me. My eyes were barely open, and no amount of Red Bull could summon the road awareness required for LA freeways.

This wasn't a one-off compressed season of filming. This was our weekly schedule. Our zombie-like submission was expected as the dues to be paid for promotion.

Embrace the debased, inhuman conditions and you too can climb the ladder.

I of course, seething in entitlement, rapidly losing any post-college interest I had in exploring working in the entertainment industry, and feeling I was owed at least as much sleep as the star's terrier, promptly jumped off the ladder. But what haunted me is the thought of what became of those that stayed. What happened to those who paid those dues to climb that ladder? It's a rare human that would ascend by those means and then expect something different from those whom they were now above.

"I paid my dues. If you want to get where I am, you can start paying yours."
And the cycle spins on.

While it's been a bit, we all heard about the tragic and disheartening episodes that came to a boiling point in the wake of Covid restrictions and requirements for airline travel. My heart sank as I read the horrific behavior of passengers feeling entitled to their rights of mask-free travel or a round of booze while they fly. Their preoccupation with what they were owed gave way to viciousness, and passengers were literally assaulting flight attendants. I'm over masks as much as the next guy, but irrespective of the case for or against the validity of masks or removing alcohol from flights, the people showing up to a job and awkwardly trying to enforce rules they didn't make were subjected to the breakdown in civility that comes when we're so blinded by our rights that we can no longer see the basic human rights of others.

A grown woman assaulted a flight attendant, broke her teeth, and lacerated her head solely because she felt entitled to her "right" to fly mask-free. A grown man punched a flight attendant in the back of the head because he felt he was owed a cup of coffee.

Entitlement tears people apart, literally.
Basic kindness is nowhere to be found. Civility is gone.

We're blinded by an obsession with our rights and literally *cannot see* the reasonable rights of others. While no man is an island, entitlement isolates us in our self-righteousness and makes sharing the same land ridden with strife.

As hosts and creators, when we are driven by a desire to prove our value, it's not just ourselves and our collaborators that get pulled into entitlement. It's also those that receive whatever we're offering. Those to whom we present our craft, our creations, our ideas, and our work. They could be customers or clients or they could be friends and family members. Let's follow their journey in the vicious cycle.

THE VICIOUS CYCLE CONTINUES

In the previous chapter, I mentioned that the cycles are not a formula to be followed but rather a dynamic to be observed. As I reflected on the model when it first came to me, one of the most profound realities was the way the cycles could transform others. While it might sound exaggerated at first, I realized that my energy had changed the way people behaved, and I too had changed my behavior in different settings, based on the behavior of others.

What we now know is acknowledging that our feelings and actions are impacted by the feelings and actions of others is not a matter of opinion. It's science. Thanks to the breakthrough discovery from neuroscientist Dr. Giacomo Rizzolatti, we now have a term to describe the reality when we mimic what we see in others: mirror neurons.[3]

This invisible but powerful energy that moves in the space between people can be an asset or a liability. In the vicious cycle, observing how these mirror neurons bring out the worst in others is cause for both concern and reflection.

Let's start at the top of the right side of the cycle.

3 Winerman, Lea. "The mind's mirror". *APA Monitor,* October 2005. https://www.apa.org/monitor/oct05/mirror

THE VICIOUS CYCLE OF ENTITLEMENT

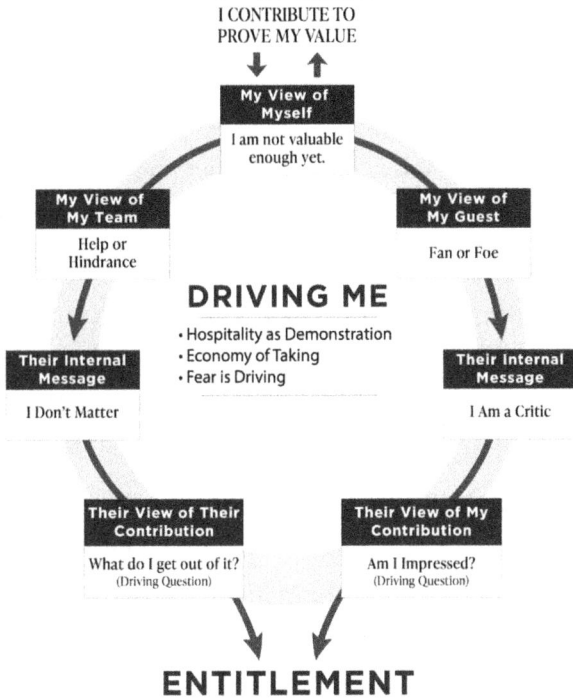

I CONTRIBUTE TO
PROVE MY VALUE

My View of Myself

I am not valuable enough yet.

My View of My Team

Help or Hindrance

My View of My Guest

Fan or Foe

DRIVING ME

- Hospitality as Demonstration
- Economy of Taking
- Fear is Driving

Their Internal Message

I Don't Matter

Their Internal Message

I Am a Critic

Their View of Their Contribution

What do I get out of it?
(Driving Question)

Their View of My Contribution

Am I Impressed?
(Driving Question)

ENTITLEMENT

VIEW OF MY GUESTS (CLIENTS/RECEIVERS): ARE THEY A FAN OR A FOE?

When I create something or offer my skills to others, driven by a desire to prove my value, I see my receivers (guests, clients, customers, friends) as a fan or a foe.

In needing to prove my value, I'm attached to the feedback regarding what I offered. The stakes are high, and as we saw in the previous chapter, because something is unsettled in the way I see myself, I need constant reassurances that my place in the world is secure. That attachment to reassurances actually transforms me from being a creator to a performer.

And when my offering becomes a performance, I'm looking for applause. I'm scanning your response for validation. And because I'm looking for your praise, I see you as a potential fan. But if you withhold your praise, you become a foe. I may be threatened, confused, disheartened, offended, or saddened by the affirmation you withheld. But mostly in the vicious cycle, when affirmation is withheld, I feel *disrespected.* Whatever I'm feeling, your lack of affirmation has confirmed the very message I'm endeavoring to silence: You don't see me as valuable as I want to be seen. And you sent me that message. You are, therefore, a foe.

I am certainly not suggesting that this is the mindset of *professional* performers. The relationship between a performer and their fans is something wholly different. There is a mutually understood agreement between performer and audience and everyone is very clear on the expectations and rules of engagement.

Being a professional performer and being co-opted into a *performance mentality* due to proving our value are entirely different. This is part of the viciousness of the cycle. It bypasses our conscious minds and hijacks us, coercing us into a way of being and seeing that we didn't intend. Professional performers are totally conscious of their role and their hoped-for outcome. The rest of us believe we are just bringing our craft, skill, product, or knowledge and offering it to the world. But when the issue of our value is at stake, whether personal or corporate, our attachment to your response frames you in the light of a fan or a foe.

What does that mean for businesses? Isn't prevailing business wisdom to create raving fans? Aren't applause, validation, and accolades in business equivalent to revenue or customer satisfaction? Can a business be insecure?

As a business owner, I will tell you unequivocally: yes.

Just like people, a business can have its question of value unsettled. Businesses are just groups of people, aligned around a common goal, and the energy of those people translates to the collective energy of the company. And when a leader of a business is trying to prove their value, their clients become fans if they applaud and foes if they don't.

Compare that with the virtuous cycle. When a business values *both* the bottom line and a better world, it sees its clients and customers as valuable people. You may or may not love the world domination achieved by Starbucks. And to be sure they've had some ups and downs, but you can't open over 35,000 stores in eighty countries without a wide circle of what's important: humans (the employee, the guest, those that like us, those that don't). The Starbucks mission statement, "To inspire and nurture the human spirit – one person, one cup and one neighborhood at a time," has fueled an operation that rides the waves and keeps growing. The corporate drive affects how it sees a customer. If their goal is to value people, then *everyone* is valued—those that applaud and those that don't.

In the vicious cycle, when business owners are trying to prove that *they* are valuable, their customers move from being seen as universally valuable to either fans or foes.

I know. I embodied it.

My business model is built on helping people celebrate some of the most important occasions of their lives. And we swing for the fences in making sure every single event we do exceeds expectations. And most of the time, we're applauded. That's why in the early days of my company, I didn't see the vicious cycle.

Because as long as the space between company and client is smooth, it can be hard to detect a problem. But the strength of a relational bridge is often only discovered when things go wrong.

Other than running out of a first-course soup sixty guests of one hundred and fifty in, things rarely went terribly *wrong*. But what I noticed when the vicious cycle became clear to me was an honest inventory of how I *felt* toward our clients that weren't jumping up and down with affirmation for us or, worse yet, didn't applaud at all.

As a student of hospitality and fostering a deeply held belief that hospitality is just the art of making people feel cared for, I realized that I would violate my own principles every time a customer withheld their applause.

I would lecture my staff about valuing our customers. And

then if a customer was high-maintenance, dramatic, difficult, or unhappy, I would roll my eyes and complain about these "damn clients." Forgetting that these "damn clients" were the ones putting food on my family's table.

Like I said, these cycles not only revealed things in me; they also gave a name to so many experiences I had engaged in with other people and businesses. They showed me how I was operating, how others were operating, and for my part, how I wanted to change.

My last job before starting my own company was with a national fine dining restaurant group. The attorney who represented the founder of the restaurant group worked in downtown LA in a building next to the restaurant I worked in and would often come in. When I started doing the pop-up winemaker dinners to launch roomforty, I still needed to keep bartending shifts to make ends meet and for a while was working two jobs.

Through a serendipitous twist of events, the attorney found out what I was building and took an interest in representing me.

Me?

I was flabbergasted.

I was one of 30,000 employees in the nationwide restaurant group. This man represented the *founder*. He had represented some of the most famous chefs and restaurateurs in the country. And he had taken an interest in my deal.

I interpreted his interest as confirmation I was finally on the right professional path and concluded his endorsement and involvement would fast-track the road to opening.

There was one slight hitch: the retainer to *start* his involvement was $25,000. He made clear that wasn't a guarantee of anything. That was a signing retainer to confirm that I was in fact his client, and if I could find investors, he would structure the relationship between them and me.

The problem was: I was a bartender. My wife Nicole was pregnant but still working, and I was making between $2,500 and $3,000 a month. $25,000 was more than seventy percent of my annual salary. I would never have the money.

One of my bar patrons that had started coming to my winemaker dinners also believed in what I was building. She wasn't by any means wealthy. She was an educator who was financially conservative and saved her money. She lived in a high-rise next to the restaurant and would often eat dinner at the bar, and we would talk about the business. Even though I had worked in restaurants for two decades, she and I had about the same amount of knowledge regarding restaurant openings and investment structures. But we both recognized that the clients this attorney represented had a track record of critically acclaimed restaurants. She agreed to loan me the $25,000 to retain the attorney, and both of us swallowed hard in his office when she wrote a check larger than either of us had ever seen.

To say that I had put this attorney on a pedestal is an understatement. He was the sage of restaurant openings, and I was the young grasshopper, eager and enthusiastic. I was in every way a fan. Consequently, basking in my worship, he was nice to me. But as time went on, I started to have rumblings of discomfort. Times where he would be unreachable or confusion on my part about his role or the timeline of his deliverables would leave me unsettled. He had been paid most of what I made in a year, and it felt like we weren't making any progress on my project.

As fans often are, I was intimidated. Especially when I compared the reputations of his other clients to mine. But I was also working hard to build a future for myself and my family. I summoned all the courage I could find and called to ask about the status of my deal.

He must have detected, for the first time, something in my voice other than adulation for his service. Because by question two, this attorney launched into a tirade the likes of which I had *literally* never experienced and to this day never have again.

He screamed at me.
Screamed.

He told me how ignorant and presumptive I was and how unreasonable my expectations were. He told me I was utterly clueless about the ways restaurant deals happen and to pull my head out of my ass. He insulted me, patronized me, verbally assaulted me, and reminded me that his retainer came with no guarantee of services. If I didn't like it, I could find another attorney.

I was speechless.
I had no words or response.
I realized in that moment the attorney I'd idolized was actually a bully.

And being bullied was a familiar reality for me.

That same childhood feeling I'd had when Luke dented my new car and then looked at me with fire in his eyes, screaming, "What are you going to do, shrimp?" came flooding back.

I felt helpless.
And trapped.
And small.

This attorney was mainlining the vicious cycle. He talked about his banner deals and star clients all the time. And the gentlemen's clubs he was part of. And the Supreme Court justices he knew. He was out to prove his value. And because of that, his view of his clients was that they were fans. And if for some reason they hinted they might not be fans, these paying clients suddenly became foes.

And woe betide the person who was that man's foe.

He felt entitled to unquestioning submission from me as his client, and suffice it to say, I felt entitled to better service from someone whose *partial* bill was close to my annual salary. It was a vicious cycle.

I never opened a restaurant, we parted ways, after years of saving I paid my benefactor back, and as luck would have it, I found an attorney who operates very much on the virtuous cycle. Turns out she's equally, if not more, respected in the industry, but her way of showing up is the opposite of what I'd experienced. Her generosity comes through not just in her approach to details like billing (which can often be a funny one with attorneys) but in offering clients like me the thing my previous attorney could never offer: a space to have hard conversations.

Let's move to the next phase of the cycle.

THE VICIOUS CYCLE OF ENTITLEMENT

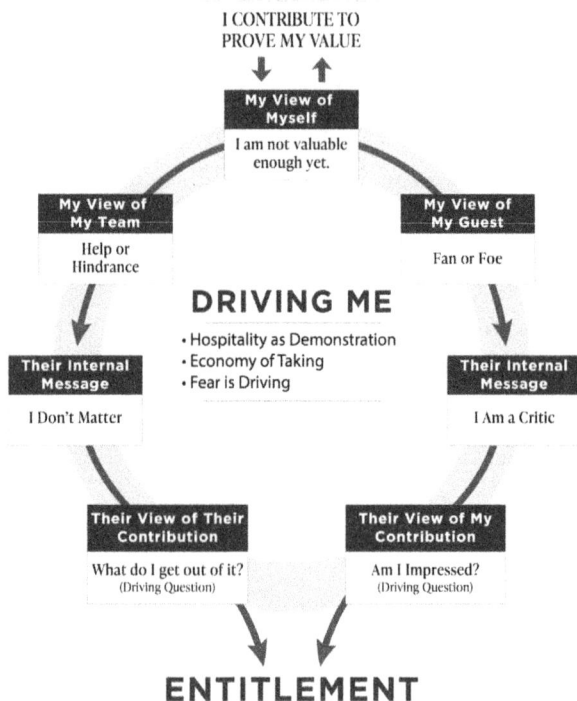

I CONTRIBUTE TO
PROVE MY VALUE

My View of Myself

I am not valuable enough yet.

My View of My Team

Help or Hindrance

My View of My Guest

Fan or Foe

DRIVING ME

- Hospitality as Demonstration
- Economy of Taking
- Fear is Driving

Their Internal Message

I Don't Matter

Their Internal Message

I Am a Critic

Their View of Their Contribution

What do I get out of it?
(Driving Question)

Their View of My Contribution

Am I Impressed?
(Driving Question)

ENTITLEMENT

THE INTERNAL MESSAGE OF MY RECEIVERS: I AM A CRITIC.

Moving to the middle of the right-hand side of the cycle,

when we view our receivers as fans or foes—whether they be clients, customers, or friends—we transform them into critics.

Remember the power of mirror neurons and the ways feelings moving through the cycles can change the mindset of the people around us? How is it that those that show up to receive what we offer can be transformed into critics?

Because it starts with us as hosts. When we're trying to prove our value, we become performers, presenting our approach to those we hope will be fans and applaud.

"I'm the smartest guy in the room."
"My style is the most current."
"I'm the parent, the teacher, the boss."
"My cocktail is a work of art."
"My social media feed is more engaging."
"I'm more of a creative than them."
"My approach to parenting is much more effective."
"I'm the chef."

Something subconscious changes in people as they observe someone performing in a context other than an actual stage. They realize (again, typically subconsciously) that what's being offered to them isn't actually about them. It's not for them. They're "users," or datapoints of feedback. It's about the craftsman, the company, the influencer, the executive, the designer, the educator...it's about playground dynamics of popularity. Their reputation and portfolio are what matters, and the customer, observer, follower, friend, or receiver is expected to applaud.

Those rules of engagement turn people into critics. Whether or not they're conscious of it, they begin moving from experiencing to *critiquing*.

And what is the primary question a critic asks?
Am I impressed?
Let's move to the next phase of the cycle.

THE VICIOUS CYCLE OF ENTITLEMENT

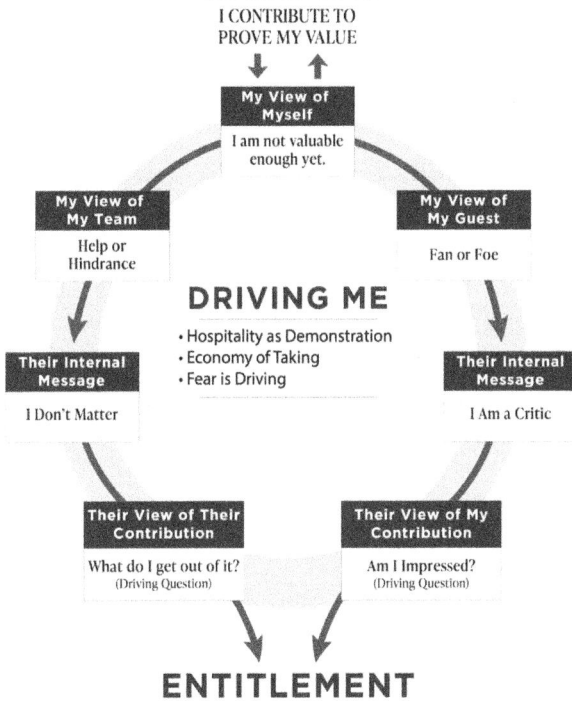

I CONTRIBUTE TO
PROVE MY VALUE

My View of Myself

I am not valuable enough yet.

My View of My Team

Help or Hindrance

My View of My Guest

Fan or Foe

DRIVING ME

- Hospitality as Demonstration
- Economy of Taking
- Fear is Driving

Their Internal Message

I Don't Matter

Their Internal Message

I Am a Critic

Their View of Their Contribution

What do I get out of it?
(Driving Question)

Their View of My Contribution

Am I Impressed?
(Driving Question)

ENTITLEMENT

THEIR VIEW OF MY CONTRIBUTION: AM I IMPRESSED?

As customers, clients, and people receiving the service of others, when we engage in experiences with the driving question of whether we're impressed, we become entitled.

We focus on our right to be impressed and what we're owed as customers. The intention of those that serve us to take our applause for their own reassurance of worth has changed us from being gracious recipients to analytical critics.

Think of the times you could tell the purpose of someone's offering was only to care for you. A birthday present, a warm meal, a painted picture, or a ride when you were stranded. It wouldn't have entered your mind to criticize. Even taking into consideration author Adam Grant's groupings of people into givers, takers, and matchers, when we have been the recipient of generosity, *most* of us become grateful and generous in return.

Giving promotes giving. And conversely, taking promotes taking.

This is partly why the space between companies and customers can become so fraught. Remember, we cannot be effective at making others feel valued while trying to *be* valued at the same time. Like breathing, you have to give it away to get it back. Once people lose the plot on valuing others and are more concerned with proving their own value, we shift into a taking economy. We don't exist in this taking economy if we're experiencing an economy of giving from our customers.

Taking from people is wrong. But it's also a *very* bad idea in today's communication ecosystem. When we begin taking from people, they will not hesitate to take their pound of flesh back. A quick perusal of business reviews on Yelp or one of the *fourteen* other business review sites will show that an offended customer will not hold back feeling entitled to their critique when triggered.

This vicious cycle that starts by trying to validate our value, seeing those we serve as fans or foes, transforming them into critics, and then everyone feeling entitled to something better happens in more than just businesses. It can happen among friends, families, and communities.

When my wife Nicole and I were first married, we were part of a small community of people, consisting of a little over a dozen couples and families. Los Angeles can be a hard place to find your people. So, among us there was intentionality to be there for each other and to, as we often said: live life together, in a city that can be very isolating.

The problem that took us over a decade to recognize was that during our entire time there, this community as a whole was totally fixated on proving to themselves, as well as any potential would-be members, that *our* way of doing community was the right way. They were trying to prove their value. Instead of just being a community, the biggest topic among us was the way *we* did community and often how it was a better approach than other communities.

From the way marriages functioned to parenting, kids' schooling, leadership models to conflict resolution—there was no end to the opinions of "a better way" that this group of thirty people had discovered in Northeast Los Angeles.

It's sad because I'm sure their hearts were in the right place. And without a doubt, they intended to be generous and sincerely be there for one another. Remember how I said the vicious cycle often exists on the level of the *sub*conscious, beyond our awareness, and can coexist with our best intentions?

The unintended impact of constantly trying to prove their value became the exact outcome of the vicious cycle model. Members were constantly being evaluated as to whether they were on the same page (fans) or not (foes). The people that took issue with the community quickly became filed into the foe category and were seen as a threat. People who had felt a warm welcome now felt a sudden distance from others, justified by some nebulous violation of community codes. This obviously resulted in people being shocked that they had been moved from "in" to "out" by the sheer nature of disagreeing with a position.

When we are trying to prove our value, we can't help but feel threatened when we hear a message that conflicts with the one we are living to confirm.

In the whiplash of a rapid migration from the inside to the outside, the people that had been filed as "foes" turned on the community and became mercilessly critical (critics). The community didn't realize that by unwittingly using the currency of criticism of others to validate itself, this approach would backfire. When its members had issues, they would use that same currency of criticism against a group of people they had once loved. Nicole and I watched baffled as people who had helped one another settle into new homes or watch each other's kids now were in vicious fights over violations of the community code.

This dynamic became personal to us, as we were openly criticized for seeking couples therapy from a professional, instead of having the community leaders provide their own version of marriage counseling. Somehow they felt threatened, second-guessed, or unappreciated for the ways they had supported our marriage, and believing the survival of our marriage depended on outside help, we were utterly bewildered why we were criticized for finding the help we needed.

Like many before us, those that had been filed as community foes for the choices they made became critics of the community. The newly created critics felt entitled to be heard or to raise concerns. The community leaders and other members felt entitled to more loyalty, alignment, or appreciation from the people they had aimed to serve. And the vicious cycle spun on.

As I've said throughout my confessions, transformation only begins to happen when the finger-pointing takes place in a mirror, rather than a window. Long before I became an unintended victim of the vicious cycle of this community, I was a perpetrator. And my energy today is spent trying to be aware of how I can operate differently.

In summary:

When we share our craft, skill, product, or offering with the drive to prove our value, it creates a vicious cycle. While suffering our own internal crisis of worth, the way we view our collaborators makes them feel devalued and results in them looking out for themselves and what they're owed. Which lands them in entitlement.

As we seek trophies for what we bring, we operate in a performance mindset and view those we aim to serve as fans or foes. Perceiving that what they're being asked for is their applause, our recipients become critics and trade appreciation for expectation, gauging whether they are impressed. Which lands them in entitlement.

The vicious cycle exists.
Everywhere.
And in the snap of a finger, we can find ourselves on it, in any one of the roles.
It isn't some methodical agenda that we're conscious of.
It's the movement of feelings that happens within the interactions of relationships.

Look in the Center of Cycle. This is the atmosphere that is created by this energy spinning:

THE VICIOUS CYCLE OF ENTITLEMENT

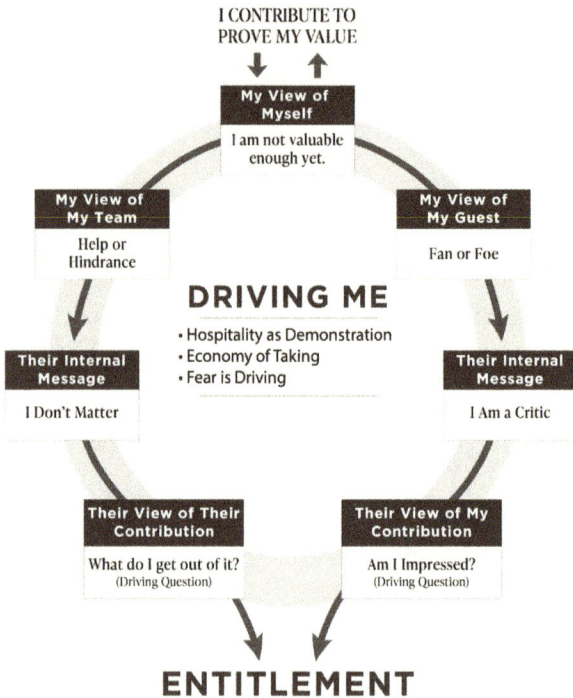

I CONTRIBUTE TO
PROVE MY VALUE

My View of Myself

I am not valuable enough yet.

My View of My Team

Help or Hindrance

My View of My Guest

Fan or Foe

DRIVING ME

- Hospitality as Demonstration
- Economy of Taking
- Fear is Driving

Their Internal Message

I Don't Matter

Their Internal Message

I Am a Critic

Their View of Their Contribution

What do I get out of it?
(Driving Question)

Their View of My Contribution

Am I Impressed?
(Driving Question)

ENTITLEMENT

IT'S ABOUT ME: DEMONSTRATION, TAKING, AND FEAR

Where the virtuous cycle is about *us,* the vicious cycle is about me.

Where the virtuous cycle is an invitation, the vicious cycle is a demonstration.

Where the virtuous cycle is animated by empathy, the vicious cycle is animated by fear. Fear that we're average. Fear that we're not seen as valuable enough.

The world resists the energy of the vicious cycle.
Because in the long game, the world resists a show-off.
Trust me.
I've been one.

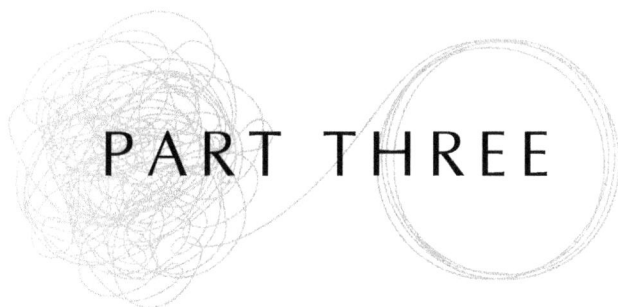

PART THREE

CHAPTER SIX

A BETTER WAY

Pause for a moment, if you will, and think about the most profound experience of beauty you have ever encountered.

The beauty was so compelling, so enveloping, that you felt frustrated by the words', or the camera's, woeful insufficiency to convey the impact.

If you're a parent and you've had the privilege of seeing your child come into the world, then maybe that's the moment. Parents always talk about the newborn cry that *breaks the silence.* What is that silence? That split second where the screams of the mother's effort or the calls of the nurse to push for just a moment…stop.

The world stands still.
Watching.

Silent.

It's only for a second.

And it's a lifetime.

It's the moment in between.

What was, and what will be.

Something about those moments feels totally *other*.

They feel holy.

Sacred.

We feel something we don't normally feel.

We feel awe.

A silent reverence for something that is loving, yet serious.

What is that thing?

That's Life.

We are witnessing *Life* emerge into existence.

And something about that moment connects with something deep within *us*. It's not just this little person that has us frozen in wonder. *It's the process of what we're witnessing.*

The power of those moments is the connection we have to something mysteriously other than us and at that same time totally part of us. There were two of us in the room. But now there are three, and no one walked through the door. Life came into existence, and we realize that whatever mysterious force caused this little thing to take its first breath is the same force inside of us causing us to breathe.

That's generativity.
It's generating life.
We're witnessing creative force.
In an instant it reframes our ideas of power.
It's power of a different sort.
It's the power to create.
It's loving. And it's strong.
It's so…different from our normal day-to-day experiences.
Even if you're not a parent, you've still had those moments.

Where *Life* and seeing the power of creative force broke through your normal receptors, into a much deeper place than your eyes and mind.

It touched something we don't totally have words for.
It got through to our existence…
What the mystics call our soul.

Maybe it was in nature. Watching how a river feels infinite. Our minds know there's a beginning and an end to a river and a finite amount of water, but in the pause of just looking at the water move, something about the river feels infinite.

And we don't know why, but that makes us feel something. We might not have the words to say that the infinity of the river connects to the infinity in us, but we just feel...struck.

Or maybe it was a moment during a concert. Where the whole stadium was singing, and something about the melody felt like it was *in* you. And even if you don't fancy yourself a singer, you found yourself singing, and something about the sound you could feel in your body as you sang, and the sound you heard in your ears as thousands of other voices sang felt different from all the other moments in the concert. The artist had the wisdom and insight to tell people to put their phones down and for a second to *just be* in that moment. Instead of trying to capture it, or memorialize it, you *lived* it.

What was the thing you felt?
That's generativity.
That's creative force.
It's that thing inside of everything that breathes.
Because it's *Life*.

In that moment, no one is bowing to the modern distinctions of who's *"a"* creative. As created beings, we're feeling the flow of creative force through us and are drawn into the unity of that experience.

It's that moment Chris Stapleton hits the chorus chords and melody of "White Horse" and in the audience a tough trucker from Arkansas will put his hands in the air and sing at the top of his lungs while standing next to a woman from California who teaches kindergarten and who is singing just as loudly.

Or when Chris Martin sings: It's true. Look at the stars. Look how they shine for you.

And for a moment, responding to the invitation, you stop looking at Chris and you actually look at the stars. And as you look, you find yourself singing your heart out. And you feel huge. And tiny. And connected. You feel *so* good. And *alive*.

That's the power of creative force, generativity.
That's why generosity is so compelling.
Because generosity *creates*.
It connects.
It taps into the life force inside all of us.
And we're drawn into a flow.
We feel something beautiful emerging in us.
So we express something beautiful in return.
And the cycle spins.

It's generous.

It creates.

It's about *us*.

It unites us to the people around us.

And to this thing outside of us and inside of us at the same time.

That's the virtuous cycle.

Those moments of birth, in nature, and the magical moments in concerts stick with us for a lifetime because the virtuous cycle is on level ten. It's like an explosion of beauty that grabs us and casts us into an all-consuming ocean where the cares and burdens and lists and divisions and categories and conflicts, for a moment, fade away.

But like welcome synapses, we get sparks of it in less grand moments.

Those little encounters where we felt something kind or gracious come toward us. And with gratitude we return the kindness. And then we feel this little moment of afterglow and think to ourselves, "That was nice."

The driver behind us lets us into their lane.

And we offer a little wave acknowledging the gesture.

The person in the elevator who sees us running toward them and holds open the closing doors.

And we thank them for their kindness.

The teacher who takes extra time to make sure our kids understand the homework.

And we send them a gift card to express our appreciation.

The airline employee who went the extra mile to make a difficult travel experience a little less painful.

And we were compelled to take the time to actually fill out the auto-sent survey so a good review might come their way.

The server who made us feel like they were genuinely happy to make our night special.

And we go overboard in return and tip thirty percent.

That's the virtuous cycle.

We feel someone's generosity toward us.

And our reflex is to be generous back.

And it feels good.

It feels good because generosity *generates*. It creates.

It's the antidote to the vicious cycle of entitlement.

It's the soil from which big solutions to bigger problems grow.

It sets the environment for us creating something together.

It's needed like never before.

Let's dig into the model.

THE VIRTUOUS CYCLE BEGINS

Feeling valued by others is a basic human need. We all want the same thing. The mysterious secret hidden in plain sight is that the way to feel really valued by people is to value them first. We have to give what we want. It's not psychology; it's ecology. It's a cosmic pattern. Like plants growing, dying, going to seed, and growing again. It's just the way it works.

As we value others, they value us in return, and a cycle of generosity begins to operate. Generosity feels so good because it's a life force; it's a creative energy flowing through us as created beings and is literally *life giving.*

To solve what faces us, we *need* that creative life force. Solutions and resolutions aren't found any other way. That's what's so exhausting about so much of our discourse and approaches to navigating existential issues. Do we actually believe in the binary, zero-sum narratives around big problems, that one side is going to be debated or dominated into conceding they had it all wrong and we had it all right? *You know what? You're totally right. I've been wrong all along. My bad.*

That's the urgent opportunity for recovering hospitality as a virtue that promotes as its sole north star: valuing others. One that sets a generous tone. And that tone becomes the required fertile soil from which the solutions to all the challenges we face can grow.

From the big problems we face as a species or a nation to problems we face at work or in our relationships, if we want solutions created, a virtuous cycle of generosity has to be present for the seedlings of these solutions to sprout. As I said, once I saw the cycles at work in me and in my industry, I saw them literally everywhere. I've begun sharing them in limitless contexts, professional and personal. Just from presenting these ideas in conversations, a few podcasts, and a few articles, people are asking to hear more. I've shared this model with creative agency teams and C-Suite executives. I've shared it with women about to become brand ambassadors for a clothing line and medical professionals leading teams of doctors and specialists. I've shared it with friends building communities and people navigating family dynamics. Everywhere I share this, I'm encouraged to see the "aha!" moment when people start to make connections, find their place in the model, and have words that name an energy they've experienced.

The virtuous cycle is not a formula for actions to take. It observes feelings that are created in our interactions that draw us to others and create good things. As these feelings are evoked, we are compelled. We like what we feel and respond accordingly.

Remember that hosting is the universal space I hold for you to receive something from me. Everyone is a host. Hosts enlist the help and involvement of others in their work, their *collaborators*. And throughout our day, we all receive what someone is offering.

The virtuous cycle of generosity starts with the intention of the host.

Let's start by looking at the top center of the cycle.

THE VIRTUOUS CYCLE OF GENEROSITY

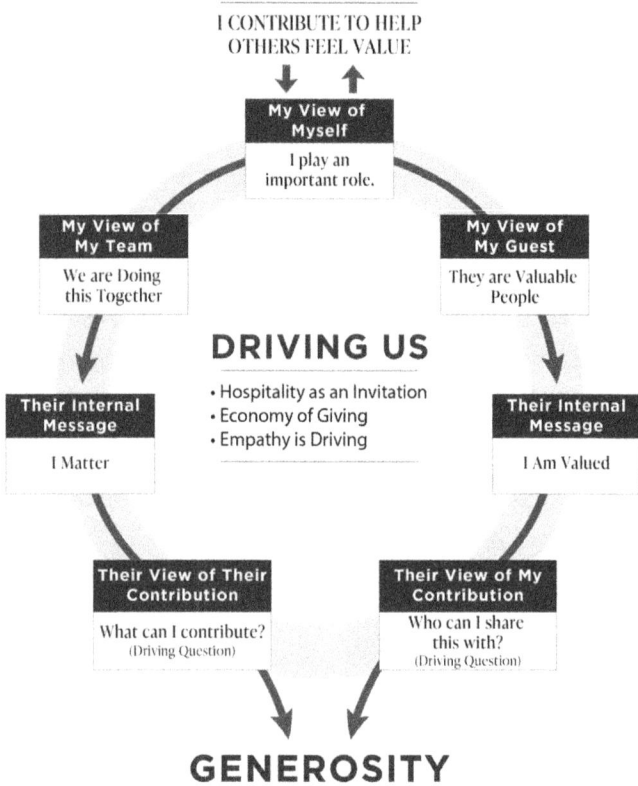

I CONTRIBUTE TO HELP
OTHERS FEEL VALUE

**My View of
Myself**

I play an
important role.

**My View of
My Team**

We are Doing
this Together

**My View of
My Guest**

They are Valuable
People

DRIVING US

- Hospitality as an Invitation
- Economy of Giving
- Empathy is Driving

**Their Internal
Message**

I Matter

**Their Internal
Message**

I Am Valued

**Their View of Their
Contribution**

What can I contribute?
(Driving Question)

**Their View of My
Contribution**

Who can I share
this with?
(Driving Question)

GENEROSITY

MY DRIVE: I CONTRIBUTE TO HELP OTHERS FEEL VALUED

It's the motivating drive behind our creation, presentation, or our offering. Motives are dicey little buggers. They can be mixed, they can be subconscious, and they can change. They can be collective, and they can be individual. But setting our intentions is kind of like dropping an anchor. We might drift from time to time, but once that anchor goes down, we aren't straying too far from where we're planted.

Valuing others is good for relationships, good for business, and good for the world. When we set our intention—that whatever we create or offer others is anchored in a desire to make them feel valued—we've planted in fruitful soil.

Companies, like people, have personalities. And as a reflective, emotional species, we respond accordingly. As varied and complex as our preferences are, the universal behavior of valuing others engages us at a deeper level than just observing. Sure, the mavens of the attention economy can be masters at getting us to look, but the amused swipe or momentary click are different than feeling *drawn*. I look at a car crash as much as the next guy, but if there's help on the scene, I don't pull over and get *involved*.

When companies set their intention to make others feel valued, they increase our involvement. We invest in them. We give them our time, our business, our friendship, our careers, our loyalty. Their corporate intention shapes their actions, and they deliver compelling results.

We're now accustomed and have come to expect companies to demonstrate an allegiance to a greater "why" than just their profits, but considering how long companies have existed, this intention is relatively new. Grocery store freezers are now packed with artisanal ice cream options. But recollect when Ben & Jerry's first came on the scene. They started a revolution. They not only had a product and economic mission but a social mission to use their company in innovative ways to make the world a better place.

Before Ben & Jerry's, people had favorite ice creams. But they weren't religious about it. The cultlike following Ben & Jerry's enjoyed wasn't just due to their creative flair and funky flavors. They decided to value others (in their case— *the world)* and the world returned the favor and valued them back. Passionately.

Look at the virtuous cycle created by Patagonia. From the beginning, their founder, Yvon Chouinard, set out to make a great product, a positive company culture, and a better world. Where many apparel and retail companies have come and gone, Patagonia has grown steadily for over fifty years.

For the cynic that might have wondered if all their talk about valuing the planet was just branding and marketing rooted in boosting their steadily increasing bottom line, in a truly unheard-of stroke of generosity, the company dedicated all its profits (you read that right) to help the planet. As their website so poignantly states: "Earth is now our only shareholder."

Whether you're a corporate executive wanting to solve big problems, a recent transplant looking for better friendships, a spouse looking to solve conflict in the partnership, or a diplomat looking to avert a crisis, a virtuous cycle of generosity is what creates the conditions where your hoped-for outcomes are much more likely to occur.

And it starts with you.
You're a host.
Set your intention to be in the hosting space with the intention of valuing others.
And it begins.

The intention becomes not just what we do, but on a level deeper, *how we see.* A virtuous cycle of generosity starts flowing with how we see ourselves. Consequently, it becomes intrinsically related to how we view others.

Remember in the vicious cycle, when we're trying to prove our value, our view of ourselves is that we aren't valuable *enough* yet. That sets us on an encoded trajectory that can only see people as a help or hindrance to our agenda.

Let's start at the top of the model:

THE VIRTUOUS CYCLE OF GENEROSITY

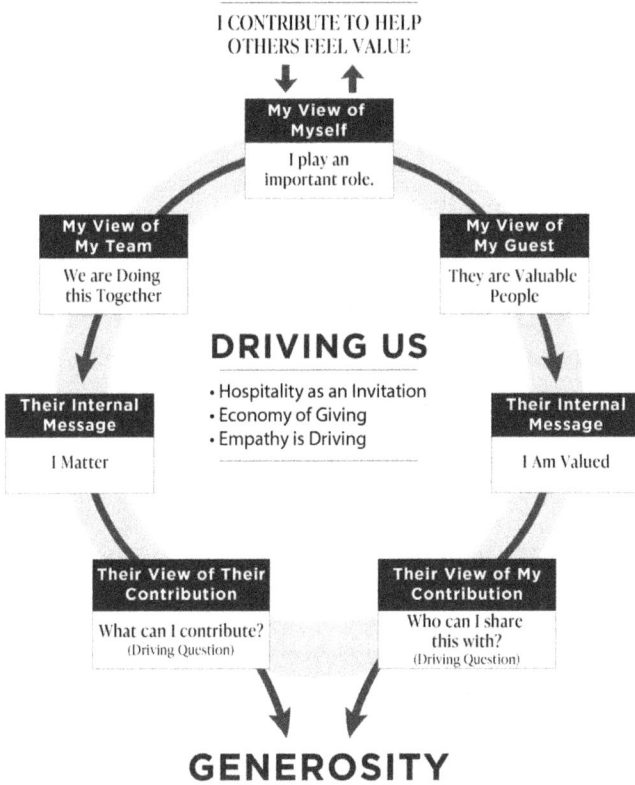

I CONTRIBUTE TO HELP
OTHERS FEEL VALUE

**My View of
Myself**

I play an
important role.

**My View of
My Team**

We are Doing
this Together

**My View of
My Guest**

They are Valuable
People

DRIVING US

- Hospitality as an Invitation
- Economy of Giving
- Empathy is Driving

**Their Internal
Message**

I Matter

**Their Internal
Message**

I Am Valued

**Their View of Their
Contribution**

What can I contribute?
(Driving Question)

**Their View of My
Contribution**

Who can I share
this with?
(Driving Question)

GENEROSITY

MY VIEW OF MYSELF: I PLAY AN IMPORTANT ROLE

In contrast to not feeling valuable enough yet, when we are

driven by a desire to leverage what we do to make others feel valued, we know something about ourselves: that we play an important role. We are aiming not just to meet a *want* of others; we're aiming to meet one of their most basic *needs*. That's important, and we feel settled in the goodness of that cause. We're grounded, confident, and honest, partly because we trust ourselves and our motives.

A great example of this is the founder of Homeboy Industries, Father Gregory Boyle. In a time when we've all seen religious voices use their platform to build their personal brand, for fifty years, Father Boyle has served what he calls the "homie" community in LA, with one mission: to show them they are valued. As the founder of the world's largest gang intervention and rehabilitation program, he's known as a straight shooter and for being the patron saint for second chances and humility. Father Boyle knows he's playing an important role in this community's life.[4]

You don't have to be the founder of a world-class community rehabilitation program and seen as a patron saint to see your role in valuing others as important work. When my wife Ni-

---

4 Lopez, Steve. "Column: 50 years as a Jesuit priest..." *LA Times,* November 2022. https://www.latimes.com/california/story/2022-11-02/lopez-column-father-greg-boyle-homeboy-industries-50-years-jesuit-priest

cole became pregnant with our first child, she was trying to figure out the best doctor to help navigate her through the new and deeply fragile journey of childbirth.

I will never forget sitting in the office of the first doctor as Nicole nervously tried to ask the right questions. She wanted to get a feel for how the doctor would approach the relationship with her along the pregnancy and delivery journey. Somewhere in the middle of her third question, the doctor cut her off and snapped: "Look, the most important thing is a healthy mom and healthy baby, and whatever we've got to do to ensure that, that's what we're going to do."

"Check, please."

Then we found Margo Kennedy. Margo is a sage of pregnancy and delivery the likes of which I've never seen. We would meet with Margo, and she would calmly ask questions and then sit and listen to the answer. Her questions were intuitive. She would read Nicole, perceiving when she was anxious, or be creative in offering an idea to bring comfort that she thought Nicole would respond to. She knew she was doing the ultimate important work of bringing life into the world. She had the confidence of someone who had done over two thousand home births, but she spoke truth gently.

She knew the health of the fetus and the delivery experience were directly related to *how Nicole felt*, and her sole aim was to bring attuned guidance, while making sure Nicole felt seen and cared for in the process.

When we set our intention to make others feel valued by what we offer, we've tapped into a universal need of those around us, and consequently, we see ourselves as doing something important and vital in the lives of others.

Let's move to the next phase on the left side of the cycle.

THE VIRTUOUS CYCLE OF GENEROSITY

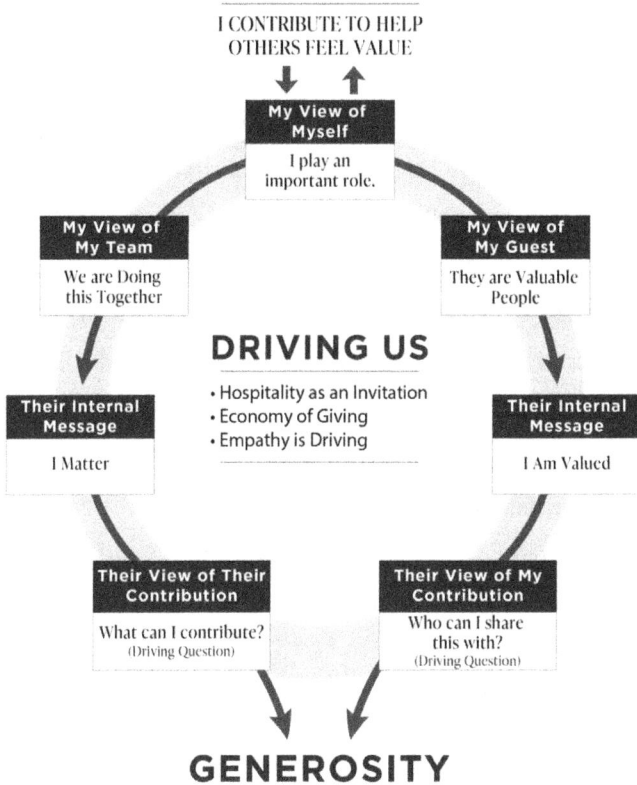

I CONTRIBUTE TO HELP
OTHERS FEEL VALUE

My View of Myself
I play an important role.

My View of My Team
We are Doing this Together

My View of My Guest
They are Valuable People

DRIVING US

- Hospitality as an Invitation
- Economy of Giving
- Empathy is Driving

Their Internal Message
I Matter

Their Internal Message
I Am Valued

Their View of Their Contribution
What can I contribute?
(Driving Question)

Their View of My Contribution
Who can I share this with?
(Driving Question)

GENEROSITY

VIEW OF MY TEAM: WE ARE DOING THIS TOGETHER

As hosts, if making others feel valued by what we offer is our goal, we see the people around us, our collaborators, as doing something *with* us. We're doing this together.

As a lifetime member of the hospitality industry, I was thrilled when years ago, one of my heroes, Danny Meyer, founder of Union Square Hospitality Group, published his book *Setting the Table*. Having newly started my own hospitality company, I read the book cover to cover, scanning for insights. What immediately stood out was, where most organizations had their investors as their top priority, Danny flipped the ladder and said the employees were the top priority. What he understood was that by valuing employees, the customers would be the beneficiaries of better performance because the employees felt taken care of and, consequently, revenues would continue to increase, which would provide a return to the investors.

Especially in business settings, if I want my end user or customer to feel valued, with all the levels of personnel between me and them, I need that value to carry through the ranks of my team—we're doing this together. Like Danny recognized, the servers, bartenders, and cooks *have* to feel valued in order to fulfill the company mission of valuing customers.

As a catering company and venue owner, we work very closely with event planners. We provide catering and spaces, but the event planners are the maestros that meet with couples, hear their vision, and then pull together florists, photographers, invitation makers, hotels for families, bands for dancing, and caterers for food to execute that vision. It's a dizzying scope of work.

Having worked with literally hundreds of event planners over the last eighteen years, one of the things I can tell immediately is whether an event planner values their team. Not just the team on their staff, but the team of vendors they've assembled to serve *their* clients.

Working events in Los Angeles, we are often serving a high-profile or celebrity clientele. In the name of pleasing those clients, some planners make the lethal mistake of thinking they will achieve the trophy of a successful event for their clients by berating their team of vendors into excellence.

Lisa Vorce isn't one of those planners. Her list of clients reads like a who's who from the titans of film, music, and professional sports. I will never forget the first event we catered with Lisa in the home of John Legend and Chrissy Teigen. As our team arrived, I braced myself for the heat that I've seen come from event settings like that.

Lisa was as kind as could be and cool as a cucumber. She's intuitive enough to know that when hourly-paid servers walk into the private home of a recognized icon to work…it's unsettling.

A server with even the slightest degree of humility and self-awareness is going to feel nervous. Who wouldn't with Quincy Jones sitting on the flipping couch? Far from putting our servers on edge, she put them at ease. She's smart enough to know that if she wants to make her world-renowned clients feel valued, the best way to achieve that is to make the staff that's serving them feel valued as well.

That's the compelling cause and effect of valuing others. Making others feel valued isn't void of self-interest. It isn't some altruistic, unrealistic forfeiting of our interests. It's actually *the path* to our interests. It's *good* for business. Lisa knows that, and so does Delta Airlines.

Delta knows that the thousands of people who make decisions about which airline to fly are going to be directly influenced by their experience with the people on the phone, the baggage handlers, the staff at the gate, and the flight attendants on the plane. The leaders of the organization know that when the Delta staff participates *with* the company to accomplish its goals, they grow revenue and stay at the top of the competition.

Let's move to the next phase on the left side of the cycle:

THE VIRTUOUS CYCLE OF GENEROSITY

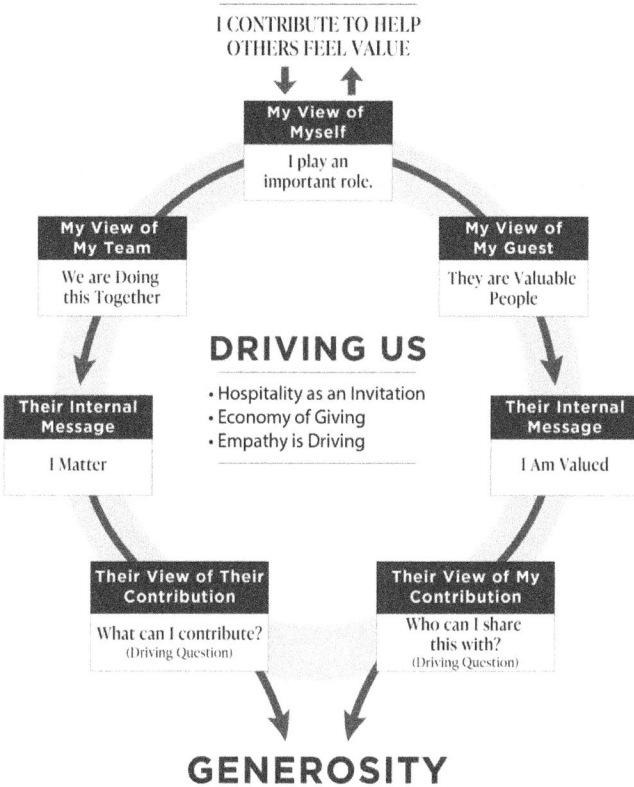

I CONTRIBUTE TO HELP
OTHERS FEEL VALUE

My View of Myself
I play an important role.

My View of My Team
We are Doing this Together

My View of My Guest
They are Valuable People

DRIVING US

- Hospitality as an Invitation
- Economy of Giving
- Empathy is Driving

Their Internal Message
I Matter

Their Internal Message
I Am Valued

Their View of Their Contribution
What can I contribute?
(Driving Question)

Their View of My Contribution
Who can I share this with?
(Driving Question)

GENEROSITY

MY TEAM'S INTERNAL MESSAGE: I MATTER

When people feel like they're doing something *with* us, as opposed to for us, they sense a critical internal message: I matter.

No one wants to feel like they matter to us more than our children. And when I engage our kids in doing something important, together with me, their hearts swell with a sense of pride. As a parent of three, who is sometimes frayed at the edges from working hard to lead a business while being a present father, I can feel the temptation to focus on the outcome and just get the job done. Friday night is pizza and movie night at our house. Most Fridays I come home excited to make pizza with the kids and settle down to a family movie after a long week of work.

But some weeks, by the time Friday comes around, I'm out of gas. On those nights it can be hard to wait for my six-year-old daughter to slowly roll out the dough with her hands and try unsuccessfully to throw it in the air. I can feel the words "let me do it" wanting to erupt out of me. But I can see her come alive when I check my need to get to the finish line and have the patience to show her we're making a fun dinner together. Even with making pizza, when I set my intention to make my kids feel valued, I see my role as a father as important, and I see my kids as doing something *with* me. And when I show up that way, I feel more at peace with myself, confident in my parenting, and my kids feel seen and consequently grounded in love. They know they matter. Even in those little private moments, I can tell in some small way, I've made the world better.

Let's move to the bottom left of the cycle.

THE VIRTUOUS CYCLE OF GENEROSITY

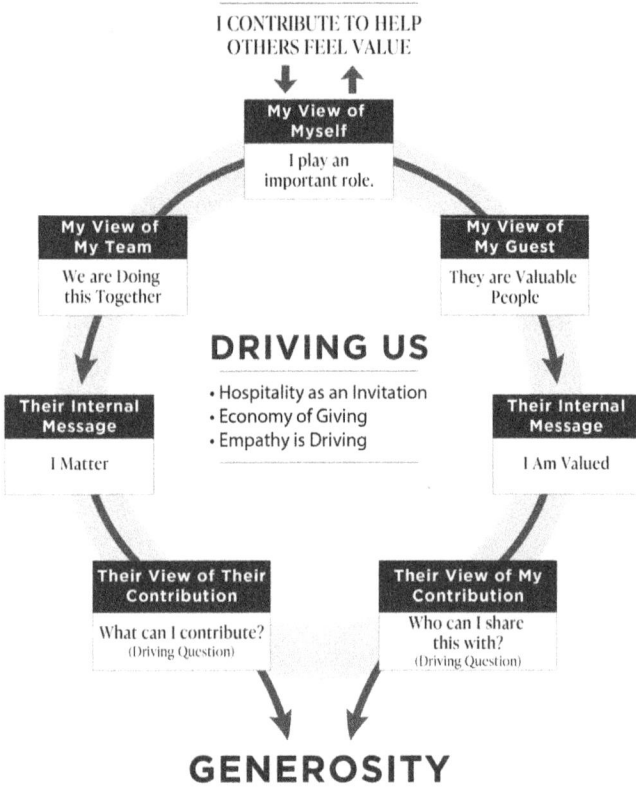

I CONTRIBUTE TO HELP
OTHERS FEEL VALUE

My View of Myself

I play an
important role.

My View of My Team

We are Doing
this Together

My View of My Guest

They are Valuable
People

DRIVING US

- Hospitality as an Invitation
- Economy of Giving
- Empathy is Driving

Their Internal Message

I Matter

Their Internal Message

I Am Valued

Their View of Their Contribution

What can I contribute?
(Driving Question)

Their View of My Contribution

Who can I share
this with?
(Driving Question)

GENEROSITY

VIEW OF THEIR WORK AND DRIVING
QUESTION: WHAT CAN I CONTRIBUTE?

When we as hosts have set our intention to value others with what we offer, we see ourselves as doing something important and our collaborators as working together *with* us in our efforts. When that's how we see our collaborators, they can feel that they are seen in that light. Their view of themselves *and* the work is that both matter. And when collaborators feel like they matter, they begin to ask a question that changes the game:

What can I contribute?

They start to think of ways they can go the extra mile, offer the extra idea, or rally the extra effort. When our collaborators start asking what they can contribute, it lands them in generosity. They're not just generous with their efforts, they're generous in how they treat others. And creativity begins to flow.

This is where the magic condition of the whole being greater than the sum of its parts begins to manifest. Something better emerges by the conditions we've created. It's progress by multiplication, instead of addition. Generosity is like a superhighway to creative flow, and as creative beings, when more than one person starts tapping into creative flow with a tone of discovery, something bigger than just one person's ideas starts to appear.

When people start asking what they can contribute, how they can help, they feel the permission of *what if?* It creates the condition for imagination, and any entrepreneur, artist, child at play, therapist, teacher, or couple navigating an impasse will tell you when imagination is welcome, something beautiful emerges.

As a musician, I've got a lot of friends that have made music their life's work. I shared my story of hoping for a record deal, only to be told I should lean into a career in hospitality. The implied conclusion was that while I had seen some momentum in my music, a safer bet was a skill set that tapped into the natural gifts I had that stood out as extraordinary. I've written some songs and can play and sing okay, but some of my closest friends have a gift for music that is from a different universe.

My dear friend and groomsman in our wedding, Busbee, who passed away way too early, was one of the most prolific songwriters I've ever known. It was like he intuitively understood how the architecture of songs works and could generate a hit in a couple of hours. From his song "Try," that the artist P!nk covered, to songs covered by Maren Morris, Rascal Flatts, and Lady Antebellum, whatever he wrote just worked. My friend Tom Crouch, who plays lead guitar for the Jonas

Brothers, can make his guitar and his voice find melodies that make you feel something deep. My brothers from another mother, Jonas and Brock, have both written songs that have literally *millions* of downloads.

It would be easy to compare and despair at my perceived mediocrity in an area of passion that has been with me since I was born. Yet all those guys have generously invited me into the musical creative process with them. They understand how creative flow works and know that while skill has a seat at the table, when they create the conditions for someone else to contribute, something else beautiful might be discovered.

As a Santa Cruz native, raised among redwoods and waves, adjusting to living in the city has been hard. After nearly two decades of building the business, we were able to get a vacation home in Montana where we can escape the noise of LA life and return to nature. As I write this during a beautiful Montana autumn, Brock and I have just finished writing a song together that we love. He was generous, invited me to contribute, and a song we both created was better than the one we would have written alone.

I always find so much encouragement in the way Bono, the lead singer of U2, refers to this process. Dozens of times in interviews he's referenced that alone: that the four members of U2 might not be the best at their individual musical skill. But when they come together and contribute what they have to offer, the whole is greater than the sum of its parts. And forty years later, they're still creating music and the world sings along.

As a host, when you treat your collaborators generously, they *look* for ways to contribute. They feel permission to tap into their own creativity and imagination, and the virtuous cycle spins, creating life-giving energy. Conversely, when this is your show and your collaborators feel like a cog in your wheel, they look for entertainment on their phones in the momentary gaps.

Let's look at what happens to those who receive what we're offering in this virtuous cycle.

THE VIRTUOUS CYCLE CONTINUES

Mirror neurons teach us that what is inside us creates mimicked responses from those on the outside. That's the power of the virtuous cycle. We can *affect* how others respond, bringing the best out of them, just by setting our intention to value them with what we offer. It isn't a guaranteed outcome. People have bad days, they misread us, or they may be too preoccupied by their own stories to read anything other than themselves.

But for the most part, whether we are receiving a product, mission, service, dinner, or advice, when people or companies, as hosts, intend for us to feel valued by what they offer, we're drawn to them.

Look at the top right side of the cycle.

THE VIRTUOUS CYCLE OF GENEROSITY

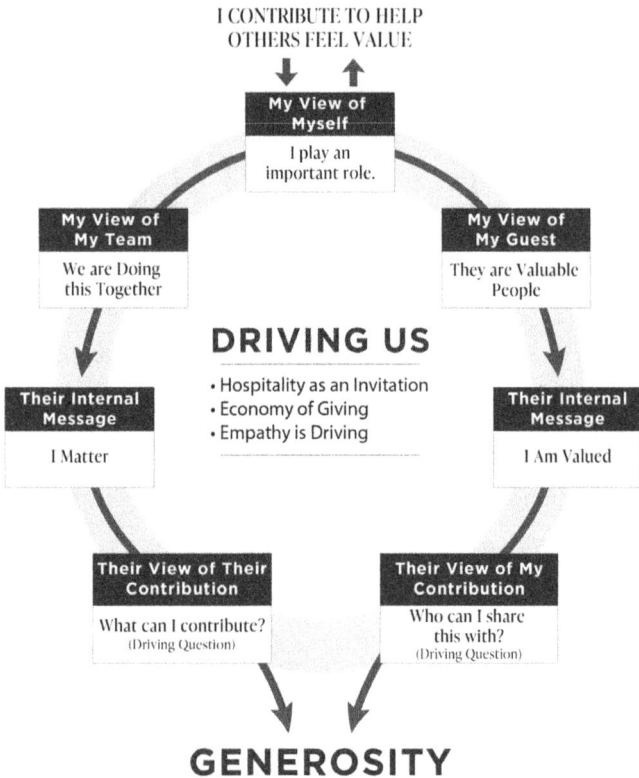

I CONTRIBUTE TO HELP
OTHERS FEEL VALUE

My View of Myself

I play an important role.

My View of My Team

We are Doing this Together

My View of My Guest

They are Valuable People

DRIVING US

- Hospitality as an Invitation
- Economy of Giving
- Empathy is Driving

Their Internal Message

I Matter

Their Internal Message

I Am Valued

Their View of Their Contribution

What can I contribute?
(Driving Question)

Their View of My Contribution

Who can I share this with?
(Driving Question)

GENEROSITY

VIEW OF MY GUESTS (OR RECEIVERS): THEY ARE VALUABLE PEOPLE

When hosts have set their intention to value others, they see whoever is receiving their offerings as valuable people. That may sound simplistic, but in our programmed reflex of doing laser-fast assessments of where people rank in our conscious and subconscious hierarchies, to see value in everyone we encounter is actually quite revolutionary.

I mentioned my experience at eating at a hot LA restaurant and feeling immediate disdain from the hostess. We had barely spoken two sentences—how could I already sense that I wasn't valued? Because I didn't have a reservation or a recognized name or a VIP pass or whatever social currency is valued, I lacked value in her eyes. Our lowest human tendencies are susceptible to ranking our fellow humans. It's playground dynamics that we have to leave behind.

People and companies that see inherent value in others create beautiful outcomes in their worlds. It's not that they don't have boundaries or different levels of access or rules of engagement, but as the cycle illustrates, when they see those that receive their work as valuable, the receivers internalize a message that they're valued. And they respond in kind.

Let's look at the middle of the right side of the model:

THE VIRTUOUS CYCLE OF GENEROSITY

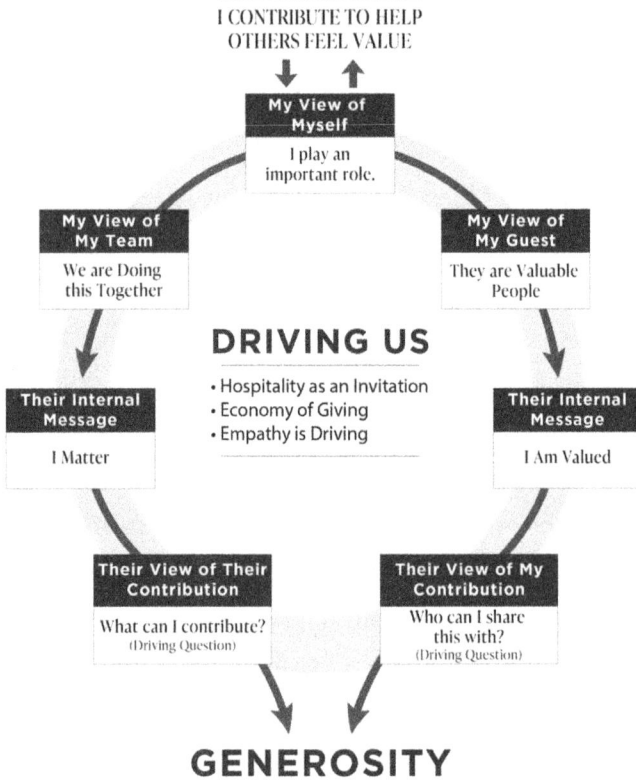

I CONTRIBUTE TO HELP
OTHERS FEEL VALUE

My View of Myself

I play an important role.

My View of My Team

We are Doing this Together

My View of My Guest

They are Valuable People

DRIVING US

- Hospitality as an Invitation
- Economy of Giving
- Empathy is Driving

Their Internal Message

I Matter

Their Internal Message

I Am Valued

Their View of Their Contribution

What can I contribute?
(Driving Question)

Their View of My Contribution

Who can I share this with?
(Driving Question)

GENEROSITY

MY CLIENTS' (OR RECEIVERS') INTERNAL MESSAGE: I AM VALUED

When people set out to make us valued, it translates. We feel it. Have you ever left a conversation with someone that made you feel valued? Maybe you felt seen, understood, or empathized with. Maybe you felt respected. We've all heard the stories of high-profile people that simply remembered someone's name. We all experience value in different ways, but the remembrance of those encounters stays with us.

Feeling valued is universally compelling. It's something all of us want. It's hardwired in our DNA. We can't help ourselves; it quenches something our souls thirst for. People and organizations that seek to provide something we're all seeking have looked deeper than the level of our wants; they've mined down to the level of our *needs*.

We might want a lot of things in our lives—great features on our phone, interesting content, good benefits packages, or new adventures—but we need to feel valued. That's what keeps us coming back. In his book *Start with Why,* Simon Sinek compares Apple's iPhone to other Android phones. He notes that based on features and functionality alone, the iPhone is arguably *not* the best phone. Yet none of us have ever seen a line out the door to get the latest Samsung phone. Why is that? He notes that Apple has mined down deeper into the levels of what people *need* to feel in their relationship with a company's products. Apple asks better questions about not only what people want from their products and service experience but what people need, thereby keeping their "why" as a driving force in their operation. And as a result they've created more than a list of products; they've created a movement for how we interact with technology.

From the moment we take our first breath, those early messages of value shape our lives. Those that feel seen and valued in those crucial formative years form secure attachments with their caregivers, which becomes the launchpad for showing up securely in the world. Tragically, those that missed out on those messages form insecure attachments and have to spend a lifetime finding what was lost.

Value extraction is a human reflex. But when we never pause to reflect on how value is actually *created*, we take and take, until there's nothing left, as Shel Silverstein's *The Giving Tree* so profoundly illustrates. A tree willingly shares what it can offer the boy in the story, and the boy willingly extracts the value being offered. But the boy never pauses to ponder, *how did the tree actually come to be?* He takes and takes, until a stump is all that's left of the tree. There is nothing left to take.

Value extraction never balanced by value *creation* creates a barren wasteland of lost relationships, lost customers, lost partnerships, and lost natural resources. When we set out to feel valued by looking for this emotion *from* others, the program breaks. Trying to extract this need from others makes them feel taken from. And as we learned from our very first playground sagas, we all hate it when someone takes something from us. We want something, we don't get it, so we try taking it, and when we're denied, collectively we spin in a vicious cycle of conflict.

When we set our sights on making others feel valued, it shapes everything we do. It shapes *how* we write the benefits package and how we hold a conversation. It isn't any one thing. It's the *tone* of our offering, more than the content itself. We can offer a friend a burrito or a five-course meal, a download of insightful advice, or a quiet listening ear; it doesn't matter. When we set our intention to make someone feel valued with the burrito we made them, it comes through.

The world's largest medical association of musculoskeletal specialists, the American Academy of Orthopedic Surgeons, has tens of thousands of members. They know that together, they do the important work of fixing our bodies when they break down. In thinking about their patients, tapping into the imaginative ideas that emerge when we create virtuous cycles of generosity, they came up with a creative way to make one of their primary clients, children, feel valued.

They came up with the idea to have the surgeons come to their annual conference a day early, so they could build new and safe versions of the place where many of our younger bones break: the playground. Surgeons wanted to look for ways they could contribute beyond their everyday work. As a result, trading scalpels for hammers, a community of doctors have donated time and resources to build playgrounds all over America, for no other reason than they wanted to find ways to make the world safer for their patients.

They could have focused solely on value extraction and concluded that more broken bones means more clients. But by tapping into the virtuous cycle of valuing their clients, they make their clients feel like more than mere users of their service. The patients feel valued by the physicians that are hosting them for critical surgeries, and the organization keeps growing from the loyal following of its valued patients.

Now let's follow further down the bottom right side of the cycle.

THE VIRTUOUS CYCLE OF GENEROSITY

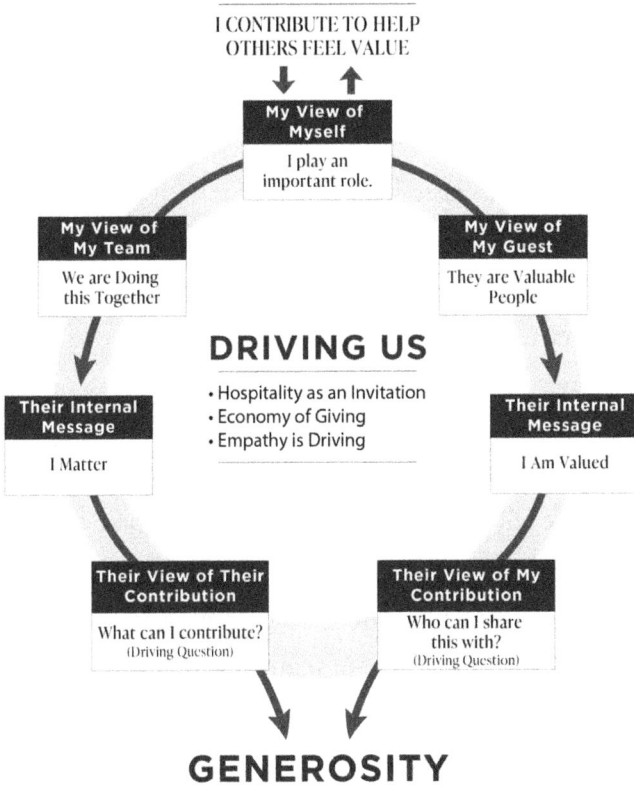

I CONTRIBUTE TO HELP OTHERS FEEL VALUE

My View of Myself
I play an important role.

My View of My Team
We are Doing this Together

My View of My Guest
They are Valuable People

DRIVING US
- Hospitality as an Invitation
- Economy of Giving
- Empathy is Driving

Their Internal Message
I Matter

Their Internal Message
I Am Valued

Their View of Their Contribution
What can I contribute?
(Driving Question)

Their View of My Contribution
Who can I share this with?
(Driving Question)

GENEROSITY

MY CLIENTS' (OR RECEIVERS') VIEW OF MY CONTRIBUTION AND DRIVING QUESTION: WHO CAN I SHARE THIS WITH?

When people feel valued by what they've received, they start asking a really exciting question: *Who can I share this with? Who can I bring along?*

They may be our customers and clients or they may be our friends or loved ones. When our craftsmanship, creation, or offering is presented with the intention of making people feel valued, they feel it. And the universal response to that feeling? They express their gratitude to us, and they want to share the experience with someone else.

Whether we tell everyone we know how a company or person treated us, invite someone to come with us the next time we visit an establishment, or just keep coming back for more, when we feel taken care of, we want to share that with others. When we feel valued, we don't have to be asked to share our experience; it's a natural outflow.

Viewing what we or our business contribute as an opportunity to host with hospitality applies to any industry, even auto mechanics. There's a unique kind of misery that comes with car trouble. Our routines are decimated when we're left stranded and held hostage by the mechanic's schedule or inability to find the problem. As we all know, finding a reliable mechanic is like the holy grail; once you've found one, you never let go.

Our mechanic Hrant is unlike any mechanic I've ever met. Somehow after fifteen years of taking our cars there, his process hasn't deviated once. It starts with him always answering the phone, "Hrant Auto, go ahead" and then asking a series of questions. He gives you a specific time to bring your car in, starts the diagnostic when he says he's going to, tells you what time he'll call with a diagnosis, calls you at the time he said he would, has your car ready when he said it would be ready, walks you through how the problem was fixed, notes the little things he went ahead and fixed without charging, and outlines the maintenance steps that should be taken in the future, finishing his service with his consistent "Sign here and here."

Every.
Single.
Time.

He values his customers like no other mechanic I've ever encountered. We all know what's often pinned up on the walls of a mechanic's garage. You can't even see Hrant's walls; they're literally *covered* with thank-you notes.

Thank-you notes?
Who writes thank-you notes to their *mechanic?*

Hrant's customers. That's how taken care of they feel. It's that natural reflex we see that happens when people feel valued. From time to time, I'll look and read what was said. And it's always the same thing:

"Thank you so much" and…
"I'm going to tell everyone I know about your service."

In fifteen years of taking our cars there, I've never once seen an empty stall. He's valuing his customers in an uncommon way for his trade, and his customers return the favor by generously spreading the good news.

When we make people feel valued, they become our salespeople and our evangelists. Delta Airlines has been voted the best workforce in the US airline industry multiple years running. There's nowhere in their customer correspondence where they ask me to be an ambassador for them or where they mention a referral program where I get a discount if I refer a friend. Their staff just makes me feel like a human who's being taken care of. Probably because *they* feel like a human who's being take care of. And as a result, I tell everyone I know that I think Delta is the best airline and that I'll fly a longer route if it means I can get to my destination with them.

As meaning makers and tellers of stories, we humans naturally want to share our enjoyable experiences. It's why we invite people to our birthday parties or bring our friends to the places where we're "regulars." When we feel seen and valued, something cellular rises up inside us that says, "I want to share this with someone." It's not marketing, it's biology. There's something automatic in our response that wants to bring people along with us to share that experience, which, like the doctors building playgrounds, is also a generous act.

Even people with massive public profiles can position their messaging in a way that makes their followers feel valued. And doing so grows their engagement.

Outside of the typical business, even in the one-way dialogue of sharing on our platforms, the tone of the content can set out to value the followers. My wife Nicole follows the social media posts of an author, podcaster, and thought leader named Jen Hatmaker. Besides her posts being hilarious and beautifully authentic, one of the main things she does is make her viewers feel valued. She has this beautiful way of knowing who she's talking to, while seeing them, and making them feel like she gets them and they matter. I can tell when Nicole reads her posts, she feels known and cared for in an inspiring way by someone she's never met.

Guess what Nicole does with those posts?
She *shares* them.
With me, for one.
Jen Hatmaker and I don't have a lot in common.
She's a mom with five kids who talks about everything from her mama-bear heart to her hair.
I am not exactly her target audience.

Yet Nicole shares those posts with me because she feels understood by Jen's words, and that makes her feel valued. And she wants me to share in that experience. She knows we become closer when I experience the things that make her feel uniquely noticed.

Making people feel valued doesn't just build our brands, it builds our legacies, as those we have valued return to express gratitude for the role we've played in their lives. Think about the stories we share about our favorite teacher or professor. It's rarely because those educators blew our minds with their mastery of a subject. Usually, the stories we share about the teachers that shaped us center around the fact that, in a classroom full of people, those teachers had the ability to make us feel uniquely valued.

As a high schooler from Santa Cruz, I spent way too much time surfing and not enough time doing my homework. In typical teenage fashion, I dismissed the reality that high school was wrapping up and my college prospects of tomorrow would be shaped by my actions of today. Sometime during my junior year, I was on a surf trip down the coast of California, and from my surfboard perch, looked up from the waves and saw buildings sprawled on a coastal mountainside.

I asked my buddy what the buildings were.
"That's Pepperdine University."
"I have *got* to go there."

The problem was my grades up to that point were mediocre at best and Pepperdine was hard to get into. I got my act together the rest of my junior and senior years and begged Pepperdine to notice my improvement. They granted me conditional admission, along with thirty-nine other applicants that were late to the game. We attended a two-month probationary period before our freshman year called Summer Bridge.

I wanted to do right by the opportunity and needed to pass the classes to be granted admission, but the freedom of my newfound independence left me a little rambunctious in the classroom. Basically, I was a disruptive pain in the ass for my professor. He was constantly trying to get me to settle down, wait my turn to speak, consider others, and all around just mellow out. He had every right to fail me and jeopardize my ability to go to college. Instead, he told me that if I wanted to pass his class, I needed to meet him at the university pool every day, one hour before class. And there he and I would swim laps for an hour.

A fifty-something-year-old professor saw something in me beyond my bad behavior, and donning swim trunks and goggles, invested an hour of his time, every single day, to make me feel like I mattered. He didn't sit on the deck, watching me swim under his command. He swam *with* me. His sage idea worked. I arrived at class exhausted and blissfully calm after having swam laps for an hour. And when the stories of teachers that shaped us come up, I share with every single person I can how Doug Cazort made me feel important, and I'll never forget him.

The words we summon when we feel valued are generous words. Whether they're typed in a review, spoken at the table, shared online, or shouted from the rooftops, when businesses and friends, doctors and teachers, attorneys and airlines, teachers and baristas, mayors and mothers make us feel like we matter to them, we talk about it. We can't help ourselves.

This is *virtuous* hospitality. It's a virtuous cycle of generosity. It begins when we recognize our role as hosts and commit to extend the virtue of hospitality by making those around us feel valued. Our collaborators ask what they can contribute, our receivers ask who they can bring along, and a beautiful chain reaction that includes everyone involved in what we're offering begins to spin and make the world a better place.

Life itself is a product of relationship.

From the human level to the molecular level, literally everything that lives forms from the relationship of two or more forces coming together. That's why hospitality is existential—and urgent. It creates the conditions where relationships flourish. There's a word we have for something that grows without a symbiotic relationship and spreads to its community of neighbors: cancer. With its voracious appetite for its own expansion, cancer devours and chokes out all other life around it. We watch with horror as what once flourished withers away while the creative life is destroyed by the inhospitable stranger who wants only to take for itself. It's a cycle that is in every way vicious.

We're in this thing called relationship whether we like it or not. And relationships will forever need solutions for mutual coexistence.

We have a choice. We can cling only to what we're owed, in the name of our sole interests, taking for ourselves, blind to what the other person, community, gender, generation, political party, nation, or planet is equally owed. And we can watch as our unchecked entitlement chokes out the life of what could flourish.

Or we can acknowledge the cosmic patterns, like breathing, where you have to give away what you want to receive, extend hospitality by valuing each other, and watch nature in motion as she does her beautiful work.

PART FOUR

CHAPTER NINE

THE GRIP MATTERS

Once we identify the cycles operating, what do we do so we see more virtuous interactions and less vicious ones? Thankfully, there actually is a framework that when followed leads to generous encounters.

The structure of the framework is a combination of four principles, each accompanied by a couple of practices that help move the principles from concepts to habits. Like any good human design, there are steps to take and behaviors that will follow. But before we dive into the framework, we need to understand how to hold the framework. The grip matters.

If I asked you to speak about your happiness, memories, or your future plans and then asked you "Are those *real?*" you might find that an odd question. Of course, they're real. But if you were on the operating table and you asked a surgeon to locate your plans or your happiness and place them on a table, they would obviously view that as an equally odd request.

Real things can be invisible.

We've used words like "atmosphere," "environment," and "energy" to describe the feelings the cycles create. When we use the word "cycle," we intuitively associate it with movement. So, as we speak about the vicious and virtuous *cycles*, what is actually moving? It's that ever-present but always invisible concept called energy. The label isn't important. What matters is that we acknowledge the energy that exists in our interactions is real *and* it's invisible. You couldn't grab the energy and put it in a petri dish, but you can listen to words and watch body language, which leads to behavioral choices, and cite with certainty that something is moving between us within our interactions.

In this book, we've spent some time exploring the energetic chain reactions that are sparked by our intentions. And we've noticed how different the experiences can be, based on the initial motivation that fires up the cycle. In a word, we've explored the "what."

So now to the "how."

But before we jump into "how" we can have more generosity, less entitlement, more virtuous and less vicious interactions, a critical reflection is needed. We need to reflect on how to *hold* the how. I know that sounds like some woefully broken hai-ku, but something that's taken me a lifetime to learn thus far is that the grip matters. It matters just as much as what we're holding. Call it a map or steps or a framework or a collection of concepts that leads to our better outcome; the point is we might love holding the tools that get us where we want to go. But like any good golf coach will tell you, how you hold the club makes all the difference.

I'm going to show you a framework for how to spend more time on the virtuous cycle of generosity and less time on the vicious cycle of entitlement. But before we dive in, I want to offer insight on the grip you should use while holding this tool. The best way to hold frameworks like these is with the hands of paradox.

Franciscan monk Richard Rohr said it best:

"Reality is paradoxical and complementary. Non-dual thinking is the highest level of consciousness."

The craving for clarity and absolutes is hardwired into our

human instinct for survival. Knowing how to protect themselves from a saber-toothed tiger or light a fire kept our ancestors safely tethered to all-or-nothing thinking. The problem is that today, wisdom, relationships, growth, life, reality itself is found in paradox. We eat food from the paradox of death and life. A plant grows, it dies, goes to seed, falls to the ground, a new plant rises, and fruit comes. As life coach Jay Shetty has pointed out, early-stage romance, or what we call "the spark," is itself a paradox of attraction and stress. "I'm crazy about her. I'm stressed that she's not as crazy about me." Muscles grow from the paradox of damage and healing. And when it comes to the realm of frameworks in our interactions, there is a beautiful paradox that calls for our surrender: design and mystery.

I first started thinking about the paradox of design and mystery in the world of events. After thirty-five years in the hospitality industry, I've catered literally thousands of weddings, birthdays, and milestone moments. And because the nature of these events is that they are urgently special, no effort is spared in designing every detail of the experience. Having been blessed to work with some of the world's top event producers, it can be dizzying to behold the sheer volume of details that go into a thoughtfully curated event, well beyond just the catering. In concert with the client, world-class event producers have literally designed *everything*. It isn't just the big-ticket items like the flowers, décor, music, and menu. It's the less obvious items, like how the sun's arc will affect photography or the type of hand towels guests will use in the restroom or something meaningful left in the car by the valet so you feel the afterglow as you drive away.

I've witnessed phenomenal event design in action firsthand. In whatever American city hosts the Super Bowl, the NFL builds a "pop-up" hospitality center called NFL House that's open the week of the game. The center hosts all of the NFL's VIPs, guests, players, coaches, and corporate sponsors. When Super Bowl LVI (that's fifty-six for the Roman numerically challenged like me) came to Los Angeles, our catering company was awarded the contract to cater for the event. Over the course of Super Bowl week, thousands of people, all highly valued by the league, would come through NFL House, which was open twelve hours a day. The scale was dizzying. Watching the creative agency who had been hired to execute the event, to transform four stories of an industrial building into a world-class experience, was a sight to behold. From hanging wallpaper to building coffee shops, juice bars, souvenir shops, comfortable boardrooms for meetings, and game rooms for the kids, from installing lounges that looked like old Hollywood Art Deco to installing airport level security, there was seemingly no limit to the details that needed to be designed. For our company, the requirement of delivering nine different menus per day (breakfast, lunch, dinner, and three snack menus) per floor, with no items repeated throughout the week, and building satellite kitchens on each floor with a headquarter kitchen across the street required planning and design that would bend the mind of the most seasoned event professionals. After the collective effort of literally hundreds of people, watching the guests come in and be thrilled by the long anticipated Super Bowl festivities was so deeply rewarding.

Without question, great events are designed.
And here's the thing:

The *best* events have something no designer could have orchestrated. It's an element no one could plan *but everyone feels*. It's a mystery, the magic stardust that came from all our efforts. I've spent a lifetime studying the architecture of memorable moments and know the "it" factor that is the difference between a great event and the best events is a magic stardust that no professional can bottle. It's a mysterious, unspoken buzz that awakens something in the hearts of everyone there, that invites their second self—the person enjoying the experience so much that they can't help but *notice* themselves having the time of their lives—to emerge. If you're an event professional or musician, public speaker or professor, or anyone who plans then delivers, you know the alchemy of which I speak. The magic that will not be mastered. We can cross every "t" and dot every "i"; we can rehearse the chords and finalize the timelines; we can know our lines and recite them verbatim, but sometimes the best-designed execution, despite our best efforts, lacks that mystery that makes the things we remember beautiful memories. But when we feel the buzz that won't be captured but can't be ignored, we never forget it.

Design and mystery.

Truth be told, I prefer design. I can study and learn and practice and forecast. I love the clarity and progress I feel when I've learned a new design. I can recognize and appreciate and anticipate once I know the design. I find design very much a chicken soup for my chaotic soul.

There are patterns that thoughtful seers, innovators, and designers have recognized and shared with us that have provided immeasurable help, insight, and progress. Human designs and patterns are literally everywhere.

Our hospitality company runs on a framework designed by entrepreneur Gino Wickman called EOS. I found ways to help identify new business ideas by using the formula introduced in the book *Blue Ocean Strategy.* I referenced earlier Jim Collins's groundbreaking framework shared in his book *Good to Great.* Charles Duhigg's *The Power of Habit,* on the cyclical patterns of habits, helped me break and form habits. Brené Brown's book *The Gifts of Imperfection* showed me ten "gifts" that help me be more wholehearted. The Enneagram's eight personality types have revolutionized how I see myself and others. Most of us know someone whose life was saved by following Bill Wilson's Twelve Steps. And whether you credit him or not, Joseph Campbell's recognition of the pattern in the hero's journey has infiltrated how the world over tells stories.

Designs in behavior and thought matter. And they help us. They shape our actions and give us something to sink our teeth into as we pursue the sometimes nebulous "better."

AND...

Wisdom would say that, in the realm of relationships and the interactions that make up a life, a promise of a formula that "guarantees" better results would accurately be called snake oil. Try as we might, life cannot be controlled. And that can frustrate the "can-do/by my bootstraps" mindset that many of us in the US operate with. As the American Zen author Adyashanti says: "The more you try to control life and others, the more out of control you feel."[5] We might agree that human patterns and design are everywhere. Here is the harder side of the paradox to hold: mystery is also everywhere. And to the human mind, especially the Western one, the concept of mystery is sometimes offensive.

The modern mindset of the West likes to believe that everything can be engineered. But *reality itself* is paradoxical. Death leads to new life. The more you fail, the more you are likely to succeed. If you want to hold on to something, let it go. And when considering growth, there is design we can learn, and there is unknowable mystery behind growth.

I am not hedging or giving a disclaimer on what I know will be the results of your interactions if you put what I'm about to share into practice. I believe wholeheartedly in the framework I'm going to present in the following pages. I've spent thirty-five years living the proof of concept.

But here we come to another confession:

---

5 Adyashanti. *Falling Into Grace: Insights on the End of Suffering.* Sounds True, 2013.

There is a nuance that has also taken me most of my life to see. Sometimes the *urgency* directed at pursuing growth and change is the very thing that needs to "grow and change." My sense of urgency has helped me; it has helped me accomplish building a better marriage, a better family life, and a better business; it has picked me up when I'm down and kept me going when there was nothing left in the tank. It's also been affirmed by those around me. So, when this urgency has been the subject of criticism or a source of conflict, I've felt protective of what feels like a core aspect of my identity.

In the spirit of confession, I must admit that there have been times I've discovered frameworks and human patterns that resonate with me and then become obsessed with strictly following every precept. It's like the formula becomes a bat to beat myself and others with into fundamental adherence. And when faced with understandable resistance from others, I interpret it as quenching my fire for growth, and my defenses instantly flare, revealing my all-or-nothing, duality-based thinking. "I don't want to put out my fire! Champions are relentless in their pursuit of better! I've accomplished what I have by being uncompromising!"

Yes. True.

If you resonate with being a highly motivated person, valued for your drive, and have suffered the confusion of having the impact of your drive on others be a source of conflict, take a breath, stay curious, and keep reading.

As I quoted in the introduction, Alan Watts once said, "A pin can feel everything except the prick of its own point." And sometimes the growth opportunity for us is to reflect on the pins we use to tack up our latest process to achieve better. In no way am I espousing complacency. I have the words "a rage to master" tattooed on my wrist. My desire to master myself and pursue mastery in several areas goes beyond an urge; it's a rage. *And* I've found my fire is channeled into much more effective results when I embrace mystery and don't try to force everything.

I watched this beautifully displayed during an Amazon special that featured a conversation between NBA star Draymond Green and scientist and author Deepak Chopra. Green is known for being the unapologetic fire-starter of the multi-NBA champion Golden State Warriors. He's also known for allowing the fire of his temper to cause unintended destruction to himself and his teammates. In the most sage, gentle way, Chopra didn't tell Green to tone it down or to not care about winning. He validated the driving passion for excellence that Green held in his heart. He just tweaked how he held it so he could be more effective. The grip matters.

Brian Chesky, CEO of Airbnb, cites the paradox of "belonging *anywhere*" as the mission that drives Airbnb. I mentioned that I first started thinking about the paradox of design and mystery when pondering what makes a great event. While no one can engineer that mysterious, invisible buzz the most memorable events have, if I were to use one word that everyone was feeling at the best events, it would be: present.

With the rise of Eastern wisdom bringing a needed ingredient to our culture's recipe for life, terms like mindfulness and presence have become common recently. But we should be on guard that familiarity with the terms doesn't breed contempt. "Presence" is not some esoteric concept reserved for the aspiring urban mystic. Simply put, being present is the opposite of being distracted. When we are present, our minds and our bodies are in the same place. Who of us hasn't experienced the strain of having our body do one thing while our mind is utterly elsewhere?

As a father of three children, I'm often approached by older parents who look at me with our kids and wistfully advise, "Cherish these days. They're gone too fast."

I sometimes wonder if that is the regret of distraction speaking, a longing to return to those moments and be present in them. Of doing something important, like life, but being driven by something urgent, like work, and missing out on key moments as a result. I'm often sadly baffled when I'm out in the world and see how many of us are staring at our phones, ignorantly presuming that a life is made up of what we watch, as opposed to what we do. I know of no greater thief of our attention than our phones. They literally consume our awareness.

Life is a collection of moments—mostly mundane, and a few of them deeply special. My career has given me the privilege of helping design those special ones. And the irony of special moments is that they are hardwired to preoccupy us with distraction. Because in the planning of them, we're thinking about a million little details. We're not just thinking, we're being *driven* by the details. Micro details like which forks to use, and macro details like starting on time and hoping it doesn't rain. And by some miracle of mindset, as the moment of planning ends and the event begins, we're supposed to shut off the NASCAR race of preparation that has been in our minds for months and just *be present in the moment*. It's a tall order, even for the most mentally disciplined of us.

Maslow's hierarchy of needs provides some explanation for this distraction. When my wife Nicole and I were first married, we both worked. I was a bartender, saving my cash tips in envelopes for our monthly budget, and doing occasional pop-up dinners for what would become roomforty. She was a corporate executive making nearly three times my income. Our combined earnings were still just enough to get by. As I mentioned in my origin story, when Nicole got pregnant with our first child, her intention was to return to work. And nine months later, when our sweet Sofia entered the world, Nicole took one look at her and said: "I can't go back to work."

It was sink-or-swim time. I was either going to abandon my entrepreneurial moonlighting and opt for as much financial security as I could find or go "all in" and figure out some way that this barely begun new business could provide for my family. To say I was preoccupied by economic survival is an understatement. Every conversation, every email, every phone call, *every minute* was a potential brick in the wall of safety I was trying to build around my family. The problem is, for first-time builders, construction projects are all-consuming. And the wall I was building wasn't just surrounding my family, it was surrounding me. Two kids later, and our business still far from an empire but safely providing a living,

Nicole looked at me, still utterly distracted by financial security, and said: "What are we doing?"

I was given the gift of a life partner who wanted nothing more than presence from me. It wasn't that she didn't appreciate a nice home over an apartment and a washing machine over a laundromat, but she didn't need those things at the expense of a present husband and father.

I was missing the very lives I was trying to provide for. My body would be at my son Dario's birthday party, but my mind was on my work, hoping the next deal would close. In no way am I minimizing how all-consuming the pressure to provide can be. That hierarchy of needs Maslow introduced teaches us that at the bottom of the hierarchy, our needs are physiological: food, water, shelter, clothing, sleep. As we move up toward the middle of the hierarchy, our needs change to love and belonging: family, friendship, intimacy, and a sense of connection. Once we've reached the top, our needs focus on reaching our potential for creativity and discovering our purpose. And you can't move up the hierarchy until the needs at each level are met.

What I'm confessing is that, long after I had climbed a few rungs on Maslow's hierarchy, I had cultivated the *habit* of being distracted. I was well on the way to losing what I could never get back: a chance to embrace and be present for the brutal but beautiful season that is having young children. I'm proud to say I've made some significant adjustments in my mindset and habits. Thanks to the gift of our third child, Giovanna, I've had a third chance to be much more present in her precious early years. While I know this season of cultivating the lives of our kids will end far too soon, today I drink the marrow of these moments, *even the mundane ones.*

We had our babies at home, and while Nicole is the unrivaled star in the process, I was privileged to play a distant second fiddle and pull each of our kids into this world. Watching them open their eyes for the first time, raising them, and then one day having to watch them leave is a mystery I can't fully understand. But if there's one thing I'm committed to, it's fighting to notice what we're doing together and giving them my attention, instead of letting it be stolen by an iPhone.

While there is a framework for steps we can take to exist on the virtuous cycle of generosity, the critical key is to be aware—to pay attention to what's driving us. Awareness, mindfulness, presence—they're all terms that are saying the same thing. Setting our intention to use what we've been given to value others, being aware of the gravitational pull to prove our value instead and then making a corrective adjustment is the crux of this work.

For those that can achieve presence and maintain the ability to observe themselves—aware of their thoughts and their actions being aligned—they reach beyond all the life designing we employ and tap into the mystery of what makes life moments memorable.

Relationships are like life, comprised of a million momentary interactions. And in these moments, we're often driven by a cellular need that is hardwired into our DNA: to be valued by others. And therein lies the invitation for how to hold the framework we're about to see.

But like any honest student and teacher of growth, I won't guarantee results. If you're present in these interactions, if you try to notice what's driving you, if you can "work the steps" while at the same time noticing your intention shifting from a proving energy to a valuing energy, you'll be tapping into the wisdom that reality is paradoxical and growth is a combination of design and mystery. I wholeheartedly believe you are going to like what you see. When it comes to frameworks, the grip matters. Hold this framework honoring the paradox of design and mystery. Now to the steps.

CHAPTER TEN

PRINCIPLE ONE: SPEAK THE GOOD

PRACTICE ONE: SPEAK KINDLY TO YOURSELF

The first principle to move from an energy that seeks to prove our value to an energy that values others is to speak the good. The negative bias of our minds programs us to see the bad, and consequently our words reflect this negative data. As we begin to program our minds to look for the good instead and then call out what we see, we move from being entitled to being generous. Growth and direction come from what we do, not from what we don't do. "Anti" corrects but it doesn't direct. It doesn't build. *But* if this step were to be framed in "anti" language, it would be: don't be a critic. The problem with that phrase as a principle is that we don't change our energy solely by *not* doing something. Like Charles Duhigg's brilliant habit hacks show us, willpower alone has scientifically proved incapable of changing behavior. We must replace what we stop doing with something we start doing. If we want to create virtuous cycles of generosity as opposed to vicious cycles of entitlement, we must stop being a critic, and when that urge or "cue" comes, replace our tendency toward criticism with a new routine of speaking the good. And the first recipient of that affirmation is ourselves.

My favorite place to have a meal is in a home. Our catering company roomforty was created by bringing restaurant-level services to the warmth of homes, before the creative wave of blending fine dining with fun, non-restaurant spaces became commonplace.

Nearly two decades later, we've catered in every type of venue, and now there is a large team of people that participate in making our clients' dream events come to life. But occasionally, I return to the place that started me on this wild ride in hospitality and host an intimate gathering all by myself in the homes of my friends. My favorite part of those nights is spreading my hosting wings and creating more than a menu—I get to create a conversation. When it comes to the meal, I involve everyone in the process and will have them join me in plating dishes or making cocktails. Everybody has a blast learning new tricks of the trade.

One of the most memorable of those gatherings was years ago at a friend's house in Nashville. The lasting memory isn't what happened at the event; it was actually the epiphany that came after the event and how that revelation became the starting point for moving from a vicious cycle to a virtuous one.

In an earlier chapter I referenced how my wife Nicole and I had been part of a small community of friends for over ten years. We came to the sad realization that we were spinning in the vicious cycle and ultimately decided to cut ties with the community. That conviction might sound noble, and to be sure it was the right decision, but make no mistake, it was brutal. We went from having a community of friends we saw multiple times a week to seeing no one. During the lonely vulnerability of that fragile season with no crew, I went to Nashville on two separate occasions to attend a marketing seminar as well as a therapy retreat center. Both of those experiences led to new friendships and new experiences with the people I met there. Nashville is a long way from LA, but my new friends were intentional in keeping the connection going. We could all travel, and I was relieved that, by all appearances, a fresh group of friends was forming for our family.

I booked a trip to return to Nashville and planned one of my hosted gatherings at a new friend's house. I pulled out the stops, served six courses of edible greatness paired with epic wines, after-dinner craft cocktails, and thoughtfully prepared questions to start honest dialogue. I love when conversations move beyond the surface into the authentic realm where connections are formed. I believe a meal is one of the most effective tools in accomplishing that type of connection, so I always want the gatherings I host to go well. But the stakes felt uncomfortably higher this time. These were new friendships, I was in a relationally bruised place, and I was longing for community. There was also an added element to make things a little more complicated: some of the new friends were "famous adjacent."

We've catered for US presidents, Jay-Z, Beyoncé, every other music titan I can think of, and a solid handful of movie stars. This crew wasn't in the same neighborhood of fame as those types, but they were only a few neighborhoods over. It wasn't household name fame, but enough where you could feel the influence differential between them and you. All this combined led to nerves I wasn't accustomed to on nights like this. And here's the confession: Yes, I wanted the evening to go well, but what I really wanted was for this group of people to like me. Wanting to be liked is an all-too-familiar, deeply insecure feeling. Like scratching an embarrassing itch, my knee-jerk reflex when I feel the uncomfortable urge of wanting to be liked is to show off.

As stand-up comic Brian Regan's hilarious bit on the "me monster" so poignantly exposes, showing off is something we've become accustomed to. We don't usually call it that; we just find ourselves thinking, "geez…that person took up so much space in the conversation." But here's the part that feels like torture: now that I've recognized the vicious and the virtuous cycles operating in me and have set my intention to value others instead of proving my value, if I start showing off, I catch myself doing it, every single time.

As I did a postmortem on this gathering of new friends, I was gutted. Maybe it was that the stakes felt higher, or maybe it had always been this way but up until now I hadn't noticed. But my inner critic unleashed a verbal lashing that would be best described as an assault.

"You're *such* an idiot, Steve."

"You tried way too hard; you took up *way* too much space. Your jokes weren't funny, your vulnerability was awkward, and honestly, man, the halibut was overdone."

"Did you see how quickly Joe said goodbye? He was desperate to get out of there."

"Nice going, wise guy. You just ruined everything."

And on and on the tape rolled.

Then the strangest, most unexpected thing happened.

By some mysterious grace, out of seemingly nowhere, in the middle of my silent internal diatribe, a picture of my sweet son Dario's adorable face flashed before my eyes. Like, literally. I saw the innocence in his golden-brown eyes. I saw the vulnerable earnestness of childhood…how one word from me could make him feel like a superhero and another word could make him feel absolutely and utterly worthless. I saw the softness in his face looking at me in a way he looked at no other human, because I'm his dad.

I viscerally could feel the love I have for him and the role I play in being his champion.

And then I imagined speaking to my son the way I was speaking to myself. I imagined looking at that innocent, earnest human, that was part of me, that I loved beyond words, knowing the power of my voice in his soul, and using my voice to utterly berate him, demean him, and humiliate him. If a gun was pointed to my head, I wouldn't speak to my son the way I was speaking to myself.

And then something happened that broke me open.

I saw myself in my son. I saw the part of me that was earnest and vulnerable, just like him, wanting to belong, and trying to make new friends. I saw the part of me that was nervous and still doing my best. Someone once said greatness is in the trying. And I saw that I was summoning courage, during a hard season, and just…trying. I saw my own innocence.

And I wept.
And wept.
And wept.

In the 1980s, American psychologist Richard Schwartz developed a hauntingly effective mode of therapy called Internal Family Systems, or IFS. Schwartz's model proposes that our identities are actually a family of individual personalities or "parts." He suggests that the more we exile certain parts—by shaming them, hiding them, accusing them, or denying their existence—two things happen: the louder they scream, and the more divided (or disassociated from our authentic, integrated self) we become. In a true spirit of hospitality, IFS says when we welcome *all* our parts to the table, when we tell them they belong as they are, when we ask them what they need, they feel hosted and return the favor. They stop raging like disgruntled guests; they calm down, ask for what they need, and become integrated, helpful members of the internal "family" of parts that make up our personality. *That's* how we become our authentic and genuine selves.

Witnessing how we speak to ourselves doesn't always come naturally. For me, this graceful interruption to the tirade I had directed at myself was a first. I imagine, justified by my desire for constant improvement, I had been berating myself for a very long time, unaware of the tone and the result. There's a very specific reason the first practice of creating a virtuous cycle of generosity says to *speak* kindly to yourself. Part of the reason why we don't witness our tone with ourselves is because our internal dialogues are rarely spoken. They're silent thoughts in our minds. Someone once said our minds are like trees with a thousand screaming monkeys in them. Identifying one thought can be as challenging as hearing what one of our monkeys is saying.

But when we speak...

When we open our mouths and use words—words that build, words that encourage and affirm the best in us, that call out our good intentions, that welcome all our parts to the table, even the ones we feel a little embarrassed about—we start to feel at home in our skin. And if ever there was a prerequisite to making *other* people feel at home, it's feeling at home ourselves. Speaking kindly to ourselves, out loud, especially to a part of ourselves that might have just embarrassed us, is the first step in the quest to make ourselves at home in our skin.

Many of us have witnessed the shouting athletic coach whose aggressive methods seem to extract greatness. Sadly, in my early days, I witnessed too many screaming chefs trying to do the same. The end (excellence) justifies the means (berating), or so the narrative goes. First, it's a flawed philosophy of sustained growth. Secondly, when our internal voice adopts the merciless tone of an external voice, we've landed ourselves on the long and certain road to a vicious cycle.

I'm pushing against a widely accepted practice among high achievers, so let's dissect this further. It bears mentioning that a quantitative accomplishment, like winning a game or getting an award, is very different than a qualitative intention, like *feeling at home with ourselves*. I would argue that even with quantitative accomplishments, a long-term practice of using shame and anger as motivators will eventually backfire. Additionally, scientific study and everyday life experience both show us that *sounds affect growth.* From plants hearing classical music as opposed to heavy metal to babies hearing cheering parents as they take their first steps, it's grace and encouragement that produce long-term growth.

Remember that old hymn? "Amazing grace, how sweet the sound."

As Bono reminds us, grace is a sound.

Shifting a lifelong habit of proving our value by what we do to valuing others with what we do is a fundamental, foundational shift. Like a baby walking, it's hard; it's awkward and new. And the part of us that is trying to do something hard, awkward, and new needs to hear the *sound* of grace.

Practice one: speak, out loud, kindly to yourself.
"But Steve, people who talk to themselves get locked up."
Really?

People who *scream* at themselves and punch the air while spitting…those people get locked up.

Watch any athlete on the field, singer before they take the stage, orator before they deliver their speech, or mother who is summoning her highest self's response after the tenth tantrum, and you'll witness a human talking to themselves. Rallying our better angels, bringing our courage to the forefront, cheering the champion inside to rise up and try again requires the most important voice in our souls, our own, to speak the words that quiet the merciless internal critic.

We've been tricked into thinking that constructive criticism is the same as being a critic. It's not.

Critics
Don't build.
Anything.

Critics tear things down from the cheap seats. As Theodore Roosevelt's "The Man in the Arena" speech articulates with timeless wisdom, the person who counts is the one in the arena, trying, failing, and trying again. The critic is the one who collapses on the couch, out of breath from walking to the fridge, who opens another beer, and lobs judgmental condemnation at the professional athlete on TV who has made mastery of their craft a lifelong pursuit.

The critic's voice is the voice of "anti." It speaks what it's against, what is wrong, what not to do, where not to go, what not to try. It speaks the bad, not the good. This has an occasional place, but you can't build something based on what you're not. You can't go somewhere by only knowing where not to go.

So, do we silence the internal critic? Careful there. Notice I said speaking kindly to ourselves to *quiet* the internal critic, not silence it. Remember, the wisdom of the Internal Family Systems therapeutic method says that the voices we try to silence only scream louder. All our internal voices, or parts, are calibrated with one goal: to help us and protect us. And when we try to shut them up, they revolt, and their agenda becomes a dominant voice inside. Through the help of my therapist Susan, I've learned to be a good host, invite my critic to the table, acknowledge his helpful intention, and try to listen to what he's saying.

"Bakersfield is lame. It's boring, hot, dry, and desolate!"

"I hear you saying don't go to Bakersfield. Got it. Is there anything else you're trying to say to me?"

"I'm just really trying to warn you about going to Bakersfield.

Your air conditioner doesn't work, and you'll be too hot, and your car will overheat, and there's long stretches of road with no service, and you'll be stranded."

"I hear you. You're really trying to protect me by warning me against going to Bakersfield. Thank you, critic. Now I'm going to speak with my internal navigator to explore how we get to San Diego."

The nuanced paradox hidden in plain sight is contained in one word: *constructive* criticism. To criticize something is to point out what's wrong. To construct something is to build it. The purpose behind constructive criticism is to build something *better*. Most of us have a rather talkative internal critic. Which means most of us are hearing what's wrong with our efforts. Speaking kindly to ourselves, out loud, is turning up the volume on what's right with our efforts. Like a parent cheering on their baby's awkward first steps, it's verbally affirming the good, the progress, and the intention, knowing that's how growth happens.

Looking upon ourselves with the same kind affirmation we use toward a child isn't easy. I was given a gift of seeing my son, in the middle of berating myself, and imagining doing that to him. Then, seeing that the young part of me, earnestly trying something new, was a lot like the face of my son. Now, I speak to myself every day. I've got a picture of myself in Little League on my phone's home screen. And when I blow it or fall short of what I wanted, I speak, *out loud,* the way I would speak to my son, Dario.

Remember how we saw that reality is paradoxical? Grace is like that. Grace doesn't lie and say you won when you lost. Grace is strong enough to hold two things. Grace can encourage us when we've failed and turn our focus to see the good that exists. And when we see the good, we get back in the game. Grace can exist in paradox. Speak kindly to yourself with the sound of grace.

"I see you, buddy. I see you're trying. That wasn't the outcome we were going for. But guess what? What do we always say?"

"Greatness is in the trying."

"That's right...greatness is in the trying. At least you're trying. You're in the arena. Right now, you're looking ahead at how far you've still got to go. Let's look back for a second and see how far we've come. Dude...that's some crazy progress you've made. Yeah...last night was hard, and the halibut might have sucked, but that dessert? That dessert melted their faces."

Here's a secret: hospitality, *real, virtuous hospitality,* the kind of hospitality that makes people feel at home…it's an inside job. It's not a demonstration of our skills to others. It's an invitation for others to join us in the life-giving spaces we've created for ourselves. Sadly, we've co-opted it and commoditized it and applied the "Do you see me? What do I get out of this?" mindset to everything we do. But when our mindset shifts to "I see you. How can I help?" people feel like curling up on our couch and never leaving.

If you want to move from a vicious cycle of entitlement to a virtuous cycle of generosity in your interactions, notice the interactions you're having with yourself, and speak kindly.

Principle One: Speak the Good

Practice One: Speak Kindly to Yourself

Principle Three

Principle Two

Principle Four

PRINCIPLE ONE: SPEAK THE GOOD

PRACTICE TWO: SPEAK KINDLY ABOUT OTHERS

The second practice is to speak kindly *about* the other. Notice I didn't say speak kindly *to* the other. Obviously we want our words to others to be kind. But what we say to others usually (hopefully) has some filter of good manners applied. It's what we say *about* others that is unfiltered and becomes the largest indicator of how we treat them. Just like the proactive practice of "speak kindly to yourself" has the corrective language of "don't be a critic," the opposite of speaking kindly about others would be criticizing and complaining about others. The client, the company, the customer, the child, the colleague, the co-parent, the community member, the competitor; when we use the power of our voice to complain about others, instead of speaking kindly about them, we fire up a truly vicious and destructive cycle of entitlement.

Fire is the best word to use for the energy of unchecked complaining and criticizing. Fires spread, they consume, and the bigger they grow, the harder they are to contain. Speaking the good about the other is like opening a spring that becomes a brook, then a creek, and eventually a river. It creates life and draws us and others into a generative flow. It gives, to us and to others. Speaking our complaints and criticisms about the other is like lighting a fire. It consumes life, contagiously spreading and choking out new chances of growth. It takes, from us and from others.

Like so many listening to our political discourse, I've moved from shock at what I'm hearing to embarrassment that these are our supposed "leaders" to desperation for something better to resignation that it might never change. It's hard to even reference recent political discourse. Going back a few years, amid an endless sea of disappointing and devastating sound bites, one ninety-second clip from the presidential campaign of 2008 stands out like a trickle of water in the middle of a raging forest fire.

Against all odds, Barack Obama had become the Democratic nominee and was competing against the heroic lion of the Senate, John McCain. The gloves-off vitriol of presidential campaigns had reached a new low as Obama's race, religion, patriotism, and even citizenship became "fair game" for those opposed to his presidency.

During a town hall meeting McCain was hosting, the ways the conversation among some of McCain's supporters had devolved from differences around policy to conspiratorial personal attacks against Obama was palpable.[6]

Instead of asking a question, one supporter told candidate McCain:

"I've got to tell you, we're scared. We're *scared* of an Obama presidency."

As we know, even though it creates a vicious cycle, fear is an *incredibly* effective motivator, as witnessed by how much of our media, news, and advertising aims to get our attention and our dollars by scaring us. Instead of capitalizing on fear as a motivator and using it to his advantage, McCain demon-

---

6 Associated Press. "McCain Counters Obama 'Arab' Question". October, 2008. Originally seen on YouTube, https://www.youtube.com/watch?v=jrnRU3ocIH4

strated presidential-like wisdom and spoke good *about* his opponent.

"First of all, I want to be president of the United States and obviously I do not want Senator Obama to be. But I *have* to tell you, I have to tell you, he is a decent person and a person that you do not have to be scared of as president of the United States." McCain's response was met by an ocean of boos and shouts of disdain among those supposedly supporting him.

Riding the conspiratorial wave, another McCain supporter got up and told McCain: "I can't trust Obama. I've read about him, and he's not, he's not...he's an Arab." The woman intended to keep going, but McCain, sensing that the fire building could quickly blaze beyond his ability to contain it, had to shift from speaking about his policies to becoming a fireman, putting out what he knew was becoming a needless and dangerously destructive inferno.

Grabbing the mic from the woman and shaking his head, McCain cut in: "No, ma'am. No, ma'am. He's a decent family man, citizen, that I just happen to have disagreements with on fundamental issues and that's what this campaign is about. He's not. Thank you."

I wonder if McCain sensed that the way Sarah Palin spoke *about* his competitor was igniting an inferno of destructive distraction from substantive policy debates. I would have no way of knowing but watching that video, as well as his concession speech where he chose to not have her speak, I wonder if her chosen approach of demonizing the other and the ensuing chaos led him to regret his selection of Palin as a running mate.

I try to keep a safe distance from the divisive realm of politics, but from an outsider's perspective, the ancient question comes to mind—what does it profit a man if he gains the world but loses his soul? I wonder if, in refusing to win through fear and vicious criticism of the other, McCain lost the world but kept his soul. Though destroying the character of an opponent is sadly a commonplace attempt in the political sphere, McCain chose to focus on what he was trying to build in the country with his vision. As the swan song to the testament of his character, it bears mentioning that as the architect of his own funeral, McCain chose his political opponent, whom he lost to, to deliver his eulogy. Those days feel so long gone. We can find them again, personally and collectively, if we check how we speak *about* people.

How we speak *about* the other has power. There's an ancient proverb that conveys the weight of our words best: "Death and life are in the power of the tongue." Ponder those words for a moment. Take thirty seconds, put the book down, and repeat slowly:

Death
and life
are in the power
of the tongue!

When that truth moves from the crowded mental aisles where the endless stream of Instagram inspirational content gets stored and drops down into our heart, I promise you, how we speak will change. Life and death are in our words.

For me, that dropping down came when I saw the image of my son, innocent and vulnerable, while silently berating myself and imagining verbally assaulting him the way I was myself. I *felt* that my words could have built him or destroyed him. And it scared me.

It scares me to think of what we kill with our words.
And it excites me to think of what we can create with our words.

What makes it all so precarious is that we have a choice. The provocative challenge "say that to my face" illustrates how much easier it is to be unfiltered when we can speak to each other anonymously. When words about others are spoken behind their backs, from the stands, or in the comments section, the gravitational pull to criticize just feels easier than choosing to build. That is the zero-sum deceitful premise of our ego. Its base state is eternally threatened. If you win, I lose. When we encounter conflict with others, given the easy choice of saying something *about* them or anonymously commenting, instead of the harder path of saying it *to* them, gravity falls. We're tempted to take the easy road of criticizing or complaining about whoever might have rubbed us the wrong way.

Speaking the good about others isn't a saccharine attempt at creating a land of unicorns and rainbows. It's a move away from the false self of our ego into our authentic self that is accepted, accepting, and unafraid. It's also a substantive acknowledgement that while others may not hear what we say, *we* hear what we say. And what we say becomes a self-fulfilling prophecy. Words create. And words destroy. Sage wisdom and the practical reality of engineering remind us that you can't do both at the same time. You can't deconstruct and construct at the same time. Fire and water are opposites.

This practice of speaking the good about the other doesn't just apply to how we speak about individuals we know well; it also applies to how we speak about groups of people—like our companies and our clients.

In the world of special occasions, there can be the occasional unspoken but very apparent two-word mantra dominating the client's mindset: "my day." The term "bride-zilla" was birthed from the collective experience of vendors trying to serve clients who were mainlining that energy and using it as a bat to impose their will on those serving them. As a vendor in high-stakes transactions, I understand being on high alert for customer abuse. I also understand the gap in expertise and wanting to protect clients from a decision that might sabotage their best interests. But after having served literally thousands of clients on special days, I've found the vast majority of clients are absolutely lovely and a pleasure to work with. The sad impact of the bad apples that were nightmares to work with and abused their vendors is that, unchecked and behind the scenes, the conversations among the vendor community can sometimes devolve into complaining about our clients.

Complaining about our companies or our clients is both contagious and counterproductive. It positions us as victims and others as villains. It is a presumption of perspective that keeps us from creating and discovering. The novice believes he sees everything clearly. It is the sage that knows we don't see things as they are; we see things as *we* are. Adopting a beginner's mindset and humility of perspective, the sage rejects the arrogance of the self-described "expert" and as a result never stops growing.

Like him or not, it is hard to dispute the singularly unique accomplishment of Tom Brady as a professional competitor, smashing every record for Super Bowl victories. What strikes me about him is that he embodies that sage mindset of continuous learning. In an interview following his seventh Super Bowl win, he was asked about his plans now that he had done the unimaginable and won a championship with a new team. All he focused on was how he wanted to improve his game, things he wanted to dial in, and progress he wanted to make. Even as the most accomplished quarterback in the history of the NFL, he didn't presume he knew everything there is to know.

I'm someone who thinks a lot about words and what they mean. The word "addiction" is a term and a state I've felt safely defended against. I have friends who have wrestled with various addictions and, while feeling empathy and support,

I didn't identify with their stories. Then I started learning about the concept of "attachment" as the universal state of the ego and discovered that attachment is just another word for addiction. The confession is, that while I might not be attached to a substance, I was helplessly addicted to my way of thinking (more on that later). And when the guaranteed moments of friction came with a company or a client or a community member, I would belly up to the bar of my perspective and drink it to the dregs.

That's what complaining and criticizing the other does: it deepens our addiction to our way of seeing. Remembering that words create realities, our critical words about the other reinforce the veil of our own blindness. In his profoundly wise commencement speech turned book, *This Is Water,* writer David Foster Wallace illustrates this point perfectly:[7]

> "There are these two young fish swimming along and they happen to meet an older fish swimming the other way, who nods at them and says: 'Morning, boys. How's the water?' And the two young fish swim on for a bit, and then eventually one of them looks over at the other and goes, 'What the hell is water?'"

---

7 Wallace, David Foster. *This is Water: Some Thoughts, Delivered on a Significant Occasion, about Living a Compassionate Life.* Little, Brown & Company, 2009.

Like us, a fish exists within the reality it knows and might never have stopped to observe it as something incomplete. That is until the crisis of being out of the water comes. Then, suddenly and brutally, a fish is facing the truth that water isn't the only reality, it's just the one they've known their whole lives. Sadly, it usually takes some sort of crisis for us to move past the conditioned reflexes of presuming our way of seeing is best. Wallace continues:

> "Everything in my own immediate experience supports my deep belief that I am the absolute center of the universe, the realest, most vivid, and important person in existence. We rarely think about this sort of natural, basic self-centeredness, because it's so socially repulsive, but it's pretty much the same for all of us, deep down."

I've felt the suffering that comes when I act like the center of the universe and presume I'm seeing everything clearly. And I've felt remorse when I see that I haven't seen as clearly as I assumed. Through all the couples therapy navigating us through the hard season I mentioned, even though my wife Nicole and I have been married for almost twenty years, we often say we are on our second marriage to the same person. In my experience, trying to get someone to see things the way I see them is a hard, brittle battle that often breaks the bridges between people. What softens that space and builds bridges is when, while holding my perspective, I acknowledge that you have a perspective that is equally valid.

That's why empathy hovers in the generous cycle, where fear hovers in the vicious one. It's a generosity to concede your perspective as subjective and partial. That's what speaking kindly *about* the other does. Often it's a leap of faith. It's recognizing that every viewpoint is a view from the subjective point we're standing on and still choosing to speak the good, when maybe all we can see is the bad. It's choosing to focus on the times I've been the client and felt stressed and then choosing to verbalize a charitable assumption in those moments when my clients are making me crazy. It's choosing to speak generous words about how hard it must be to run a great company and looking for how I can make it better when I'm tempted to feel like a victim of my company's shortsightedness. It's bringing to the forefront of my mind all the ways my spouse has shown up for me and speaking about their support to my crew of confidants when I'm feeling maxed out and alone.

Again, nuance and paradox must be acknowledged in the wisdom of this practice. I'm not saying there aren't certain situations that require us to "call a spade a spade" and name what *is.* Those times absolutely do exist. Can we hold seemingly conflicting perspectives? Recovering virtuous hospitality in our interactions, where we experience a virtuous cycle of generosity, calls us to speak the good, to verbally call out kind words to ourselves and about others. *And* there are also times of reckoning when we summon our courage, address the elephant in the room, confront who must be held accountable, or speak truth to power. There is a time to tear down and a time to build up. Words have power. If you want to exist in interactions that build, speak the good. As a master of holding that tension, one man deserves the last word:

> *"When evil men shout ugly words of hatred, good men must commit themselves to the glories of love."*

Martin Luther King, Jr.

Principle One:
Speak the Good

Practice One: Speak Kindly to Yourself

Practice Two: Speak Kindly About Others

Principle Three

Principle Two

Principle Four

PRINCIPLE TWO: HONOR THOSE YOU SERVE

Motives in our conversations are like undertows in the ocean. They're invisible, but they pull us. When our motivation is to prove our worth and value in a conversation, it pulls us and others into entitlement, where we're all distracted by what we're owed. Conversely, when our motivation is to make other people feel valued, it pulls us and others into generosity, where everyone is present to how they can contribute, wanting to be helpful and share the experience with others. The second principle that helps manifest this virtuous cycle of generosity is honoring those you serve. And the first practice we embrace to do that is mining for the gold in others through curiosity.

Words make us feel something, even when we're not always able to name exactly what we're feeling. For example, the word "patriotism" has come to mean different things to different people. For many, the words "honor" and "serve" are like that. They bring up feelings. For those that have bravely served in the military or law enforcement, perhaps those words bring pride. Or maybe you've had experiences where you felt obligated, exploited, or demeaned in your service, and when the call comes to honor those you serve, something viscerally recoils. However you experience those concepts, some context for how to interpret them in a way that can help improve our interactions will be helpful.

Before we get to interpretating the words "honor" and "serve," there's a horse of a word that must precede the cart. It's a concept that totally shapes how we perceive honoring and serving others. Reflecting on this word is potentially more radioactive, but it's a crucial first step in mindfully noticing how we respond to the call.

What feelings come up when you hear the word *power?*
Do you see it as a good thing?
A bad thing?
Do you crave it?
Do you despise it?

Do you feel the conflict of wanting it but feel ashamed of your desire?

Do you feel ambivalent to it?

Who's the first person you think of when you hear that word?

Do you admire them?

There's a minor but mighty misquote of the ancient proverb about money. Some say, "Money is the root of all evil," forgetting the actual quote is "The *love* of money is the root of all evil."

Do you see power as the real root of evil?

Or the love of power as the root of evil?

Or as a necessary evil to accomplish good?

Whatever the word makes you feel, power is powerful in our collective psyche.

As one of the big three human drivers (sex, money, and power), there is much we associate with that word.

There may be other words subtly different in their technical definition but closely related that we're more comfortable with, like "strength," "influence," or "agency." Or maybe we prefer how the word "empowered" sounds and can accept that expanded version as a universally desired state. But deny as we might, there are associations each one of us has with the word "power."

My confessions and rumble with that word could be (and may one day be) the subject of an entire book. As you might imagine having read some of my story, of being bullied and over*powered*, I have spent a lifetime wrestling with the concept of power. Identifying with the Enneagram Type 8, I have a sixth sense of power dynamics and can literally feel them operating in a room.

As a male, historically described as the "alpha type," not wanting to apologize for my gender or personality, simultaneously wanting the best for my strong wife and two strong daughters, while also trying to model manhood for my son, my desire to get masculinity right has been deep and challenging. I confess I've reacted, been ignorant, overcompensated, made mistakes, and hurt those I care about in the quest of finding my way. Often the search for how to gracefully and maturely walk in the energy of our gender is a fraught process, especially when it comes to power.

Regardless of how you gender identify, the differences in gender *energies* complicate how we navigate our own personal journey with power.

Both the masculine and feminine are invited on a journey of discovering power as a blessing. The end of that journey lands the masculine and feminine energies in a place that is complementary and united, wielding power in a generative and integrated way. But the journey to that common destination takes a very different path for each.

My quest to get it right also exposed me to the writings of Father Richard Rohr, whose work on the subject I found unspeakably helpful. Believing that immature and ultimately toxic masculine energy is one of the greatest cultural threats of our time, Rohr has done a deep dive on the journey of male energy throughout the ages.

His thesis on the subject is that throughout history, the practice of male initiation has been a component of all indigenous cultures. He describes the universal process of elders taking boys "out of the camp" for a series of rituals as a rite of passage into manhood. As Rohr studied historical (and current) rites of initiation throughout all societies, a common theme arose that boys encountered their own powerlessness through these rituals. The elder men made sure that each boy experienced the depth of his own powerlessness, *so that* he would have a redeemed and renewed relationship with his own power and strength. *That one renewal* transformed the boy into a man. Like the chrysalis emerging into a butterfly, having been softened by viscerally touching his own powerlessness, the man now used his power and strength on *behalf* of others, *with* others, where the boy had used his power and strength over others, against others.

In a profound cultural critique, Rohr's work on the male journey observes that Western societies have abandoned ritual rites of passage to our peril. And as a result, the havoc wreaked is not the work of men but of boys in men's bodies. He notes the fatherlessness multiple generations of men experience and, in the absence of elders and male role models, the existential question of what it means to be a man leaves males confused and misdirected. Rohr adjusts the understandable feminine exasperation to not be directed at male energy but at boy energy, mainlining the uninitiated purpose of power.

I am both inspired by and the beneficiary of the way Father Rohr didn't stop with observation and cultural critique. Fueled by hope for change, over cynicism for what exists, Rohr created a series of rituals that could be applied in a Western context called Men's Rites of Passage, where men can go on a retreat with other initiated men and experience their powerlessness, to redeem how they hold power.

One cannot achieve manhood vicariously by studying, listening to podcasts, or proclaiming it in isolation. The boy has to hear "you are a man now" before he can say to himself, "I am a man." It must be bestowed by other men who have redeemed their rumble with powerlessness to living their lives using their power and strength as a blessing to others. Resonating with this timeless truth deeply, I went on this retreat at the age of forty-one and was one of the youngest attendees by far. Men of all ages, from all walks of life, religions, races, and sexual orientations had found community in Father Rohr's retreats and gathered around one common quest to answer: "What does it mean to be a man?" The initiated elders spoke about mature masculine energy as being neither abdication nor domination, but generative. In their own words, they talked about the vicious and the virtuous cycles and the difference between a giving energy and a taking energy. They talked about how when the male and female energies have both redeemed their concept of power, the integrated expression is beautiful and a blessing to all.

The retreat ends with the elders holding each of the initiates by the shoulders, looking them square in the eye, and saying: "When I was boy, I thought like a boy. But now I'm a man, and I live as a man." The sight of seventy-five-year-old newly initiated men, who had felt fatherless and confused their whole lives, weeping with joy is a sight I will *never* forget.

I won't begin to presume I have walked the feminine path toward redemptive power. But as a sojourner toward the place of seeing power as a blessing, I will say the inspired women voices I hear in our culture resonate with the concept of a power that neither abdicates or dominates but is generative, integrated between the genders and a blessing.

Influence, strength, agency…power.
Like yeast in the dough, these words become something in the bread of our lives. For better, or for worse, they grow.
They confuse, they inspire, they build, they break.
Gandhi had power.
So did Hitler.
I've had moments where I was a victim of power being misused against me.
And moments where I was the villain misusing power against others.
I've had moments where I was the beneficiary of redeemed power being used on my behalf.

And moments where I was able to use the power I've been given on behalf of others.

My journey through power has changed me from being a mindless expert with ignorant opinions to a lifelong mindful student trying to learn. I'm far from finished in my learnings, but here's what I've learned so far:

I've learned that power is neutral. As Martin Luther King Jr. so poignantly defined for us all, "power is the ability to achieve purpose." As a neutral force, power is neither bad nor good. The purpose of power, and how power is used, determines whether it goes in the good or evil column.

I've learned that *real* power is a deeper magic, and the power of the sage is a thousand times stronger than the power of the "influencer" leveraging their fifteen minutes. The games of power culture plays, and those we believe are winning, are literally child's play. Holding our attention, influencing our spending, occupying the headlines, or stirring us up for a season is power of the playground type. Creating life, leaving lasting change for the better, and walking in love no matter what is power of a completely different dimension.

I've learned that power is a mystery. There is no formula that the cosmic force of power will be mastered by. Who deserves it, who ultimately gets it, who uses it for good, who uses it for evil? These are all questions that are above my pay grade.

And I've learned that whether our relationship to the concept of power is front and center, on the back burner, or somewhere in between, to be human is to navigate this concept in some capacity.

You may be wondering how all this talk of power has anything to do with honoring those we serve and existing on the generous cycle of valuing others. On a macro level, over the last decade, the service industries have been rife with conflict between company and customer. The foundation of this conflict is squarely rooted in the power differential. Whether reacting to an overabundance of it, compensating for a lack of it, or pursuing the balance of it, power and the struggle for it between company and customer has been front and center. In my own industry of hospitality, thanks in large part to the culture of chefs as celebrities, I could never hope to count how many restaurants I've visited as a customer and encountered a server who made it clear that the power is held by the chef. Within minutes of arriving, the practice of hearing instructions of how chef "would like you to order" has become so common, we no longer flag it as odd. On the other side of the line, I have an equal number of episodes as a company and owner where we've tried to navigate a complex situation with a customer, only to hear their determination that they hold all power as our customer and demand we fall in line. In short, when it comes to companies serving customers, the power struggle is real.

On a more individual, micro level, we might not realize it consciously, but our interpretation of the word "serve" is directly related to how we interpret power. When we interpret power as a force used over us or against us, we will see "service" through the lens of a power differential, having felt the sting of misused and abused power. It leaves us in a push/pull relationship with both concepts—pushing for situations where we *feel* powerful and pulling away from situations where serving makes us feel powerless. If we interpret power as a force used with us or for us, we experience being the beneficiary of power and consequently are more likely to see service as our agency in motion.

Find a person in any position of influence or authority, who seems to have lost the plot in serving others—whether a minister or a police officer, an executive or a teacher—and you will find someone who misunderstands the purpose of power. Perpetuating the vicious cycle, the victim endures their turn, climbs, and in time becomes the villain. Look elsewhere and find someone who seems to serve with joy, and you'll see their resources come from motives other than fear or obligation. This is the person who has perceived that the greatest power is in giving life to others. It's the difference between stimulation and impartation. Feeling the perks of our position can be stimulating. But leveraging our position to *impart* something that gives life to the hopes and dreams of others is the purpose of our power, wherever we exercise it.

The sages of our time have all understood that even in leadership, their call was to service. I once had a professor that said leaders lead by serving and serve by leading. It takes that wise perspective to walk this way, but when we begin to see our role with others as service, the virtuous cycle of generosity begins to emerge in our interactions. Reframing our post as one of service isn't confined to those in conventional leadership positions. Nor is it confined to history's heroes like Gandhi who brought conventional power to its knees through the power of service. Seeing opportunities to serve those around us in everyday encounters is how we experience more fulfilling relationships.

When the parent sees that their influence or power is a service to their child's well-being or the officer takes the words on the squad car—to protect and serve the community—seriously, their interactions change for the better. When the executive sees good leadership as a service to their direct reports and the architect sees their creativity as a service to the excited home builder, a cycle of generosity starts to operate. When I first started working in restaurants I was leveraging my homegrown skills as a way to make money, but my heart wasn't in it. I saw service as the undesirable consequences of weakness, the tasks as menial, and authority as a privileged graduation from feeling powerless. Like I've shared in previous chapters, life offered shifts in my mindset, and I began to see the nobility and joy in serving and nourishing others. If you hold a similar perspective, that serving anyone other than those you love indicates low status on a class system of your own making, you'll need to engage a similar mindset shift to adopt a new paradigm of serving others before you'll experience the virtuous cycle.

Remember that hosting is the universal space between creators and receivers. Whatever you are creating, whether it be a vanilla latte or a bedtime routine for the kids, you are hosting whoever receives what you've created. Much like the word "service," the word "honor" can mean different things depending on our experience. The definition of honor is to treat someone with admiration or respect. I like to think of honor as elevating the dignity of others. To honor those we serve is to raise the dignity of those we host. When our offering is one of service and our view of those we serve is that they have dignity, the virtuous cycle of generosity is set in motion.

There are two legitimate obstacles to the principle of honoring those you serve: how do you authentically honor someone you don't know, and how do you honor someone who isn't acting honorably? As we've all seen and know, the customer is *not* always right. Whether the "customer" is a disgruntled guest or your tantrum-throwing colleague, honoring those you serve and being genuine about it can be hard. The principle's first practice helps us over the hurdle: mine for the gold by being curious.

PRACTICE ONE: MINE FOR THE GOLD WITH CURIOSITY

As we saw in an earlier chapter, curiosity is the energy of mastery, because it's manifesting "I don't know everything." Those on the path of mastery have a beginner's mind, or the mindset of discovery. They talk more about their learnings than their expertise. We don't readily admit to being "experts" on other humans, but when we presume we see them clearly and profess to know their intention, it shuts down curiosity. We've applied a tourniquet to the flow of curiosity, which leads to learning and growing.

One of the most common places this absence of curiosity shuts down a virtuous cycle is in close relationships, especially marriage. After years of living with someone, we're so familiar with their habits, responses, behaviors, and personalities that it can be hard to suspend assumptions of the people we know best. I've learned the hard way, through working tirelessly on my marriage, that the million presumed conclusions we make in our daily interactions with those we live with will often lead to fights that devolve into a vicious cycle.

As part of an organization that supports CEOs and founders called Vistage, I attend monthly meetings where the heads of companies vulnerably shine light on our biggest issues, for input and perspective from other leaders in the room. The difficult task of facilitating a productive meeting among twenty CEOs and entrepreneurs is one I do not envy. Our local chapter's facilitator, Don Riddell, is a seventy-five-year-old sage and has been wrangling, optimizing, challenging, focusing, and improving the lives of these leaders for over twenty years. As one of the longest-serving and most successful facilitators in a global network, Don is often asked for the secret to his success. He will answer with one word: curiosity.

The diverse talents and challenges in our group are vast. We have CEOs of two-hundred-million-dollar companies and five-million-dollar companies. We have one of the largest egg farmers in the US, whose business was nearly wiped out by the 2022 avian flu. We have leaders that are financial and tech geniuses, like my friend and co-member John Delbridge, who runs Mimeo, one of the largest online digital printers. We also have leaders like Steve Schwartz, who started a company called Art of Tea. Steve spends half his time in the most remote parts of Japan and India, personally meeting the world's best tea leaf farmers. We have founders of creative agencies and packaging companies, a music composition company, a supplement manufacturer, and a caterer. Before being a Vistage chairperson, Don was a restaurant manager, a basketball coach, and a school principal. On paper, Don's resume isn't what one might expect to see for the leader of our group. Yet to a person, every one of us would cite Don as a voice of wisdom and guidance in our lives.

How does that happen?

Because Don sees his role as one of service to us and he reminds us constantly how honored he is to walk with us. Practically, he is relentless in his practice of curiosity. Don has mastered the art of the question, and during the time he spends with us individually, he comes with curious interest over microwave-ready advice. After walking closely with nearly every type of business leader, both personally and professionally, for over twenty years, there isn't a lot that Don hasn't seen. I'm sure by now, when he hears the latest issue a leader is facing, he could advise numerous courses of action. But in choosing the genius discipline of curiosity over the tempting reflex of demonstrating his own expertise, Don *draws out* the inherent wisdom and value that sometimes gets buried under the pile of our preoccupations. He mines for the gold. And when we discover the gold we hold in ourselves, we see the gleam in his eye when he says "look at what you found there," when a lesser guide would say "look at what I did there."

Mining for the gold by being curious is the first practice we employ when looking to honor those we serve. And it is one of the only ways we can be authentic in honoring either those we don't know or those who we find less than honorable.

When our team is called upon to serve an American president, an industry leader, or a widely known titan in their industry, it is easy to summon honor. But how can we honor the executive we know nothing about or a bride behaving badly, without faking it?

If we agree that hosting is universal and that to host well is to serve, how do we honor the stranger at the counter, the distracted student, the disgruntled customer, the nonperforming direct report, or the dinner guest who didn't even bother to offer cleanup help? While they might not be doing anything wrong or mal-intended, if we're not curious about what's happening for them, we become susceptible to subconsciously presuming expertise on people we know nothing about. Said simpler, when we encounter behaviors that bother us, we can become judgmental.

Not all our chances to serve afford us the opportunity to ask great questions like Don. Asking a deeply probing question like "how do you experience affirmation?" might seem a bit out of place for small talk as we check the status of our client's order. Being curious about others doesn't necessarily mean we ask them questions. We can ask ourselves questions, with them in mind, and discover the same gold.

After a lifetime of serving others, there are two great questions I've found to ask myself on behalf of those I'm serving:

What do I have in common with this person?

What do I find inspiring about this person?

WHAT DO I HAVE IN COMMON WITH THIS PERSON?

Between the energy of our ego and the instinctual negative bias programmed into our brains, we are constantly scanning for the ways we are different and separate from those around us. We can swim against the current of separating ourselves by intentionally looking for common ground. At first glance, Don Riddell might not have a lot in common with the CEO of a multimillion-dollar company or an entrepreneur who has studied Vedic medicine and held fellowships with Japanese tea farmers. But instead of discounting his experience as utterly different and thus irrelevant, he asks himself, "What might I have in common with this person?"

As he does that, the floodgates of relevant common ground are opened.

"Have I ever felt overwhelmed? What helped me in that situation?"

"Do I know what it's like to struggle to find focus? What have

I learned about prioritizing?"

"How have I collaborated and coached people with a different background than mine?"

"I've lived enough life to know I'm susceptible to triggers. How have I learned to manage my big emotions?"

I've always thought catering is one of the most uniquely challenging business models, and it's very different from restaurants. The catering customer has rarely, if ever, been as invested in the outcome of the event. It's a once-in-a-lifetime or once-in-a-decade event. The restaurant customer is invested, but at the end of the day, if dinner was bad, their next one is on the house.

"I'm sorry your wedding reception was ruined, your next one is on us" isn't really going to appease an unhappy catering customer.

Beyond the gap in investment, there's the gap in income. The majority of America does not hire a full-service catering company, complete with servers and cooks, for birthday parties or social gatherings. For those that order catering outside of the once a year, once a decade, or once a lifetime, they are typically affluent.

Yet on the service side, it is a gig-based worker economy. Catering servers might be moderately invested, but they are often creative types who do not want the commitment of a full-time restaurant job, so they take catering gigs that work with their schedule. They typically see catering as a temporary way to make some money while they pursue other avenues, like acting or music. Suffice it to say, the gap in investment and affluence between the catering server and client is a wide one.

In my early days as a business owner, I tried to close the gap between our servers and our clients with a pleading sense of urgency. Knowing our young company's reputation was on the line, I would all but beg servers to care and do their best. After experiencing the layers of flaws in that approach, I now invite our staff to reflect on what they might have in common with our clients. Our client might have more money, but haven't we all had a celebration where our hopes and expectations were on the line, and all we wanted was for everyone to have a good time? Haven't all of us felt the pangs of anxiety that even though we're throwing a party, we're nervous and just hoping everyone has fun? In the face of feeling slighted, could we as a service team extend a bit of grace that maybe there's been times where our own preoccupations and nerves left us a little less gracious and considerate than we would otherwise hope to be?

As much as I don't like to admit it, I have to confess that my engines of judgmentalism rev quickly. I can go from zero to sixty faster than the latest Tesla. And the more open I've become about this tendency, the more I find that I'm not alone. Asking myself what I have in common with those that I'm serving or those that I'm in conflict with *slows my engines of judgmentalism.* As I said, like swimming upstream, looking for common ground is counterintuitive and takes the determination of intention to stay open-minded. But I find when someone has offended me or I'm serving someone that feels like an alien to me, as I start asking myself what I might have in common with this rude alien, the energy *in me* and then between us changes.

It's a key to maintaining civility and extending basic kindness to our fellow humans.

Well...there was that one time I was super rude to the Uber driver when I thought I was going to miss my flight...

Man...I was so stressed at my wedding...geez. I catered my own wedding, and all I wanted was everything to be perfect...

And when we didn't hit budget and payroll was high, I'm sure I also came off intense at our all-hands meeting...

Thank God no one was filming me at bedtime last night when my kid wasn't listening...I probably didn't look like the kind of parent I aspire to be...

I'm sure we can all think of times we weren't gracious or weren't the best version of ourselves. Ask yourself, what do I have in common with the other?

It's a practical way to honor the person you're serving.

WHAT DO I FIND INSPIRING ABOUT THIS PERSON?

In trying to authentically honor those we serve, another question we can ask ourselves is "what do I find inspiring about this person?" Often when we are so immersed in our experience, it makes honoring someone difficult, because we haven't reflected on their experience.

When our kids were younger, traveling anywhere was traumatizing. We were that family tornado walking in the airport with Nicole wearing baby three, while pulling two suitcases and holding the carry-on bags, me pushing a stroller with kid two, while also pulling a suitcase *and* carrying a car seat and coaxing kid one to walk on her own and pull her unicorn mini suitcase. In the next second, I'm grabbing the Spider-Man backpack that tantrum-throwing kid two just dropped out of the stroller, as Nicole is looking for our boarding passes while picking up the pacifier off the floor that screaming baby three just spit out, hoping that by some miracle of logistics our children and our stuff would make it to our plane on time.

Without fail, every single time we traveled, from the eye of the storm, I would peek out of our family tornado and see a single mother, with the same number of kids, the same amount of logistics, but half the support somehow making it work. Like a rookie watching a Hall of Famer, all I could do was look on in wonder and be inspired. She's alone, her hands are more than full, her kids are still being kids, she has the same complications (like her seats aren't all together or she needs to talk to the airline attendant at the desk) and still somehow keeps the kid that walks from wandering. By some miracle, she has to make it work.

The airline employee has her own stressful circumstances. She just received an email from corporate that today will require her to work a double shift due to staffing shortages. She has to scramble and figure out childcare since she's coming home eight hours later than expected. Add to that the flight has been oversold or it's delayed because of a hurricane, the man from first class who keeps using "summer" as a verb is livid because his status entitles him a reprieve from inconvenient acts of God, like the weather, there are more passengers than there are seats, and some lady is at the counter complaining that all her seats aren't together. She's lucky she has seats.

The vicious cycle needs no help to fire up in situations like these. But, if just one of the players can slow down and notice the other and set a generous intention, a virtuous cycle can emerge and change how the space between these strangers feels. Perhaps, if the airline employee who vaguely remembers hearing something in her corporate onboarding about hospitality and can set her intention to swim against the current that centers on her own experience, she might see something new. She might see how inspiring it is that, with all the stress of traveling with kids, this single mom is composed and courteous, albeit understandably hoping she can sit with her babies. Reflecting that she has childcare challenges in common with this customer due to her recent shift change and being inspired by this woman's grace under pressure, the airline attendant can authentically, through the chaos and the noise, honor the woman she's serving.

While I could never be a teacher and can't imagine the challenges of wrangling while educating, as the parent of a teenager in middle school, I have learned that middle school wasn't just hard for me, it's hard for everyone. Being a teenager is hard. By studying the work of Dr. Lisa Damour, books like *The Emotional Lives of Teenagers* and *Untangled,* I read the staggering science of what is happening in the teenage brain. Based on what teenagers are facing in the best of circumstances, due to the monumental and literal rewiring of their brain chemistry, let alone in a post-Covid, existentially confusing time with school shootings happening almost weekly, for a teenager to just show up to class at all is…inspiring.

The teacher who is trying to prove his lectures are worthy of respect might find his students more entitled than curious and end up exasperated. The teacher who sees teaching as a service, who aspires to honor his students and decides to mine for the gold by looking for something inspiring in these beautiful messy balls of internal conflict, might find his students literally pulling the wisdom out of him and be reminded of why he first fell in love with teaching.

When we're inspired by people, it changes how we treat them. And when we don't know people or they aren't behaving in a particularly inspiring way, we have a choice: we can indulge our reflexes and create a vicious cycle, or we can grab our mental pickaxes and go mine for the gold in this imperfect human by asking what inspiring nugget might be buried beneath the rocky surface.

Asking ourselves what is inspiring about those we are serving is truly mining for gold. It's not always sitting there, glimmering in plain sight. But if we mine for the gold by looking for something inspiring in those we serve, if we look long enough, we'll find what we're looking for, we will find the miner's prize.

Principle One: Speak the Good

Practice One: Speak Kindly to Yourself

Practice Two: Speak Kindly About Others

Principle Three

Principle Two: Honor Those You Serve

Practice One: Mine for the Gold by Being Curious

What Do I Have in Common?

What Is Inspiring?

Principle Four

PRINCIPLE TWO: HONOR THOSE YOU SERVE

PRACTICE TWO: APPLY WHAT YOU DISCOVERED

Once we've mined for the gold by being curious about the other person, we then apply what we've discovered. It's not that we've necessarily asked them questions; we've asked questions of ourselves with them in mind. We reflected on what we might have in common and what we see as inspiring about them. We found some nuggets. Now what?

There are two practical steps we can take that extend hospitality and contribute to activating a virtuous cycle of generosity in our interactions.

First, we proactively respond to what we found, and second, we customize our generosity.

PROACTIVELY RESPOND TO WHAT WE FOUND

Hospitable hosts are proactively responsive in their generosity. They have an internal locus of control and look for the little things that don't require permission to make others feel taken care of.

Shopping for obscure grocery items often reminds me of this lesson. There are some grocery stores where if you ask an employee if they carry an obscure item, like tahini paste, they'll answer you with an unapologetic "I'm not really sure."

Other grocery stores slightly more service-oriented might answer the same question with an answer like "Check on Aisle 9."

The first sign of a hospitality-oriented staff is that they're curious. If you look confused at Trader Joe's, many employees will ask "Can I help you find something?" And if you say,

"I'm looking for tahini paste," their response is "Come with me."

Trader Joe's employees don't need permission to break from their task to walk you to a different aisle. They're proactively responding to what they found by being curious.

Curiosity is data mining for the ways we can help others. And little acts of proactively responding to the data makes others feel taken care of. As a result, customers naturally return the favor with their appreciation and loyalty. The Starbucks barista proactively memorizing your drink and offering "the usual" when you walk in, the host using the gluten-free flour in half the batch so everyone can get cookies, the office worker opening the door for the person whose arm is in a sling, or the professor swimming laps with the hyper college kid before their lecture so he can calm down and pass their class are types of proactive things we do when our curiosity has revealed something about the person we're hosting.

It never ceases to amaze me how vicious *and* virtuous cycles can become catalyzed by acts that seem so insignificant and small. We're a sensitive bunch, us humans. And like sleepless computers, hardwired for connection with other humans, we are constantly, consciously, and subconsciously sending messages. Our greatest desire for the messages we send to others is a response. One of the simplest ways we move from a vicious cycle that is all about "me" to a virtuous cycle that is all about "others" is to notice the cues others are sending us and just respond.

When I was first learning how to serve tables, one of my managers taught me a valuable lesson. He said the best servers know what a table needs before they have to ask for it, and the way to do that is to observe and to especially observe the eyes. I learned that the eyes truly are a window to the soul. Eyes reading a menu would tell me people hadn't decided what they were eating yet, so asking them if they were ready to order wasn't an attuned question. But eyes reading a menu with a slightly furrowed brow would tell me the customer was trying to understand a dish and asking them if they had any questions would be a welcome offering of service. Eyes locked in a conversation with another diner would tell me it wasn't a good time to interrupt the flow by asking them how everything tasted. Eyes that were looking down at the plate as they placed a bite on their fork might present a better time to confirm they were enjoying their meal.

Observing the eyes and responding to what they're saying applies to more than just table service. It's a life lesson for leveling up our interactions. As an outgoing, leader-type person, I'm not someone who ever saw myself as socially anxious. But as I have begun to reflect more on the cycles of energies flowing in my interactions and slow things down, I've realized that when I am not centered, I have a harder time maintaining eye contact. I'm not talking about the creepy type of eye contact hilariously illustrated by Steve Martin's character in *Baby Mama,* where he would "reward with five minutes of uninterrupted eye contact." I'm referring to a calm, grounded ability to naturally look someone in the eyes. Some of that anxiety comes from a lifetime of hosting others and a reflex of deferring to others at my own expense. Like the flight attendants say, you have to put on your own oxygen mask before helping others find theirs.

This practical one-two step of curiously observing, then proactively responding is a simple yet powerful action that transforms our interactions for the better. Noticing the eyes is a tangible message I can observe. Cultivating this skill grows our capacity to see what other people's energy is saying to us. We spend so much time responding (and tragically reacting) to people's words, but as the eighties band Miami Sound Machine reminds us, often "the words get in the way." A lifetime of studying communication (as experienced by a lifetime of miscommunication) has shown me that aligning our words with our energy is a ninja-level skill.

Typically most of us don't communicate our simple needs when we speak. In the name of growing our language skills, we've left the innocence and simplicity of childhood communication behind. A therapist of mine, Ron, revealed how I was a textbook example of this. As I would describe an issue, I would consistently start a diatribe with "I feel like they don't really..." Over and over, he would stop me and remind me how that statement was an oxymoron.

"'I feel like they don't' isn't a feeling, Steve; it's a judgment. The moment you say 'I feel *like*' you're describing a perception or a judgment. What do you feel?"

I would squirm with exasperation under the pressure of boiling my nuanced analysis down into a seemingly oversimplified childlike statement of my core feeling. Ron would kindly hold my feet to the fire and challenge me to stop analyzing and just name the feeling. It would take a while but almost every time, when I noticed what I felt and just surrendered with a simple statement like "I feel afraid," the tears would flow.

The ego is a driven wizard. In interactions, it looks for openings to defend and promote itself with laser-fast speed. When we slow our ego's roll, we begin to see what the other person is looking for in their interaction with us, so that our response can provide what they need. That's what makes people feel valued.

Most of our interactions don't use simple statements about what we need or sound like the following:

"I'm frustrated. I need you to care."

"This means a lot to me. I feel dismissed."

"I need reassurance."

"I'm scared. I'm craving a fortune teller who can tell me how this ends."

"I'm so sad."

"I feel exposed."

"I feel regret. I stretched to do this, and I wish I wouldn't have."

"I'm afraid I don't belong here."

When we're curious, we can read what people are saying and then proactively respond. It honors them, and it improves our interactions. And there's a way we can dial our response in even further to activate generosity.

CUSTOMIZE OUR GENEROSITY

Now that we've been curious and noticed some things about those we are hosting and have decided to respond to the nuggets of information we found, we can move further into the virtuous cycle by customizing our generosity. These are not always grand gestures. And though little thoughtful gifts can be one way we customize our generosity, this step isn't limited to just gifts.

There are several movies that beautifully illustrate moving from the vicious cycle of entitlement to the virtuous cycle of generosity, and one of my favorites is a movie from 1988, *Rain Man*. Assuming his deceased father's wealth will pass to him, car dealer Charlie Babbitt is shocked and enraged to discover that most of the inheritance has been left to an autistic brother he didn't know he had, Raymond. As an entitled taker, consumed with what he's owed, Charlie begrudgingly forges a relationship with his brother in pursuit of a greater share of the inheritance. In the beginning, Raymond's autism and inflexibility are a source of exasperation and incredulity for Charlie. Tiny details, like syrup not being on the table before the pancakes come, can trigger an explosive episode that Charlie is embarrassed by. But as the relationship develops,

Raymond's autism becomes the stone that breaks Charlie's heart open, and he becomes someone who cares more about his brother than about the inheritance. As their time together is ending, Charlie draws Raymond's attention to a tiny, customized gesture he's done to care for his brother.

"Look, Ray, the syrup is on the table."

Entitlement bristles at the things we find inflexible or illogical in others. Generosity keeps our own idiosyncrasies in mind and looks for ways to "put the syrup on the table" for the sole purpose of making people feel cared for using their currency.

Most of us aspire to do this twice a year on birthdays and holidays, thinking up gifts that people will love. But gifts are expected on those occasions. It's the little unexpected gestures of customized generosity that really kick off the virtuous cycle.

I mentioned earlier about my short stint working in the entertainment industry immediately after college. As I met more people in similar positions, it became obvious that success had a lot to do with anticipating and delivering on the tiniest of preferences of those we worked for. From how drinks should be lined up in a fridge to the exact temperature of a dressing room, there was a mandate to know the preferences of the boss. Sure, that's part of the drill of working for others, and I appreciate attuned assistance as much as the next person. But running customized preferences up the flagpole isn't generosity, it's good job performance. Generosity is when we flip the flow and offer something customized to those perhaps further down the org chart, who aren't owed.

My friend Jeremy Vallerand is a master at this. Jeremy runs a nonprofit called Atlas Free that our company has been proud to partner with and serve. Beyond the typical relationship between a company and nonprofit, Jeremy and I have become close. One of the things that I am constantly amazed by is how much Jeremy is looking for what he can give, when many of his nonprofit colleagues are looking for what they can get. With a mindset that is counter to many nonprofit leaders who see everyone as potential donors, Jeremy understands the physics of the virtuous cycle. Instead of trying to prove the value of his organization's cause and feeling entitled to more from his donor base, Jeremy looks for what he can give to his donors, and it creates a powerful cycle of generosity.

I understand that after our company has donated a dinner and helped raise funds for his organization, Jeremy is most likely going to pass along some sort of "thank you" gesture. But what makes Jeremy's generous acts so memorable is that they're customized. It would be faster and easier to send me a gift card to a restaurant or a bottle of wine that his local shop could ship. But Jeremy has gifted me with a Japanese chef knife, a shop apron to wear in my woodshop, and knowing Montana is my happy place, a custom-made hatchet for chopping wood. Opening Jeremy's gifts makes me feel seen and understood by him in a unique way, and all I want to do is return the generosity.

As I said, it's not just material things that we can offer people in our attempts to customize our generosity. Sometimes one of the most helpful things we can offer someone is an introduction that would be meaningful to them. Knowing I'm an entrepreneur looking to learn and grow, Jeremy's generosity hasn't been limited to epic gifts. In a truly generous and unselfish act, Jeremy introduced me to Curt Richardson, the founder of Otterbox, who has become a mentor and friend. Curt is known for being generous with both his time and investing insight with younger leaders. Since Curt represents a strategic relationship for Jeremy, Jeremy could have understandably wanted to protect access to Curt. Instead, he has initiated and blessed me speaking with Curt independently of him.

When, like Charlie Babbitt, we look for what makes people literally tick and then "put the syrup on the table," something inside them feels seen and cared for. Something that has helped me is realizing we don't have to be void of self-interest to be generous. This virtuous cycle is not the pattern of the altruistic ascetic who wants nothing for themselves. Rather, it's the pattern of the wise person who realizes that in life, just as in gardening, we reap what we sow. If we plant apple seeds, we pick apples. If we plant generosity, we get it returned. If we plant entitlement, we get that returned as well.

When medical professionals worry more about their patients feeling cared for than protecting themselves from malpractice suits, creative ideas emerge. I know of a hospital that bakes fresh cookies for their patients, knowing a warm cookie might bring some much-needed joy. When patients feel valued by their physicians, they offer their trust and loyalty instead of their suspicion and skepticism.

When as an executive you don't just tell your assistant your schedule but also know enough about *her* kid's sports schedule to let her leave early on a game day, your assistant feels seen and valued and you get those hours returned fivefold.

If instead of telling customers how the chef wants them to

order, you document the order and offer something custom to their preferences the next time they dine, you've made a customer and an ambassador for life.

Honoring those we serve is a key principle in creating a virtuous cycle of generosity. Before we can do that, philosophically, we have to reconcile our idea of power differentials and see service as a strength. Once we've done that, then we mine for the gold by being curious and then respond to what we discovered. Like the gardener enjoying the fruits of his labor, when we take these steps, we don't just enrich the lives of others, we enrich our own lives.

Principle One:
Speak the Good

Practice One: Speak Kindly to Yourself

Practice Two: Speak Kindly About Others

Principle Three

Principle Two:
Honor Those You Serve

**Practice One: Mine for the Gold
by Being Curious**

What Do I Have in Common?

What Is Inspiring?

Practice Two: Apply What You Discovered

Proactively Respond

Customize Your Generosity

Principle Four

PRINCIPLE THREE: EARN THEIR RESPECT

PRACTICE ONE: STAND IN THEIR SHOES

In the last chapter, we put a few words under the microscope to see the layers of meaning and feeling they evoke. The words "power", "honor," and "serve" are weighty words worthy of reflection. We humans are meaning makers. We find more meaning in our stories than in data or definitions. We may hold Webster's definition of a word in our heads, but if I ask you what a word means *to you,* the meaning you hold in your heart will be connected to your experiences with that word. As we look at the next principle that helps us move from a vicious cycle of entitlement to a virtuous cycle of generosity, there's another word whose meaning we have to reflect on: respect.

Let's get the dictionary definition out of the way so we can mine deeper into the stories we hold with that word. Oxford defines *respect* as both a noun and a verb:

noun

noun: **respect**; plural noun: **respects**

> a feeling of deep admiration for someone or something elicited by their abilities, qualities, or achievements

> "the director had a lot of respect for Douglas as an actor"

verb

verb: **respect**

> admire (someone or something) deeply, as a result of their abilities, qualities, or achievements

> "she was respected by everyone she worked with"

That's the technical definition of the word, but to experientially define the word, we return to the wise place of paradox.

As a noun, respect is something we have. As a verb, respect is something we do. In noun form, paradoxically, respect is defined both as a feeling we have and a regard for the feelings of others. It is a feeling of deep admiration for someone or something elicited by a person's abilities, qualities, or achievements (I respect how hard how they've worked). *And* respect is also defined as due regard for the feelings, wishes, rights, or traditions of others (kids should respect their parents). In verb form, respect means to admire someone or something deeply, as a result of their abilities, qualities, or achievements (he was respected by everyone on the team).

Moving from the head down to the heart, once again, I would ask what feelings come up when you hear that word. What stories do you hold that shape what that word means to you? Like power, our relationship with respect infiltrates the moments that make up our days. The big ones and the little ones. In some environments, our awareness is heightened to the presence or absence of respect. As someone who surfs and trains in mixed martial arts, I've learned that respect is literally the price of entry. Show up without it, and you'll be shown to the mat (or the sand). Being a parent and the owner of a company are also places where being respect-aware seems obvious. But noticing the vicious and virtuous cycles operating in the interactions between all people, not just those we know, has shown me that little moments carry a barometer for respect as well. Observe the average driver on the road with other drivers, and you'll be able to quickly determine their relationship with respect.

The thing that makes respect so pervasive in our lives is that it acts like a plumb line, measuring the depth of our hypocrisy. It's something all of us want from others, all the time. Yet if we're honest with ourselves, it's not something we readily give to others, all the time. I'll go first with the confession: I hate how my own hypocrisy gets exposed when thinking about respect. Entitlement has me fuming when I'm disrespected, totally consumed with believing I'm owed something better. But as it so masterfully does, entitlement also blinds me to the times I didn't offer respect, didn't give something someone else was equally owed. That's the insidious nature of entitlement. It is the consummate hindrance to perspective.

Montana is our happy place. But it's also wild and should be respected as such. We once had an unforgettable experience with bats. Every night at dusk we would see bats flying back and forth under the eaves of the exterior roof, looking like they'd made a home in the space between the exterior and interior walls. The bats had been getting in through a tiny crack in the outside wall. We learned the hard way that not all wildlife experts are exactly "experts." The first person we called came and plugged the hole, telling us the bats would die of starvation when they couldn't fly out at night to feed. What he didn't keep in mind is that the fight for survival is innate, so in a desperate fight to live, the bats found another tiny crack in the crawl space between the roof and the interior ceiling and were now coming inside the house. The peak of the nightmare culminated with sixteen bats flying in the living room and bedrooms while the five of us ran screaming for cover. The second wildlife specialist we called revealed the stupidity of the first guy's strategy as evidenced by the real-life horror movie we were living. Then he drilled a hole in the outside wall and installed a one-way trap. When hungry, bats could get out into the night sky to feed, but they couldn't get back in.

Entitlement is like that. It's a one-way trap that lets our perspective out, but it doesn't let other perspectives back in. And often, it is our experiences with respect that serve as a spotlight, revealing entitlement in our lives. Entitlement is undeveloped or immature perspective. Ideally as we grow in age, we hopefully grow in awareness, and in a perfect world, experiences of ourselves and others mature our perspective. Sadly, blindness doesn't have an expiration date, and we've all encountered people who have ignored the lessons life offers that would've raised their maturity and lowered their entitlement. If you want to take a measure of your entitlement, the fastest way is to notice your response to being disrespected. No one likes it, of course, but there's a difference between feeling discomfort and feeling an explosion. Someone once said:

> *"Maturity is when you have the power to destroy someone who did you wrong, but you just breathe, walk away and let life take care of them."*

Not only can entitled people not walk away when they're disrespected, they can't breathe. When disrespected, entitlement seethes with a hyperventilating anger.

Universally, respect is something all of us want. Full stop. And something else that's universal, whether in your office, at a store, with your partner or your child, with one of your customers or service providers, by the friend at your table, or the stranger on the road is that at some point today you will be given less respect than you deserve. You will be *dis*respected. In that very moment, your response contributes to whether you will kick off a vicious cycle with the other person or a virtuous one.

With the first principle, we noticed the wisdom of language that tells us what *to* do, where *to* go, as opposed to what *not* to do, where *not* to go. We saw that if the first principle included both directives, it would be: speak the good, *don't* be a critic. If this third principle were to include both directives, it would be: earn respect, *don't* expect it.

Recall the energies that operate inside the cycles. The vicious cycle is an energy of taking. The virtuous cycle is an energy of giving. We all deserve respect. But expecting it is a taking energy. It's like the difference between earned authority and imposed authority. The moment I play my authority card in a power struggle, I've actually undermined my authority. "Because I'm in charge and I said so" is another way of saying "because I'm at a loss as to how to get what I need from you, or I don't have time to figure it out, so I'll play the only card I have."

The transforming intention we choose with this principle is to *earn* respect as opposed to expecting it. Some might say expecting respect is a reasonable desire, especially among the power differentials we see in everyday relationships. From coach to player, parent to child, teacher to student, veteran to rookie, executive to assistant, sage to novice, customer to server, some would argue that respect is a fair assumption. The argument here isn't for what is fair and reasonable. The invitation is to see what is generous and how generosity changes the tone in relationships. The transference of respect is like trust; it's not binary. It's given, *and* it's earned. And when those that could safely presume to be respected by another set their intention to earn it, it changes the game.

The difference between expecting respect and earning it is a story that has been told for all time. Historical figures like Jesus, Gandhi, and Martin Luther King Jr. all earned the respect of the masses, enraging those with powerful titles, who expected it. Cult classic movies like *Gladiator* and *Braveheart* are meditations on that same theme. We see the obligatory, heartless homage paid to those with titles who expect and demand respect. But the inspiring respect that follows wherever it's led, sacrifices whatever the cost, marches in the face of danger, and gives generously over and again is willingly offered to those who have earned it.

My confession here is that learning this lesson has been hard for me. Progress in my growth and promotion in my leadership was something I would constantly sabotage when triggered by disrespect. No matter how many books on leadership I read or how pure my intentions, when I didn't receive the respect I expected, I couldn't bring myself to "breathe, walk away and let life take care of them." When I heard descriptions of my personality or my leadership, like the asterisk on Barry Bond's home run record, there was always a "but" to how people saw me. They would affirm my passion, vision, and ability to inspire, but in an attempt to be diplomatic, they would use a word like "intense" or "intimidating" to describe how my less than admirable reactions had surfaced in a tense moment.

The vicious cycle and the virtuous cycle that exist between people are based on choices we make, not once and for all, but over and again as we interact with the world around us. Our approach to respect is a choice. We can expect it and when we don't receive it, demand it. And the vicious cycle will be the result. Or we can earn it. And a virtuous cycle will begin. Once we're aligned with the principle of earning it, the obvious question is: how?

PRACTICE ONE: STAND IN THEIR SHOES

I've found the most profound truths that change my life are not complicated. A child could understand them. But they're hard. Standing in the shoes of others is one of those challenging disciplines that is becoming a lost art in our public discourse. A mantra of Richard Rohr's is that we don't see things as they are—we see things as *we* are. Confessing our perspective as subjective takes humility. It's a humility grounded in the wisdom that our information is always partial.

The timeless format of debate used to reveal this intuitively. In ages past, debate was a form of mining, uncovering unexposed sides of a topic so that the gem of truth could be revealed more fully. Lately, debate has become a form of verbal blood sport, attempting to eviscerate any validity of the other perspective, so a victor can hold the prized trophy of being "right."

I am not a relativist, believing that there are no absolutes. There are. What I've learned is that reality is always presenting us with opportunities to admit the limits of our perspective. Do you believe everything you think? I used to. I couldn't see it at the time, but when we operate that way, clinging to our self-penned volumes of absolutes, a subconscious barometer relentlessly measures our interactions. That barometer gauges if we're aligned with others or where they're wrong. Find someone who believes they're always right and I promise you, no matter how profound their insights, you will also find someone who is, at best, deeply judgmental and, at worst, arrogant, ignorant, and mean.

Virtuous cycles in our interactions can still stand on absolutes, but they stand on more solid ground than the sand of our limited perspective. Curiosity in the experiences of others and viewing the dignity of their journey as valid is an absolute that you can trust.

We can put this principle into practice by standing in the shoes of the other. It's a practice that asks better questions, even in the face of an overtly offensive person. Instead of asking "what's wrong with them?" or "where are they wrong?" we start to ask "what happened to them?" and "what have they experienced?"

Typically, we don't initiate this shift until we're cornered. We run on the programs of our operating system, until the system crashes. For me, my system started crashing in 2016. There had been signs that I needed a system update: tension in my marriage, conflict in my friendships, embarrassing arguments with strangers, exasperation with employees, but I chalked those up to glitches. Until I couldn't. There was too much strife and too many patterns of conflict to ignore. Signs turned to billboards, screaming for me to own my culpability in the circumstances I didn't like. In an attempt to find more peace and a desire to live up to my potential, I went on a therapy retreat called "Living Centered" where, in a group setting, we were invited to reflect on our stories in hopes of seeing and overcoming the obstacles to living, well...more *centered*.

The first day in our group, it was all I could do to not get up and walk out. Had I driven and not flown to the retreat, I would have left. I was convinced I was in the wrong place. People in my group were addicted to substances, addicted to food, unfaithful to their partners, addicted to sex, some couldn't hold down a job. I was the founder and CEO of a growing company, faithful to my wife, a loving father, physically fit, disciplined in my habits, and in my estimation (to my arrogant and ignorant mind) these people were a wreck. There were traumas mentioned I had no experience with. I had been raised by parents who loved me, loved each other, were respected in the community, provided for me, brought me to church, and sent me to a great college. Sure, I'd had some hardships, but what kid didn't? I was firmly convinced I was in the wrong place (aka at best, deeply judgmental and, at worst, arrogant, ignorant, and mean).

Over the course of the week, we began telling our stories. What was so insightful was that we were prompted to go further back than our own beginning. The human tendency to see ourselves as the lead actor in the saga of our lives was intentionally widened by forcing us to expand the saga to the generations that came before us. What did we recall of our parents' stories? And their parents'? We reflected on how that shaped our early journeys. We were shown how our paths (and often our obstacles) aren't only about what happened to us, and that the meaning we make from those episodes and how we respond (or react to them) is even more important.

As only therapy can, the space to reflect brought back buried memories. Recall in the early pages the childhood trauma from my neighbor. I remembered (yes, I had "forgotten") that I had been sexually molested as a child. It may sound bewildering and somewhat tragic that I had buried it to the point of not remembering such a traumatic event. But when it had happened, I filed it away as the older neighbor kid misbehaving when his parents weren't home. Even though I was only nine years old, I felt like I was partially to blame, so I was too ashamed to tell my parents. And equally as formative, I started to see the impact of being made fun of, bullied, and socially ostracized nearly all of my formative years.

Sometimes we have to see our story before we can tell it.

What I started to see wasn't just what happened *to* me but what happened *in* me. The episodes weren't the main dish of the work; they were the ingredients. The six-course meal was the operating system I had built in response to the episodes. As I shared my story, I softened. And what I found from these people I had so arrogantly deemed "wrecks" was reciprocated softness, grace, empathy, and understanding. We humans are way more transparent than we presume. Even though people can't read our thoughts, they can read our eyes and our body language. My guess is the judgmentalism that I brought into the room was visible to others. Regardless, those that I had presumed "beneath" me became my teachers. They showed me love and empathy. The retreat intentionally tells us to keep our careers and accomplishments to ourselves. I was experiencing love for who I was, for my humanity, for my story, without sharing one aspect of my achievements or successful accomplishments. Like a kid who has only known puddles, seeing the ocean for the first time, I felt a foreign feeling:

Wonder.

I started to feel seen in a different way than I had ever been, and it was changing something deep in my operating system.

Others started sharing their stories. Cracks in the launchpad of their lives, destabilizing blows to their agency, a lack of the foundational bonds we all need to form our sense of self. The feelings they shared were feelings I identified with and deeply resonated with. I started having thoughts like "I probably would have responded the same way if that happened to me." And then the craziest thing happened.

I saw my own addiction.
My addiction was to the way that I think.
I had a pattern of holding my perspectives as absolute.

Eastern thought uses the word *attachments* to describe the universal human tendency to form coping mechanisms for the circumstances that dysregulate us. The vocabulary of the West to alternatively use the word "addiction" keeps many of us from seeing that while there might not be a twelve-step program to overcome our patterns of coping, we all have them. My addiction was harder to discover because it is more sinister and culturally accepted. There isn't yet a twelve-step group for perspectives—anonymous, for people who are powerless over their attachment to thinking they're always right and believe they see everything clearly. When triggered, some drink, some snort, some have sex, some pick up their phones, some work, some shop, some gamble.

I analyzed.
And judged.

And filed people and situations into an intricate filing system I'd created.

My high was being "right" in my own eyes.

The epic high was when I was right in the eyes of others.

Proving and justifying became the habits to get me "high," calm, regulated, and feeling all is right with the world.

And here's where the work gets even harder.

I saw that this practice was generational.

One of those big words that has lots of facets is "religion."

I saw there is a facet of a religious mindset that links being right with existential and cosmic standing.

Keeping whatever faith practice we have but losing a religious and existentially judgmental mindset has nothing to do with getting tattoos, growing long hair, and cussing in public. It has to do with recognizing our tendency to presume that we stand shoulder to shoulder with God, as experts on the divine preferences for humanity.

Your practice may not link your perspectives or opinions with any divine source, but when they're held as absolute, the effect is the same. We presume that we objectively see Reality, capital R. Much innovation and entrepreneurialism has been born of our attempts to push against Reality. At one point, getting across an ocean in a matter of hours wasn't reality. Until someone invented the airplane. The trap is when we succeed, it blinds our ability to recognize when we've come against a wall we cannot break. There is a trail of broken relationships, failed companies, fallen icons, and disgraced institutions left by those whose track record of success blinded them from seeing when Reality held its ground and would no longer bend to their wills.

As someone who takes great pride in my ability to break through barriers, I had to learn a hard lesson.

You can fight Reality.
But Reality
Doesn't
Lose.

Seeing my inability to stand in the shoes of others' perspective as an addiction that was a *generational* burden set me on the hard work of making the following determination: things that "run in the family" will run out with me.

The work of addiction expert Gabor Maté has taught me that healing comes when, instead of seeing our coping mechanisms as something to be judged and criticized, we see them as understandable habits we formed to survive but that are no longer serving us.

The work of Dick Schwartz and Internal Family Systems has taught me that hating parts of ourselves in hopes of banishing them only drives them deeper into our shadow, where instead of quieting, they revolt and sabotage other parts of our lives. The way to quiet them and integrate them into a more mature cohesive flow is by listening to what they're saying, empathizing with them as intending to help us, and thanking them for their service.

I didn't need to start hating my mind or my perspectives or my opinions and abilities to analyze situations. I just needed to see that, like the gym rat that only bench-presses but has chicken legs, I needed to work other muscles. I needed to be able to hold two things simultaneously: the validity of my viewpoints and the viewpoints of others. I needed to do the work of standing in the shoes of others. And when I do, rather than being diminished or negated, I'm actually expanded and enlarged.

Like I said earlier, standing in others' shoes isn't complicated, but it's hard. It can be hard to bridge the gap between people, between races, genders, sexual orientations, beliefs, cultures, even generations. We make progress when we recognize our own way of seeing as subjective. Ways of seeing aren't only individual, they are collective, built on the common experiences of whatever identity groups we occupy.

As a member of Gen X, I see the world so differently than baby boomers, and as a former "disrupter," I get frustrated when I perceive rigidity in their mindsets. But Pearl Jam is no longer the voice of a generation disrupting the establishment, and as Gen X is hopefully moving into eldership, Millennials and Gen Z present my generation with the hard opportunity of standing in their shoes.

Here lies the existential hope of our collective flourishing. When we see that vicious cycles don't just take place between people but between groups, we see the invitation to a better way: a virtuous cycle. When generosity exists between generations, genders, cultures, faiths, and ideologies, like a sapling becoming an oak, we see the humble beginnings of potential for strength and stability. Reciprocal respect is the undeniable prerequisite for that potential, and standing in others' shoes is how that respect starts to be given.

To be clear, this does not mean we become void of conviction or passion. It's that we hold our zeal as roots for our own grounding, not as indictments for flaws in others. Netflix featured a documentary called *Mission Joy* that films a conversation over the course of several days between Bishop Desmond Tutu and the Dalai Lama. To know anything about either of them is to know they are men of deeply held conviction, passion, and proven dedication to their beliefs. The subject matter of those beliefs comes from the sacred well of their views about the divine and life itself. To be sure, there are vast differences between their worldviews—views on which their lives are staked. Yet to watch them interact, you see their missions transcend their positions and become a collaborative mission: joy. While holding their viewpoints, they still generously offer respect to one another's positions. And, as leaders of masses, their mutual respect models and paves the way for their vast group of followers to follow suit.

The path to earning respect from others by standing in their shoes might look different depending on the environments you stand in. In my industry of hospitality, there have been many chefs, sommeliers, cocktail experts, restaurateurs, caterers, and event planners that early in their careers were abused to excellence and in turn have adopted those practices as their initiation rites to filter out mediocrity. In the name of commitment to their craft and feeling entitled to respect, they've forgotten to stand in the shoes of their support staff and their customer. Yet little by little, signs of a sea change are afoot as both employers and employees in the service industries recognize a need for a better way.

In a recent CNN article, Michelin-starred chef Simon Rogan depicts the horrors of what many in our industry refer to as the "old school" approach to training and setting standards of excellence.[8] Rogan recalls as a young cook being expected to tolerate cuts on his hands from sanding oyster shells, followed by unbearable stinging from juicing lemons.

> "'Thinking about it now, I'm sure it was an initiation to the kitchen that said: "This is as good as it gets. You've got to earn your stripes. It's gonna be hard. We're gonna push you…" A lot has changed. I think those days (of accepting these behaviors as the norm) are gone, and rightfully so,' he says."

The widely accepted kitchen brigade system where kitchens are run like the military, with cooks shouting "yes, chef!" instead of privates yelling "yes, sir" perhaps had a place at one time. But times need to and are changing. Between the workforce taking an inventory of their own deep unhappiness in their work, collectively calling for change, and the

8 Hiufu Wong Maggie. "The Michelin-starred chef fighting toxic kitchen culture". CNN, August 2022.

often-vicious cycles between the providers and consumers of fine dining, an opportunity for a reset in the service industries is plainly before us.

Perhaps one of the most poignant depictions of the vicious cycle that can occur between creators and patrons of excellent food and beverage is the movie *The Menu,* starring Ralph Fiennes as a gourmet chef at a restaurant on a private island. It depicts a group of customers who are all self-appointed connoisseurs of the finer things having a dining experience provided by one of the world's most prestigious, acclaimed chefs and his team. While the movie includes some morbid and exaggerated elements, as someone who has worked in this industry for over thirty years, I can say that *the dynamics* at play in the characters were eerily accurate. On vivid display was how everyone involved in the exchange felt entitled to more respect and had lost all ability to stand in the other's shoes. The subsequent utter absence of joy in creating and partaking in a world-class experience was sadly palpable. Whether we are offering or receiving the best this world can offer, when we pause to take an honest inventory and see that there is no joy in the experience, the toll crushes our soul.

In a sobering example of art imitating life, René Redzepi, renowned chef and founder of what many have described as the world's (think about that: the world's) best restaurant, Noma, recently closed his restaurant, citing the financial and emotional toll.

Expecting respect is a forgetfulness of our own humanity and a blindness to the humanity of others. It creates a vicious cycle between proprietor and customer and every other group you can think of. An antidote to this viciousness is the practice of standing in others' shoes. As we do it, we flip the script to generosity and begin to earn the respect we so desperately desire.

Principle One:
Speak the Good

Practice One: Speak Kindly to Yourself

Practice Two: Speak Kindly About Others

Principle Three:
Earn Their Respect

Practice One: Stand in Their Shoes

Principle Two:
Honor Those You Serve

Practice One: Mine for the Gold by Being Curious

What Do I Have in Common?

What Is Inspiring?

Practice Two: Apply What You Discovered

Proactively Respond

Customize Your Generosity

Principle Four

PRINCIPLE THREE: EARN THEIR RESPECT

PRACTICE TWO: PURSUE RECONCILIATION WHEN OTHERS FEEL LET DOWN

Conflict is a mystery.

And a paradox.

It can't be filed neatly into one box. Labels like "bad," "good," "my problem," "your problem," "right," or "wrong" aren't the end of the matter. Conflict is exhausting. It is also instructive. It makes us tired. It makes us strong. It makes us angry. It makes us better. Whatever life metaphor you use: the weights tearing the muscle to strengthen it, the iron that sharpens iron, or the suffering that softens us…

Conflict

Just

Is.

One of my confessions is that as an Enneagram 8 with an intense personality, I've learned I might be more comfortable with conflict than others. As I age and hopefully grow, I've had to recognize that my willingness to confront and engage in conflict can make others feel uncomfortable and want to retreat. The irony is that as a highly sensitive and relational person, I'm (sometimes to a fault) deeply impacted by strain and breaks in relationship. In the aftermath of that retreat, like all of us, I'm faced with a choice: resign to the distance or attempt to close the gap by pursuing reconciliation.

To that end, I've had to learn a lot about reconciliation. What it is, what it isn't, how to do it, and how not to do it. Simply, I've learned that reconciliation is something we can only pursue, we can't mandate. Reconciliation is an outcome, and no matter how hard we try, outcomes will not be controlled, especially when other people are involved. The virtuous cycle becomes possible when despite the outcome, we at least *pursue it.*

Even though conflict as a force can't be filed into our labeled boxes of bad or good, the sad outcome of many conflicts is that they break relational connection. Yes, some relationships are best ended and in those situations, conflict was likely the battle that preceded peace. But in many cases, the broken connections caused by conflict are a less than ideal outcome. They're the tragic aftermath of a vicious cycle. To that end, reconciliation is an attempt to *restore relationship.*

Relationships are a continuum. Not all connections are created equal. The relationship we have with our life partners, our families, and our friends is obviously different than those we have with customers, employers, employees, teachers, students, or the clerk at the counter. Yet in all of those interactions, we are presented with conflicts, little or large, that can lead to the severing of those ties, no matter how significant (or insignificant) they may be. It can be hard to recognize, but as we allow a pattern of severed relational ties to go unmended, it becomes more likely a vicious cycle of entitlement will become ingrained in us, leaving us baffled and bitter by our isolation.

Remember, no one ever thinks to themselves: "I'm entitled." We usually have to listen to our language, especially how we talk about the conflicts and frustrations we have with others.

When we hear ourselves speaking about "them" and "what they did" and "what they don't see" or "their flaws" without reflecting on our own actions, our culpability, our side of the street, entitlement is taking root. Entitlement is fundamentally *anti-relational.* Connection and entitlement can't coexist. Entitlement breaks the mayonnaise.

Pursuing reconciliation is how we combat that downhill slide toward the blindness of our own entitlement. And while the relationship being restored is a great outcome, the results of our efforts to reconcile don't necessarily determine whether or not we're in a vicious or virtuous cycle. Pursuing reconciliation may change the relationship, but it definitely changes us. When we pursue reconciliation in the aftermath of conflict, no matter what happens between us, what happens *within* us is that we become more generous with others. We harvest what we plant. We may or may not reap that generosity in the given circumstance, but as increasingly generous people, we are likely to see generosity returned to greater measure in the future.

As we know, when the student is ready, the teacher appears. In my life, between business coaches, elders, therapists, mentors, and wise friends, as I processed various conflicts with them, I realized that like many of us, I had to be taught by these guides *how* to reconcile. I'm still learning, but like only the mystery of conflict can, patterns of conflict cornered me into confessing my stubbornness and embracing the teachability of a beginner's mind.

A key moment came when I learned the nuanced difference between agreeing and empathizing. Empathy is what is most needed for reconciliation, not alignment. Reconciliation is not found on the zero-sum extremes of "I see it how you see it" or "let's agree to disagree." When forced into a binary premise of either dismissing the perspective of others or forfeiting the validity of our own, the relationship loses every time.

Literal years of strife are the result of feeling trapped by that lose/lose mindset. When conflict came, I naïvely assumed people were looking to be agreed with. And if I couldn't agree with how they saw it, the requirement to deny how I saw it in order to preserve connection felt like an impossible option. The higher the relational stakes, the more untenable that premise becomes. The concept of real empathy was foreign to me. It was so freeing to be shown a third way. I learned that what people want most when they retreat or feel disappointed is to be empathized with. It's an art of the heart, not the head. Repairing broken bridges of connection comes when we identify with their feelings more than their perspective. They may hope we see it how they see it, but what they really want is for us to *feel* it how they felt it. Take it from a reformed combatant, when people feel *felt,* they drop their weapons.

Far from an abstract practice of psychobabble, identifying with how people feel can be a learned sequence of steps. A river of tears was shed on the therapist's couch as my wife Nicole and I were coached in the unfamiliar process of mirroring, clarifying, validating, repairing, and investigating in the pursuit of empathizing for the sake of reconciliation. I credit one of our many therapists, Mark Reid, for teaching us these steps, which I'm sure he learned from another source as well. Learning the steps of these conversations changed how I navigate relationships and literally changed my life.

What's amazing is that these steps of reconciliation, learned on behalf of my marriage, have translated to relatively innocuous relationships and everything in between. I've used these steps in big conflicts with my kids and co-workers, and I've also used them in minor misunderstandings with parents at our kids' school, vendors, customers, guys at the gym, or fellow surfers in the water that I don't know at all.

Conflict resolution is reciprocal hosting. When you ask some-one to listen to something you need to say, you're playing the role of host. They're receiving (hopefully) something you're offering. And even though what you're offering might not be as exciting as a Negroni on the rocks, you're still hoping it will be received. If you're the person responding, the role of host has in that moment shifted to you. You're now the one offering a response that you hope will be received. You host, I host, you host, I host. It's a dance.

At this point we're crystal clear that when we host with the intention to make the other person feel valued, we've extend-ed hospitality. What follows are steps to bring the act of hos-pitality into risky conversations. We *can* have conflict while still intending to make the other person feel valued. We can do two things at once, or we can choose to do one thing: get our point across. It's harder to do two things, and…you guessed it: it's a cycle. The harder thing—giving what we want to get—is how we arrive at our hoped-for destination. When we invite hospitality into our pursuit of reconciliation, the likelihood of success, the likelihood of *peace,* is signifi-cantly increased.

Just like meals, reconciliation conversations have levels of depth. Some meals consist of guac, chips, salsa, beer, and a paper towel for a napkin. Other meals consist of another universe of complexity and attention to detail. Effective reconciling is like that. Not everyone uses the same language around feelings and emotion, but *everyone feels*. And everyone wants to be heard. Some conversations call for a "paper towel napkin" level of depth but the steps still apply. Other conversations will require Michelin-star type attention to detail in how we speak about our feelings. Regardless, you can apply these steps in a way that fits the context of the relationship.

The first step is mirroring. Before people can feel felt, they need to feel heard. There is a vulnerable exposure involved in sharing our frustrations. Sure, there are the odd occasions of venting without caring whether we're heard (or odd ducks who make a practice of it). But typically, people are feeling a chaotic soup of emotions before they summon the courage to tell us hard things. When they finish, responding with a short "I get it" just builds the walls higher than before. Mirroring is the act of offering back to them what we've heard. To mirror, our first response should be "What I hear you saying is..." With as much neutrality as we can summon, we repeat what we heard them say. This is of course nuanced and can be weaponized. Tone matters, and if our tone reveals our contempt for what they said, hearing their own words sent back to them with a hostile energy won't make them feel heard. Knowing this tendency, in the name of caution and minimizing the chances of poor mirroring making things worse, some have created rigid approaches to mirroring. One of those practices is called Imago Dialogue, where you literally repeat word for word the exact words someone said. While I appreciate the intent of a literal repeating—keeping conflict resolution on the rails—I've found feeling heard happens in the heart. Hearing my vulnerable words mechanically repeated back to me verbatim doesn't engage my heart. I prefer a more fluid approach. But tone, neutrality, and non-exaggeration are urgent keys for mirroring that lead to reconciliation.

For example, if someone says to me, "This thing you do really bothers me," and I respond with "I hear you saying *everything* I do bothers you," that isn't effective mirroring. It's a counterpunch that only escalates the fight.

Two things help keep us from armoring up when we mirror the hard things others have said to us: first, suspending our own judgment of what has been said. We don't have to agree or disagree, affirm or deny. We just mirror what we heard. Secondly, feeling assured in the fact that in most reasonable conversations, an opportunity to present our side will come.

If done effectively, even just that first step begins to de-escalate conflict. People begin to drop their defenses when they feel heard, and that openness lays the groundwork for reconciliation.

Sometimes, after someone speaks, we can feel tempted to jump straight to apologizing. We may want to minimize drama, we might not be feeling defensive and are willing and happy to apologize, or we may want to just get the conversation over with quickly. Don't skip mirroring. When we're upset, we want an apology, but the universal desire in all of us is to be understood. When we quickly apologize after someone has spoken, the relief they experience is only partial. They may resign to end the conversation, but there is a high probability of the conflict reoccurring if they didn't feel heard. When people feel heard, they feel understood. Mirroring is a critical first step in pursuing reconciliation.

The second step is clarifying that we heard them correctly.

After we repeat what we heard, asking them "did I get that right?" gives them the opportunity to clarify. In an ideal world, we've adopted Brené Brown's brilliant practice of writing down our own "shitty first draft" *before* we come and say hard things to people so that as they are trying to contain what we're saying and listen, others are spared the carnage and potential hurt of our unedited presentations. I know. It may sound impractical and unlikely that we are going to literally write down a version of the hard things we want to say to others. I would say the higher the relational stakes and the heavier the words are, the more we should prepare. Even with an edited version, most of us stumble our way through these conversations, and as our listener puts back what they heard us say, we appreciate the opportunity to offer "that's not exactly what I mean."

If hospitality is about making people feel valued, one of the most common places people feel devalued, dismissed, and ignored is during moments of conflict (whether big or small) and conversations intended to resolve them. Restaurateur Danny Meyer calls hospitality a dialogue, not a monologue. Good conflict resolution is the same. Monologuing our frustrations in anger, dropping the mic, and receiving a post-diatribe "sorry about that" isn't reconciliation. We might feel momentary relief after giving the monologue, but as we settle down, we can feel unheard, misunderstood, shame for how we spoke, and usually more shut down by the lackluster response. Conversely, if we had to listen to the monologue, we may feel flooded by everything and like the kitchen sink just came at us.

Clarifying after we mirror that we heard someone correctly gives them the opportunity to be imperfectly human in sharing frustration and then circle back with a second chance to be clearer.

After we've mirrored and clarified that we've heard them clearly, we mirror the edited version again and then move to the third step: validating. Here's the juice of reconciliation: validating isn't agreeing. It merits repeating.

Validating
Isn't
Agreeing.

Even as different as we may be, when in conflict with someone, we summon the commonality of the human experience and ask ourselves what we might have felt in a similar situation. Emotions like anger, frustration, exasperation, and hurt are secondary emotions. We feel them *after* feeling something else. We feel disrespected and then feel angry for feeling disrespected. We feel abandoned and then we feel hurt by those feelings of abandonment. We feel tired and then we feel exasperated by being pushed when we're tired.

Conflict resolution usually starts with someone expressing

those secondary emotions first. Reconciliation comes when we as a listener get past the anger, frustration, exasperation, and hurt to validate the feelings underneath. We do that with imagination and curiosity. We stand in their shoes and imagine what we might have felt if we had experienced the same thing.

"I imagine you might have felt _____. Is that *some* of what you were feeling?"

Typically, the response will be "Yes! That's *exactly* what I felt!"

Sometimes someone may tweak our summary, but our attempts to imagine their experience usually soften their adjustment.

"It wasn't so much that I felt_____. I felt a little more _____."

Reasonable people don't need us to capture every feeling they experience in conflict. Like salt, a little goes a long way. When we accurately name just one of their core feelings, even the toughest eggs begin to crack. Then, *then* we validate that *feeling*. We don't have to validate their logic, their interpretation of a situation, or how they arrived at what they feel. We just express that those feelings are valid. Odds are we've felt the same thing at some point, and suspending any entitlement we might feel on our side of the conflict, we generously offer words that validate their feelings.

"I hear you're angry. I imagine that might be because you felt ignored by me. Is that some of what you felt? That's so hard. You make sense."

Dialogue is the key to reconciliation. Again, it's a dance: you step, I step, you step, I step.

"I'm really mad you didn't talk to me the entire night."

"I hear you saying you're mad I didn't talk to you all night. Did I get that right?"

"Actually, it's not that you didn't talk to me—I know you were with your friends—but you didn't even check in to see if I was okay."

"I hear that you're mad I didn't check in. Is that right?"

"Yeah, that's right."

"I imagine you felt ignored and uncared for by that. Is that some of what you felt?"

"Yes! That's *totally* how I felt."

"That's so hard. Feeling ignored is so hard. You make sense."

Notice-it's not necessary to agree with the perspective.

"I totally ignored you" probably isn't something you'll be inclined to say.

"You *felt* ignored. That sucks. That makes sense" is something we can bring ourselves to say.

When done well, the dance can actually be beautiful and the mystery of conflict is that as we dance, we become closer. Ever seen MMA fighters hug and kiss each other after beating the shit out of each other? They respect one another for getting in the ring and doing the dance.

Conversely, entitlement debates, denies, diverts, and defends in those situations.

"You told me to go have fun! I haven't seen those guys in years. I wasn't ignoring you. What was I supposed to do? I can't read your mind. I looked over at you and it looked like you were in a conversation. What about you? You didn't check on me either. I don't understand why you told me to have fun and now I'm being punished for doing what you suggested I do."

And so spins the vicious cycle.

It's generous to validate other people's experiences and feelings, even if the path to where they landed doesn't make sense to us. The path to their feeling makes sense to *them.* Validating isn't agreeing with how they got there. It's identifying with where they landed. And in conflict resolution, it's a must-have for reconciliation.

The next step is repairing.
Repair is where we summon two very weighty words:
I'm
Sorry.

Volumes could be written on the art of the apology, and to be sure, I'm not qualified to pen the work. However, by now you've probably gathered that my journey has included a lot of apologies. Some effective, some not so much. Like moving past the binary trap of "you're right" or "I'm right" to find the third way of empathy, I've had to learn how to apologize.

Similar apologizing mishaps have led me and many others to struggle to say the words. We free ourselves to authentically say those words when we find that third way. On one extreme is the self-protected "I'm sorry you felt that way." At best that approach falls flat; at worst it escalates conflict. We might as well just say "that sounds like a *you* problem."

"I'm sorry you felt that way" has no ownership, no validating, and no acknowledgment of our culpability in the conflict. It's lobbing a Hail Mary behind the walls of our defenses and hoping we score points. But we don't. I win, but you lose. So, we lose.

Equally, there is the other extreme: an apology that is usually impossible to summon. Where beyond identifying and validating your feeling, I feel forced to agree with your interpretation, logic, or your process. Typically, that trap comes with the threat of rejection if I fail to see it how you see it. I'm cornered by another impossible choice of violating the dignity of my perspective or risking the loss of a relationship. While these corners may not qualify as trauma, in his book *The Myth of Normal,* Gabor Maté brilliantly identifies the birthplace of trauma as having to choose between authenticity and attachment. In hopes of reconciling, I don't want to lose the attachment so I'm dishonestly inauthentic and offer an "I'm sorry, I agree, I totally did that, I meant to, I'm an idiot." You win, but I lose. So, we lose.

The third way acknowledges the impact our choice had on another person and apologizes for that impact. And reassures them that we didn't intend for them to feel what they felt because of our actions.

"I hear you felt ignored by me not checking in on you. I'm sorry that my actions had that impact. I don't want you to feel that way. Ever. I hate feeling ignored. I'm sorry."

That's repairing.

It offers an apology for something I did in fact do, that impacted you negatively, *regardless of whether or not my intentions were bad.*

Our natural defenses want to mention our intentions when we apologize. From a child saying "I didn't mean to" to adults saying "that's not at all where I was coming from," it's a human urge. But conflict is experienced at the level of our actions, not our intentions. As a well-intended yet intense person, I'm often misunderstood. It's hard to apologize without mentioning our misunderstood good intentions, but the power of repair is diminished when we add that to the back end of our apology. I'm learning to let my apology stand on its own. The time for mentioning our intentions can come when it's our turn to speak.

If you've repaired effectively with a third-way apology, you've just served up a very satisfying meal. But good meals are made great by an after-dinner drink. I like whisky. As an Italian, my dad prefers coffee to complete his meal. No matter the hour, he will drink a cup of caffeinated black coffee and drift peacefully off to sleep. (I know sleep experts are crawling in their skin to hear that.)

Mirroring, clarifying, validating, repairing. The final step of a complete reconciliation process is investigating. Like the after-dinner drink that completes the meal, investigating is what makes these conversations go from feeling pretty good to feeling *complete*. This is where we ask them important questions like "do you feel heard?" and "do you feel repaired?" or "is there anything else you need to hear?" Again, you can contextualize the language. "Are we cool?" is equally appropriate for some relationships.

Nine times out of ten, this process has paved the way for the person we're in conflict with to feel reconciled. Occasionally, when the person reflects on their answer, they might have one final splinter that's still stuck. This is a pivotal moment. We've just patiently held their space, and our sense of fairness might start to growl being asked to wait longer for our turn. My advice is to take the time to get the splinter out and go through the steps again. You just removed the big chunks, so it will be faster the second time around. It's better for them to feel purged and soothed than allow a small remnant to reinfect the wound.

It's during this last step of investigating where we pivot the focus and ask if we can take our turn. It's important we frame that as a question, as opposed to an announcement. People usually feel relieved and softened when we take these steps with them. Abruptly demanding our turn with "now I'm gonna talk" will shoot their walls right back up and your hard work will be lost. By framing our desire to take a turn as a question, we give people the chance to ask themselves if our repair has taken root and if they're now in a position to listen to us.

Sometimes when we ask to take our turn, people will request a moment to let our apology sink in. This too can be weaponized. The subtle and relentless nature of entitlement can find its way even into moments like this. When their right to be heard negates your right to be heard, entitlement is close at hand. But it's nuanced. There's wisdom in letting our apologies sink in, and sometimes that takes a moment. If someone asks for time to let your apology sink in before hearing your side, it's on them to circle back and say "I'm ready." When they do, you know you're not dealing with entitlement; you're actually dealing with someone generous who wants to take the time to drop their defenses and really hear what you're saying.

Pursuing reconciliation isn't just about how we listen and respond; it's also about how we speak about our frustrations. Voices much wiser and informed than mine have provided extensive guidance on effective language in conflict resolution. A few simple keys that I've learned are worth mentioning.

One of my therapists, Ron Frederick, gave me a valuable key regarding the language of our feelings. I know what you're thinking: *"this guy has had a lot of therapists!"* It's true and I'm not ashamed. I believe therapy is like emotional fitness. The more we work, the more fit we become. Therapy is for the healthy, not the broken.

Ron taught me a simple way to see the difference between a

feeling and a judgment. It was noticing the word "like" when I spoke about my feelings.

"I feel like they don't see," "I feel like you were...," and "I feel like she totally..." aren't feelings, they're judgments. They're the language of the head, analyzing and judging people and intentions. Judgments make reconciliation almost impossible. People can't suffer feeling judged by other imperfect people, even if we're speaking softly. Saying "I feel like you..." is the fastest way for our listener to put up their guard.

What keeps our listener's guard down is hearing our feelings. Our feelings are language of the heart, and reconciliation happens when conversations are heart-to-heart, not head-to-head. Remember, this practice of pursuing reconciliation manifests the principle of earning the respect of the other. When people feel judged, they feel disrespected. We earn their respect not just by how we listen but also by how we speak.

"I feel really mad," "I feel really disappointed," "I feel misunderstood," "I feel alone," "I feel thrown under the bus."

It's a small but invaluable tweak if we want to be heard.

"I feel *like you* threw me under the bus" will raise my defenses.

"I feel thrown under the bus" is something I can hear. I've felt that way before. The "like you threw me" assigns blame; it states a judgment. I "feel thrown" is stating our feelings.

When pursuing reconciliation, speak your feelings as opposed to your judgments and you've significantly increased the likelihood that you'll be heard.

Secondly, as prolific as Brené Brown is, I imagine there aren't a lot of people who haven't read her, but as a member of the surfing and MMA communities, and having Montana hunters as friends, I can see how a few remaining places remain where her wisdom hasn't yet descended. In her work, she references the lethal blow we deal to reconciliation when we use shame, blame, and criticism.

"What were you thinking?"
"What's wrong with you?"
"Why do you do that?"
"It's not just me that feels this way. Other people feel the same way."
"I'm tired of you doing this to me."

"People don't like it when you do that."
"You really need to get it together."
"This is why your business is failing."
"You're the reason we're in this mess."
"You have a pattern of doing this."
"You're too dramatic."
"You're so sensitive."
"You're so…"

I could go on. We've all heard it. And we've all said it. As a business owner, I've been on the receiving end of the occasional diatribe dump from disgruntled employees or unhappy customers; diatribes littered with shame, blame, and criticism. And you can bet some of my worst moments have included serving up the same things myself.

That's why Brown's practice of writing down a shitty first draft (SFD) *before* you vent your truth is so wise. When we're activated, we're fired up, not thinking objectively, and convinced of our judgments. And if we don't get them out, they find their way in, despite our best efforts. Sometimes people are afraid of speaking directly to us, wanting to avoid conflict or confrontation, and prefer writing. An equally destructive choice is to actually *send* your SFD. I've received more than one letter from people who were afraid to speak to me directly and preferred to eviscerate me with their written words. What was eviscerated was my trust in the relationship, that I replaced with very firm boundaries.

As I said, realistically, we won't take the time to write down our unfiltered feelings for every conflict. Sure, for the high-stakes conversations with our most valued relationships, we may put the time in. But when a co-worker insults us, it's unlikely we're going to pause and go grab our journals. The key is to remember that, unless you are a sage of perfectly disciplined communication, if it's your turn to speak, your unfiltered, vented versions can rarely, if ever, be digested.

Knowing reconciliation is something we can pursue but can't guarantee, it's motivating to remember that when we pursue it, whether or not someone meets us in the ring, we're likely to earn their respect. Again, these steps aren't confined to personal relationships; they apply to professional ones as well.

Reconciliation is an attempt to restore the breaks in human connection, no matter what level of relationship exists. Connection doesn't always mean deep affection, friendship, or intimacy. Basic kindness and civility are aspects of connection that are essential to our mutual coexistence with one another.

John Donne's words that "no man is an island" offend our deeply held American value of ultimate independence, but they're true. Our existence depends on relationships. A relationship isn't something solely between the people we choose to have in our lives for the long haul. We have relationships with our co-workers, our customers, our hairstylists, and strangers in the neighborhood. When we've let others down, we can't guarantee that the relationship will be restored, but we can initiate the practice of reconciliation and when we pursue it, we're behaving like adults who understand that a base level of civility is required for society to function. The attempt on our part to make peace shows a desire to earn their respect.

For those navigating relationships with customers, here's something to remember: refunds do not equal reconciliation.

There are those rare customers (usually takers) that will express their disappointment for the sole purpose of getting a refund, but for the most part, when people go to the length of expressing their disappointment, they're looking for more than just a refund.

How does pursuing reconciliation earn our customer's respect? Because it takes courage to pursue reconciliation, and people respect courage.

In our business of catering, refunds are pretty irrelevant. We can't tell a bride "I'm sorry you didn't like your wedding, your next one is on us." But in restaurants and hotels, refunding a dish, a room charge, or giving a complimentary breakfast doesn't take a lot of courage.

But hearing how our catering customers felt let down and doing everything in our power to reconcile the relationship takes an undefended, courageous posture toward them. And when we do that, our customers respect us.

For us, we've learned that special events that call for catering are high stakes, and here, there are no do-overs. For the most part, we get it right—but every once in a while we miss the mark.

Several years ago, we were catering a wedding for a couple that lived out of state. And after all the revisions and guest count changes were made, we sent them the final bill prior to their wedding, as is our practice.

Due to all the last-minute changes the clients had made, by the time they got the final balance, the couple, family, and extended family and friends had already arrived in Los Angeles.

Shortly after sending it, one of our team members realized that she hadn't included the valet charge on the final contract and needed to resend it, but with another $2,500 added.

This obviously caused a lot of whiplash to the parents of the bride.

As a result, the mother of the bride wanted to look through a long email chain that went months back, to confirm that our event specialist had informed them of the charge, that it was indeed stated in the contract, and that she hadn't already paid it.

All this going back and looking through emails took a lot of time and left the bride's mom missing a welcome brunch for the out-of-town guests.

For those of you that are small business owners, you know that when people are really upset, they contact the owner.

After the wedding, I received one of those emails that every business owner dreads, that said:

"While we understand mistakes happen, your team's

mistake resulted in us sitting in our hotel room, looking through past emails and contracts, instead of hosting our family and friends for an event surrounding our daughter's wedding."

I had a lot of choices in that moment as a business owner.

I could have been defensive and *defended* that our contract states that there are additional valet charges.

I could have *minimized* the offense and pointed out that they didn't miss the wedding or rehearsal dinner; they just missed an extra brunch they had planned.

I could have *blamed them*—I could have told them that their last-minute changes resulted in us revising their final balance way too late in the game, and they could've received the final bill earlier if they hadn't kept making changes.

I could have ignored them. Or sent a short email back.

I could have been *entitled* and fought for the right to be right in this situation. And all that would have done is left my customer feeling entitled as well—that they had the right to not be reviewing contract fine print two days before their daughter's wedding. That approach would have guaranteed a vicious cycle would have spun quickly between us and our customer.

It was hard, but I picked up the phone and used the two practices.
I stood in their shoes.
And then I pursued reconciliation.

As they spoke, I tried to remember my own wedding and how every gathering before and after felt like a sacred time to celebrate this once-in-a-lifetime event. I imagined my own daughter's wedding and how angry I would be if instead of hosting our family and friends, I was on my computer reviewing a contract.

I didn't defend our company. I stood in their shoes. I listened. And then I worked the steps of pursuing reconciliation.

After mirroring what I'd heard and clarifying if I'd heard them right, I validated their feelings. I started first by telling them how angry I would be. How disappointed I would be.

"You must feel such a sense of loss, like that moment was lost and can't be recovered. Is that some of what you feel?"

"Yes! That's *exactly* what we feel."

I utilized the third-way apology.

I didn't use the scripted "I *do* apologize" that corporate call center agents use when they couldn't care less.

Equally, I didn't lie down in utter abdication like some interpretations of service espouse (a typical misapplication of the "customer is always right" credo).

I told them I thought what happened was awful, and I hated the fact that they'd missed one moment of this special weekend because of a mistake we had made. *Regardless of whether or not I could find justification and a defense.*

"I hate that this happened. I am so, so sorry. I don't want you to feel that way. I don't want any of our customers to feel that way. I know when my daughter gets married, I want to savor every single moment. You make sense. As the owner of this company, I want you to hear sincerely, I am sorry."

Then I investigated. I asked what they needed. I asked what I could do. That's a scary question in customer service because you never know how unreasonable the person on the other end of the line is going to be.

But that's the power of reconciliation done effectively. It earns the respect of others and brings out their reasonable responses. This couple wasn't looking for a $5,000 refund; they weren't looking for a $500 refund.

They weren't looking for a refund at all. They didn't feel entitled…they felt let down.

They were looking for a human to connect with and understand their disappointment. Honestly what they were looking for was someone to own their mistake. Restoring the relationship just looked like being courageous enough to listen in an undefended way and care enough to apologize sincerely.

Here's the email I received from the mother of the bride after our conversation.

> *"Hi Steve, thanks for taking the time to chat yesterday.*
>
> *We are in Boiling Springs. If you are ever on the east coast, let us know. Gettysburg is 20 minutes from our home. Hershey is 40 minutes away."*

Notice how the episode ends in generosity. By earning the

customer's respect through standing in her shoes and pursuing reconciliation, a disappointed customer ended up inviting me into her home.

This is how the virtuous cycle wins over a vicious one. We earn the respect of others when we stand in their shoes and pursue reconciliation. Giving wins over taking. Generosity wins over entitlement. The dance brings us closer.

Principle One:
Speak the Good

Practice One: Speak Kindly to Yourself

Practice Two: Speak Kindly About Others

Principle Three:
Earn Their Respect

Practice One: Stand in Their Shoes

Practice Two: Pursue Reconciliation When Others Feel Let Down

Principle Two:
Honor Those You Serve

Practice One: Mine for the Gold by Being Curious

What Do I Have in Common?

What Is Inspiring?

Practice Two: Apply What You Discovered

Proactively Respond

Customize Your Generosity

Principle Four

PRINCIPLE FOUR: CELEBRATE AND IMPROVE

Ah, paradox.

I've mentioned it a lot in previous chapters.

We can see the word and concede the wisdom of accepting it, but concession and implementation are very different things. What makes paradox so hard to accept as a reality of our existence is that it confounds the compartments we create in our minds.

Throughout the ages many cultures have recognized that the mind, body, and spirit are equally important to human thriving. But many of us Westerners are a little late to the game and have naïvely elevated the mind as more important. To be sure, the mind is a wonderful tool, but ignoring the timeless wisdom of integrating mind, body, and spirit as the whole self hasn't helped us. Numerous sage voices in our society helping reintegrate vital parts of our lives that have long been neglected are finding resonance. A tidal wave of content on the benefits of meditation—works like Bessel van der Kolk's *The Body Keeps the Score* and Dr. Iain McGilchrist's *The Master and His Emissary*—are some of the many resources that can help us access dormant parts that we need to live up to our potential. For those of us that need science and data before we're open to the universal wisdom of incorporating mind, body, *and* spirit, I would say seek and you will find. The data is readily accessible and speaks for itself. And for those that find guidance in the stories of others, many inspiring testimonials can be found as well.

Harvard professor of psychology Richard Alpert, who changed his name to Ram Dass and became a spiritual guide to many, details one of the most moving accounts of opening up these dormant parts. In an attempt to widen his lens from seeing his Harvard intellect as the ultimate faculty, Alpert goes on a spiritual pilgrimage to India and meets the man who would become his guru, Maharaj-ji. As his guru starts to use his gift in supernatural ways and verbalize secrets that no one knew—like how Alpert's mother died—Ram Dass details the journey of new parts awakening.

> "My mind is running circles, getting nowhere…It's definitely not in the cognitive psychology textbook…My mind goes faster and faster, trying to figure out how Maharaj-ji knows this. Finally, like a cartoon computer stuck in an insoluble loop, the bell rings, and the red-light flashes. My mind just stops. I'm stuck. My rational mind gives up. It just goes, Pouf! At that same moment, there's a violent wrenching in my chest, a very painful pull, and I start to cry. Later, I realize it was my spiritual heart opening."

Like a seesaw needing two people to work as intended, the mind alone cannot discover the gifts paradox has to offer. Paradox is beyond our rational mind. It defies the categories and absolutes the mind creates. It sits deeper than rationality and dualistic definitions. Like I said about connection, not all paradoxes are created equal. The amusing paradoxes of my personality—being strong and sensitive, an entrepreneur and a mystic, a surfer who loves my Montana cowboy side—are easy for me to swallow. But embracing the lessons found in the paradox of success and failure, peace and conflict, or clarity and confusion are much harder for me to accept. Typically, we buck against the immutability of paradox when we're stuck and want different outcomes. While I hate being stuck, my confession here is that the times I've been stuck, and my rational mind can't find the solution, are usually when my spiritual heart begins to open, and I hear wisdom.

The pursuit of progress is in all of us to some degree. As an entrepreneur, longing for our company to make an impact in its industry, my thirst for progress has been deep. As a husband and father, wanting to have a great marriage and raise great kids, the longing has been even deeper.

So then, what is the recipe for progress? Do we celebrate what we're doing well? Or do we seek to improve where we need to do better? Yes. We do both. It's not "or." It's "and." We celebrate *and* improve.

It might be easy to cognitively agree with the wisdom of doing both. The invitation is to reflect on whether we walk with both of those energies in our relationships. The first relationship to audit is the one we have with ourselves. Are you the eternal optimist, embracing the power of positive thinking and rarely seeing areas you want to improve in yourself? Or are you more like me, hard on yourself, toggling between an internal general that constantly drives for better and the exhausted quitter who collapses beneath the guilt of never being enough? How we treat ourselves is how we will treat others. We may edit our delivery with more socially acceptable communication styles in speaking to others, but whatever is inside makes its way out.

In the first practice of speaking the good, remember the story of me catching myself berating myself and then realizing I would never do that to my son, Dario? It's true. I wouldn't unleash the verbal tirade to him that I was conducting internally. But the critical approach and the small comments could still create an environment of feedback that would've made him feel essentially the same: *never enough*.

Our tendency to emphasize one side of the equation is like riding a bike, only pushing one pedal. We go in circles. To go forward, we have to push both pedals. Why would we do otherwise? Our tendencies have a lot to do with our concept of *better*. In the pursuit of better incomes, better recognition, better feelings, better days, we push on the pedal our programmed reflexes have taught us will get us there.

Remember, these practices are about creating a different cycle in our interactions with people. Moving from interactions where we, and everyone around us, are preoccupied with what we're owed *(entitlement)* to encounters where we and everyone around us are more focused on what we can give *(generosity)*. Achievement can be a by-product of the cycle we create with others, but it isn't the goal in mind. Pushing both pedals of celebrating and improving leads to better interactions. Better interactions lead to better outcomes. But outcomes are the cart before the horse.

We have to identify that we are stuck in vicious cycles before we can want something better. Notice the two images on the cover of this book. One cycle produces chaos and entropy. Another engages the cosmic order of things and produces generativity. When the knot of a vicious cycle winds tighter, practicing the art of celebrating and improving is the fourth principle that untangles the hair ball and brings beauty out of the chaos.

PRACTICE ONE: CELEBRATE WHAT'S WORKING

What does it mean to celebrate? What's the point? Why do we do it, *how* do we do it? What does it accomplish?

I've spent my entire life in the celebrating business. Nearly every single time our company is called on to cater, it is for a celebration of one kind or another. We cater an average of 200 events per year, with guest counts ranging from five to five hundred people. After eighteen years in business, our company has served literally hundreds of thousands of people. I've been given a front-row seat not just to serve people but to *watch* them as they gather and celebrate.

Hosting that many people, I've learned not just about the logistics but also the dynamics at play among people at celebrations. Watching the host in the moments before people arrive, the guests as they filter in and try to find a comfortable conversation, the mingling, the toasts and speeches, the dinner conversations, the parents as they gather everyone to sing "Happy Birthday" to the apple of their eye, the fathers giving away their daughters, the grooms as they watch their soulmates walk down the aisle into their life together, the companies as they launch their new product with anticipation, it's more than parties; it's a study in architecture of the moments that mark our lives.

A valuable lesson I've learned as a host is that people don't always feel celebrated just because there's an event to mark an occasion. I've been to so many gatherings that were designed to celebrate a person, occasion, or an accomplishment, but the awkwardness, fear of embarrassment, or absence of a good emcee left the guests unsure of what to do or say. There's an assumption that the stated purpose of the gathering is enough to achieve the intended outcome just by getting people together. But in the absence of words that convey what we want others to hear and feel, the missed opportunity can be palpable.

As a business owner, I've also had a front-row seat to the dynamics of work: of what people feel, and what they need, day in and day out as they do their job. "Their paycheck is their reward" is a guaranteed way to make sure our teams are looking for other jobs in their off time.

We don't have to be orators or professional party planners. Celebrating others is just the recognition that everyone needs a moment where they feel like their efforts, their life, their vows, their holidays, their moments mean something. We can raise our voice and our glass in our own style and speak the words that let people feel cheered.

As I mentioned earlier, the magic of memorable celebrations transcends all the organization and the myriad little details employed to throw the perfect party. There is a ghost in the machine of celebrations that leaves people feeling the buzz of a good memory.

Through watching every kind of celebration, I've had the

privilege of learning that celebrating is an issue of currency. To get it right, you have to use correct currency, or you could spend your efforts in vain.

A confession here is that I learned a hard rookie lesson about currency on my first trip to play music overseas. It was 1999 and our band had been invited to play in the recently opened East Germany, to celebrate the turn of the century. The first leg of the trip was Los Angeles to Minneapolis where we would catch a flight to Amsterdam, then on to Hamburg, Germany. Except I left my passport on the plane to Minneapolis and had to watch my band board for Europe, while I was stuck in the airport in Saint Paul, Minnesota, on Christmas Eve, waiting for the plane to return the next morning with my passport. Before he left for Amsterdam, our manager handed me our itinerary, with an address in Neustadt, East Germany, and said: "Catch the free train when you land in Hamburg to Neustadt, call this number from the train station and we'll come pick you up."

I caught my flight to Amsterdam the next morning and had a few hours in the airport before my final flight. Knowing my final flight would be short, and I'd need money to make a call when I got there, I used the layover time to get a meal, freshen up, and exchange my money before boarding my final flight.

It's hard for us to remember a time before mobile phones and apps made global travel substantially easier, but this was 1999. I didn't have a phone, there were no apps that instantly translated foreign languages, and GPS was something only governments used.

I got off my final flight, alone, without a translator, not speaking a word of German, trying to find my way to reunite with my band. I was the lead singer, a day late, and knew if I didn't get there soon, we'd have a problem. I fumbled my way to the right train and boarded, saying the only German word I knew to the passengers: "Neustadt? Neustadt? What stop is Noy-Schtaaadt?"

A kind old German man used the universal language of gestures to let me know I had come to my stop. We were now far out of the city, in the East German countryside. I got off the train and arrived at a lonely, empty train station that looked like something out of a World War II movie. I was literally the only person at the station that consisted of a cement platform and one pay phone. I pulled out the phone number and walked to the pay phone to call my ride.

As soon as I put the coins in the phone, they would instantly come out the bottom. I figured it was my ignorance at dialing. Do I use a "1"? Are these numbers an area code that I don't need? I tried over and over, but I couldn't make a call. Then the panic set in. I looked down at my coins and saw the words looked different than the words on the phone. This was long before the euro. I realized I had handed over my dollars at the airport in Amsterdam and, not speaking Dutch, was too ignorant to ask for marks. So naturally the Dutch worker at the currency exchange gave me guilders.

I stood there alone, at an abandoned train station in East Germany, with money that was of no use in this country and a gig that was now hours away from starting.

I was utterly
Lost.

By some miracle, after the longest twenty minutes of my life, a taxi driver came to the train station, and though we didn't speak a common language, I handed him my itinerary, pointed to the address, and arrived moments before the gig. Our German hosts paid my fare, and I sang my lungs out with relief.

Currency represents value. Knowing a person's currency is knowing their language, their needs, what they value. When we celebrate people without knowing their currency, we're lost. We're trying, but our efforts don't connect, because the other person feels celebrated with a different currency.

On a macro level, every culture has a different currency, and in each of those cultures, every individual possesses differences that are even more personal. The roomforty catering staff had to be taught that our practice of serving "ladies first" was offensive to our Korean clients. In that culture, to show respect, the eldest man is served first. I've loved witnessing the diversity of our Jewish clients celebrating with a hora, while lifting couples up in their chairs, our Japanese clients incorporating sacred tea ceremonies, or our clients from the South doing a line dance that gets literally every person out of their chairs.

Celebrating others is an issue of knowing what makes them feel seen and acknowledged, cheering for them in their way of choice.

Remember that as hosts, we have to consider what's happening *in* us before we can tend to what's happening outside of us. Principle one showed us that you can't make others feel at home if you don't feel at home with yourself, comfortable in your skin. As we saw, the very first habit we form to create a generous virtuous cycle is to speak kindly to ourselves. This practice of celebrating adopts the same wisdom. We have to celebrate our own progress, not only the progress of others. Generosity comes from abundance; entitlement comes from perceived scarcity.

It's hard to never feel celebrated by certain people. But the sad reality is that if they're never celebrating others, it's probably because they're never celebrating themselves. The well is dry. Certain fountains only come from within, and we have to drink from those internal wells before we can quench the thirst of others.

It can feel totally foreign at first to know how to celebrate ourselves.

I'm not going to throw myself a party every time I do something good.

Heard. But this is different than speaking kindly to yourself. Speaking kindly to yourself is about affirmation, encouragement, reassurance. This practice is about giving yourself a high five. It's actually *celebrating* your progress. It's understanding our own neurology and the way our minds are hard-wired to crave *reward*. Withholding reward from ourselves is robbing our minds of critical chemicals, and we diminish.

Remember how we learned that Schwartz's science in Internal Family Systems shows us that the parts of ourselves we try to silence just rebel and revolt? Conversely, the parts we acknowledge ask for what they need and, feeling heard, take an integrated seat among the other members of our personality. Giving ourselves an *atta boy, atta girl* when we're making progress is hosting ourselves with hospitality. It's saying: *I see that part of you that just did this, that was awesome!* We're catching ourselves doing something right and making sure the part that just put out valiant effort hears our praise. That part senses our affirmation, feels the juice of a pat on the back, and then gets back in the game. If we withhold the praise, those parts of ourselves that are trying hard to make progress begin to rebel, craving credit or quitting in despair.

This practice has changed my life, especially in my personal and professional relationships. Often the progress we're trying to make is on the back of conflict or others asking us to make a change. Sometimes that request is made for years before we actually hear the urgency of the ask and commit to trying something different.

There have been so many invaluable people who run the day-to-day of our catering company. Our controller, Katrina, our director of catering, Elvira, our executive chef, Tony, our food and beverage director, Devon, our catering manager, Lorenzo, our facilities manager, Marcelino, and the prince of all things Fig House, Kevin, keep our operation running. You can bet after all that time, they've seen more of me than a lot of other people. As the team working closely with a visionary type, they often have a better gauge of what our employees or clients are feeling. I'm out looking at the horizon, and they're looking at what exists right now. They have the unenviable challenge of figuring out how to let me fly while also reminding me the status of our plane. There's been than more than one occasion where the way I'm flying is causing too much turbulence, and they've asked me to make a change.

There have been times I've worked so hard on making the changes they've made clear are critical to our safety. Guess what? My team isn't rushing into the cockpit cheering me on with every little adjustment. It's not that they don't affirm me, it's that they're tending to everyone else on the plane and our clients. And even though I'm technically "the boss," I can't deny the part of me that is earnest, that believes the best leaders are coachable, that wants to please and is looking for an "atta boy, I see you." If that part doesn't get what it needs, it could start driving conversations in an effort to look for credit (a *very* dangerous path for leaders) or resign itself to the fact that the effort isn't seen, so what's the point? (This is an equally destructive approach.) I have to provide that for myself. I have to see that part of me that is trying something new, something that worked, and give myself a high five.

You did it! Did you see that? You've always done *this* in that situation, but this time you did *that*. And it worked! Look at the different outcome. Keep at it!

Like speaking to ourselves kindly, for me, celebrating our progress is just usually saying something *out loud* to myself so it moves from being one more monkey in my head to something I actually hear.

Sometimes celebrating progress in ourselves is a course of action we take to build on our momentum. My lifelong friend Kelley worked for *Time* magazine for years, selling advertising. Her boss Ed used to tell her, "When you get a sale, don't break out the champagne. You're on a roll. Celebrate by making ten more calls. When you fall short, that's when you draw a bath, pour the champagne, and celebrate your efforts with a relaxing drink."

Celebrating our progress is even more important in the realm of our intimate relationships. When our partners and family members ask us to make changes, it's often hard because they've exposed something ingrained, that feels like part of us but needs to grow in order to flourish in the relationship. Maybe your long-held routine after a tough day is to decompress in silence and not talk to anyone. If your partner is hurt by the lack of communication and has been asking you to engage with them or the kids for a few minutes when you come home, it can feel counterintuitive and laborious. When we start making those little yet massive changes, those close to us might still be a little tentative or bruised from a pattern that's been there a while. We have to host a little celebration for the part of ourselves that heeded the plea and course corrected, or those parts will revolt in exasperated defeat and the vicious cycle wins.

I have a lot of experience working hard to change a part of myself for the better. Without careful course correction when I'm doing that work, any celebration of progress can easily be drowned out by the urgency of improvement.

I've already shared about the relentless bullying I experienced for most of my youth. As a result of those experiences, over time I developed a very strong protector part that is incredibly effective in *not* losing a fight. My therapist Susan taught me that when we work with various parts of ourselves, and the more we can see the unique identities of those parts, we can begin to understand them and ultimately integrate them with the other parts. This integration decreases internal conflicts we have with ourselves, naturally decreasing the conflicts we have with others. To help bring those unique identities to life, she encourages me to name each of my parts. Even though it sounds a little funny, it has actually been surprisingly helpful. I named the protector part of myself the Hulk, because when he's scared or threatened or sees someone else scared or threatened, he becomes very big, very strong, and can be very destructive. Similar to the way Bruce Banner's metamorphosis into the Incredible Hulk is triggered by his heart rate more than his circumstance, not all situations where I feel afraid or threatened call for the Hulk. I've had a lot of regret and grief over ways that part overreacted, scaring or hurting people I care about. Like Brené Brown so profoundly says, "I'm scary when I'm scared."

I try to practice what I preach by applying the concept of celebrate and improve to this area that needs ongoing work, but it can be counterintuitive to celebrate small steps of progress when the requests for improvement, especially from those we love, feel urgent. Nicole has asked me for years to work with this protector part—not to get rid of it, but to keep it on the sidelines until a viable threat that calls for a Hulk-level response emerges. The internal wounds that my Hulk protects are so deep and came so young, for so long, I have to confess he's a big part of me. Making changes here has been hard, hard work. Sadly, there are too many occasions to count where he did more harm than good, but one episode stands out as particularly (and now somewhat comically) embarrassing.

Our son Dario was in his second year of playing youth soccer with AYSO (American Youth Soccer Organization). Going every Saturday morning to watch little eight-year-olds run up and down the field in a chaotic but precious mosh pit, hoping the ball rolled into the goal, was, surprisingly, an emotional roller coaster as a parent. Families on the sidelines cheered on their kids with the same (if not more) passion than you'd see at an NFL game.

For the most part, the boys were roughly the same size, but every year, there's one team in the league with a player five sizes bigger than everyone else in the age bracket. On this particular Saturday, Dario was playing the team with the bearded Goliath from second grade. This kid easily had fourteen inches and fifty pounds on Dario. To say he *leveraged* his advantage, so to speak, would be an understatement. In hindsight, his eight-year-old brain probably hadn't developed enough to control his eighteen-year-old body. Regardless, he would clumsily run down the field literally trampling over the much smaller opponents, sending them flying to the ground. It was like watching a drunk elephant run through a flock of penguins.

Because the referees were all volunteer parents, the level of order and oversight varied each week based on how much experience, confidence, or morning coffee the ref-parent had. Unfortunately the parent charged with officiating Goliath versus All was either half-asleep, hungover, or scared of the sound of his own whistle. I sat on the sidelines in horror as time and again this man-child knocked Dario over, stepping on him, elbowing him, tripping him from behind, or just plowing him face-first into the field, while an utterly absent referee/dad sleepwalked through the slaughter. The sight of my son crying with pain on the ground over and over had me working hard to keep the volcano inside from erupting.

And then it happened.

One time too many, this linebacker of a kid sent Dario, arms and legs outstretched, flying, slamming him to the ground, weeping. It was too much, and I snapped. All signs of a societally adaptive Steve flipped to black, and the Hulk exploded. I charged onto the field, picked crying Dario up off the ground, and while holding him in my arms, got inches from Goliath's face and screamed: "STOP KNOCKING OVER MY SON!" so loud, with such a force of rage, that this kid (who suddenly compared to me, now looked more like a David than a Goliath) literally buckled to his knees and cracked into terrified tears.

Yep. I'm that guy. The dad who charged the field during a Saturday morning soccer game and scared an eight-year-old bully so badly, I'm sure he had to change his shorts. Instantly the boy's mom ran onto the field, shielding her son, coaches and parents from both sides joined the fray, the regional director of AYSO, seeing the commotion, came running from two fields away, and thanks to my well-intended but very unnecessary Hulk part, we had a full-fledged spectacle on our hands.

Like literally waking up from a coma, my "adult" part came to and realized what another part had done. Mortified, I knelt down, softened my voice, and said to the boy, who was now hiding behind his mother's legs, trembling, that I was so sorry. I apologized to the mom and then made my way around the field, apologizing to the parents and coaches. I was so embarrassed and had made such a scene, I pretty much just started apologizing to any human in my proximity.

Following my apology tour, an unexpected moment of vindication slightly lessened my embarrassment. With my face still red with Dad-shame, a mom grabbed my arm and said, "Thank you so much. That kid and his mom had it coming." She went on to tell me that her son went to school with Goliath, who was apparently a daily bully, and every time other parents went to the school, Mama Goliath rushed to protect him. Numerous parents were fed up with this kid's bullying going unchecked by his parent or the school.

The moment of relief from her reassurance faded fast. Yes, I had checked someone who needed checking in a way that he'll probably never forget. What lasted a lot longer, however, was the realization that this Hulk part in me needed some checking of his own. He had the ability to act in utterly unacceptable, harmful ways and, in the blind rage of protecting the innocent, could simultaneously hurt the innocent. I (or more accurately, *a part of "I"*), packaged in an adult body, with some developed muscles who trains in MMA, had screamed at a child. And a child not my own. I had embarrassed myself, embarrassed my family, shocked a crowd of people, created a chaotic melee in a family-fun environment, and scared the living shit out of a little kid. Who looked like the bully now? The need to improve this area was nonnegotiable. Yet it was hard. This part of me was created from crises that didn't offer me the protection I desperately needed. But what this part possesses in brawn he lacks in brains. He can't distinguish between traumatizing events in the long distant past and the feelings that came from those events, resurfacing in totally different, present-day realities. His overactive alert systems, motivated by protection, coupled with the futile urge my other parts feel to banish him in exile, make it exhausting to keep working with this part to learn something new. To this day, I have to train myself relentlessly to practice new habits when familiar triggers are pulled.

I confess this unflattering vulnerability to underscore how critical it is we celebrate progress in the areas we're trying to improve, especially the ones we're not proud of—what the mystics call our shadow. We're deeply uncomfortable with other people seeing these parts and would much rather keep these parts hidden in the shadows of our lives. But hiding something doesn't end its existence. Those parts are still there waiting and watching.

When the triggers get pulled, they rush into the light and run the survival programs they've practiced for a lifetime. It takes vigilant intentionality, and sometimes feels counterintuitive, to reward myself with an internal "atta boy" when the Hulk hears the alarm bells but is able to breathe, slow his roll, and stay seated. It feels more gravitationally logical to focus solely on how much he needs to improve. It feels irresponsibly indulgent to bring a cheerleader when you think a drill sergeant might produce faster results.

But even Hulks get tired. Even Hulks need to hear they're winning, making progress, and are headed in the right direction. These shadow parts don't need hatred, they need understanding, *then* guidance. As author Tina Payne Bryson teaches in her parenting work, you have to "connect, *then* re-direct." Typically, the core of the self-made monsters keeping us safe is very soft, sensitive, and filled with bruises. If you want to develop an approach for sustained growth, over the long haul, you have to learn to celebrate your own progress in a way that rewards your hard work.

You can find the internal reward systems that work for you. Maybe all you need is to hear yourself say, "well done." Maybe you need to add a "today's wins" column to your daily planner and write down every time you notice a response that reflected progress. I usually make my task lists at the end of each day for the following day. Knowing that I need to incorporate micro-celebrations to keep me in the game all day long, sometimes I'll add fun things to that list I want to research or plans I want to make. Looking for a new camping site, watching a surfing snippet, reading the fishing update, or making a dinner reservation are all little ways I give myself a high five. And of course, having a commercial kitchen at work makes edible rewards incredibly convenient.

Our brains are literally programmed to crave reward. Learning is hard work. Change is hard work. It's lonely work, done in secret, and usually unrecognized by others in the immediate. People need to experience change that has lasted before they can realize and acknowledge the progress. Hard work deserves affirmation; it deserves celebration. Sometimes celebration will look like our team members dumping the Gatorade cooler on our backs and then carrying us off the field. Other times, celebration will be more like a whisper we say to ourselves, that no one hears or sees. *"I saw what you did there. That was new! That's what we're going for! Well done!"*

Whatever your chosen method of reward, if you want to experience a virtuous cycle of generosity, remember that we all need rewards for our progress, as a host, a collaborator, or a receiver.

Celebrating isn't the same thing as indulgence or complacency. It doesn't say: "You finished!" It says: "Great play! Now let's keep going." It's a paradox. Watch the field or the locker room when the players have just won the semifinals. There's a celebration. There's hugs and high fives.

And…there's still more work to do.
There's another game still ahead.

Principle One:
Speak the Good

Practice One: Speak Kindly to Yourself

Practice Two: Speak Kindly About Others

Principle Three:
Earn Their Respect

Practice One: Stand in Their Shoes

**Practice Two: Pursue Reconciliation
When Others Feel Let Down**

Principle Two:
Honor Those You Serve

**Practice One: Mine for the Gold
by Being Curious**

What Do I Have in Common?

What Is Inspiring?

Practice Two: Apply What You Discovered

Proactively Respond

Customize Your Generosity

Principle Four:
Celebrate and Improve

Practice One: Celebrate What's Working

PRINCIPLE FOUR: CELEBRATE AND IMPROVE

PRACTICE TWO: IMPROVE ONE THING

Archimedes taught us that with a lever, we can move the world. Improving one thing is the sage wisdom of finding the next lever. We've seen that the virtuous cycle of generosity is about energy. It's a contagious, coalescing force that draws people together to create. That energy can create a pleasant moment between strangers, and it can create solutions to the world's biggest problems. The science of energy has taught us that when it is directed at one source, its power is concentrated. And amazing things happen when energy is channeled toward one place.

The moment we divide energy among multiple places, the effect is diminished. Life circumstances, scopes of work, multiple roles we play create an obvious reality where energy is going toward multiple places. That's also why we're often so tired. Because we're expending the necessary energy that life is requiring of us. We have to chew gum and walk at the same time (wouldn't it be great if it were only that easy!).

The fascinating thing about life force is that we both expend and create energy. If we only expended energy, like value extraction never being balanced by value creation, we'd run dry. If you only inhale, you run out of breath. You have to give the last breath away, to make room for more. We have to think not just about how we release energy; we have to consider how we create it.

Nearly everyone wants to improve some aspect of their lives, whether it's their communication, their relationships, their finances, their performance, their health. Growth happens in a paradox. We need to celebrate progress, and we also need to improve.

Improving something in our lives requires energy. We don't slide upwards. The act of summoning the energy we need calls on us to think about how to create the energy that's being asked of us. Focusing on one thing does that. It creates energy for the task at hand, while channeling the output of our energy into one place for better results. It's a virtuous cycle.

My confession here is that even though as a textbook entrepreneur I seem to find endless supplies of energy for new ideas, when I spend that energy pursuing all the ideas, I complete none of them, and progress is diminished.

The hardest part about a catering company is the ebb and flow of work. It's not like a restaurant that is open every day. Sure, Saturday at a restaurant is busier than a Monday, but most restaurants will still have customers even on their quiet nights. So there's always work to be done and shifts to be filled. Getting a catering company to the place where there's always *some* events, no matter the season, is a feat for the fortunate.

Our early years were brutally burdened by the peaks and valleys of event volume. In spring and fall, there were multiple weddings every weekend. During the holidays there were plenty of parties, and thanks to being in Los Angeles, February and March contain events centered around the Oscars, Grammys, Golden Globes, and Emmys. We need dozens of cooks and hundreds of servers to fulfill the demand of busy seasons. The steady stream of events during these times gives us enough work to find the gig-based catering staff we need.

But when it's a hundred and two degrees in July, no one wants a wedding. When the world is still stuffed and hungover in January, people are starting new fitness plans and projecting new annual budgets. Nobody is partying. There are no events, so there are no shifts to offer…until there are. Then we're scrambling to find the people that understandably needed an income and went to find work elsewhere. It is a vicious cycle of the worst kind.

When this challenge of finding staff first presented itself, like many entrepreneurs, I invented a solution. What if we started a lunch delivery service that had a creative twist? Lots of catering companies have diversified offerings to keep their staff employed. I came up with the idea of serving a modern bento box, with a California flair, and called it L.A. Bento. Summoning my love of woodworking (that I'd used to build the original roomforty tables) I designed a prototype of a beautiful wood bento box. I contacted my connections in the winemaking industry and found one of the companies they used to make the wood boxes for their high-end wines. I placed my first order of five hundred wood bento boxes, that had a removable cover with the words L.A. Bento engraved in it.

Each box would have an epic deli sandwich, a salad, home-made potato chips, and a homemade cookie.

Working to improve our staffing shortages by coming up with a new idea scratched my entrepreneurial itch. Knowing the elbow grease it takes to launch early endeavors, I print-ed menus and personally canvased office parks, handing out menus to receptionists. It was humbling to have gone from catering large-scale events to walking the streets passing out menus. But we'd lost most of our staff, and the company was down to me, my friend Matt, and our chef at the time, Libry Darusman. To his credit, Libry met me on the field of eating humble pie and went from cooking high-concept, beautiful dishes to making sandwiches and potato chips. Like a true master, he summoned his culinary skills and channeled his creative expertise into making a mind-blowing lunch menu. I still think about his ham and Brie sandwich with black pep-per gastrique.

We all celebrated as our first orders came in. We were onto something. If this took off, we could grow our team of full-time staff and not be such a skeleton crew when the events gradually started to come in.

But there were flaws in the model. The flow of lunch orders was more like a trickle. And I'd spent precious resources on all the new inventory we needed for a delivered lunch product. Remember how our first kitchen was one hundred square feet with one oven, one fridge, and two prep tables? When a catering event did come in, along with a small ten-person lunch order, the wheels came off. Matt, who normally wrangled all the staff and stuff needed for an event, was busy delivering boxes to a new lunch order and since we'd made expensive, beautiful wood boxes for every lunch, part of our service was picking up empty boxes from a previous order. The oven was being used to braise short ribs for a wedding, so Nicole would bake the cookies for the boxes in our apartment oven and bring them to the kitchen. The Los Angeles Health Department requires a special permit to have a fryer in the kitchen, which we didn't have, so the stove was filled with giant stock pots of boiling oil to make potato chips. And I was scrambling to get new catering clients for good-paying events, while trying to keep corporate lunch clients so we could improve our staffing challenges.

To say that we were diluting how our energy was being spent is an understatement. We were dying on the vine. It might have been a good idea, but we needed to pick one thing to improve and channel our energies toward that one place. To be sure, there was no shortage of things to improve. We needed to improve our catering sales, we needed to improve our marketing, we needed to come up with a *way* better system around the boxes, we needed to improve our processes and establish better boundaries around minimum orders, and we needed to improve our facility. But we couldn't afford a better facility without improving the other things.

That's the vicious cycle of not focusing on one thing to improve. We either burn out the people around us by driving them harder in too many directions or we burn ourselves out by never replenishing our energy resources. After months of madness, Libry finally came to me and said the hard thing. We were compromising twenty-thousand-dollar events for two-hundred-dollar lunch orders. We weren't ready to diversify our efforts. We had to pick one thing to improve and go all in.

As I shared, part of my work in self-mastery is training in mixed martial arts. Not only is it a spiritual practice for me, it trains my brain and my body to have new reflexes. As a bullied kid, in a perceived threat situation, I carried a destructive pattern of reactivity well into my adult life. Long after I was no longer at risk of being beaten up, the body keeps the score and if I felt threatened, despite my size, the part of me that still felt little would summon the Hulk.

As I train, I'm teaching my body to draw on learned technique held in my prefrontal cortex (the executive part of my brain) as opposed to reacting from my amygdala (the lizard part of my brain) where all my flight, fight, and freeze instincts are held. Both of my MMA coaches are always teaching me the wisdom of *focusing on one thing*.

My Jiu Jitsu coach Jason Parry is two hundred twenty pounds of solid muscle. He's a third-degree black belt and a world champion. When we're grappling, it feels like wrestling with an Amazonian boa constrictor made of concrete. It's scary. As the pressure intensifies, my novice tendency is to start freaking out, expending energy through literally every muscle of my body to survive. It's the wrong choice. That's the sage wisdom of Jiu Jitsu, which translates to "the gentle way." It was created by people that were smaller as kids, like me, and wanted to figure out how to stay safe when the big boys bullied. Like Archimedes, its magic is in finding the levers.

When a lever is found and all the energy is channeled toward that one lever, a man can move a mountain. Whenever I start scrambling under the intense pressure of Jason's legs or arms (or any number of mysterious other appendages he seems to summon in choking me), he always calmly asks:

"What's bothering you?"

When I calm down and take an inventory of the one thing he's doing that has rendered me helpless, I can always identify what he's doing that's shutting down everything else.

"Your foot on my hips."
"Okay. Focus on that."

Beyond being a black belt, Jason is a mountain compared to me. Even if I use every drip of strength I have, there's no way, through energy exertion alone, I'll power my way through. He can beat my Hulk. *Without using his Hulk.* I have to find the lever. I've got to improve one thing if I want to get unstuck. And when I find that lever, despite our size differential, I can move the mountain of a man on top of me.

That's what pressure does to us. It makes us feel cornered and our survival instincts scramble to get us out. We stand paralyzed, staring at all the doors, not sure which one to open. Or we expend energy running for solutions in every direction, gassing out from exhaustion and feeling like a failure. It's a vicious cycle.

What's bothering you?

Everything!

Okay, but what's the one condition that needs to be improved over all the other things?

Focus on that.

It's how we do big things, overcome big odds, find big solutions, and move mountains. But learning the wisdom of improving one thing doesn't just apply to where we focus our own efforts. It's critical to focus on one thing when we're asking for improvement in others as well.

In the chapter on pursuing reconciliation, I shared openly about lessons Nicole and I had to be coached on in our conflict resolution. Another one of those lessons that revolutionized (and probably saved) our relationship is to focus on one thing you need the other person to improve. Not ten. There is no faster way to ignite a vicious cycle and have people feeling entitled to a fairer assessment than presenting them with a barrage of things they need to improve.

Like many couples, Nicole and I had to learn how to fight fair. Rattling off a litany of issues we needed the other to improve summoned our most entitled selves.

How could someone not feel entitled to better treatment when in the heat of the moment, the baby is thrown out with the bathwater and anything good is crushed under the weight of all that needs to improve? After receiving a diatribe of needed changes, what exists underneath the anger is a broken heart. A heart that encompasses more than the last bad choice or unintended slight. Being a human is hard work, and everyone is doing their best. When we make the mistake of flooding others with the numerous ways they need to improve, they come to the sad conclusion that despite how hard they're trying, their best will never be good enough. And they pull away.

The hospitality we extend to others by creating a virtuous cycle of generosity doesn't mean we're inauthentically positive and only celebrate them. Virtuous hospitality means we're looking to create cycles of generosity. It's a generous act to consider someone's capacity and honor the law of levers. Give them one thing, *THE* thing. Even if there are multiple, find the lever, and they'll start moving. Inertia teaches us that bodies in motion tend to stay in motion. They can't move on ten things, but they can move on one. They'll be paralyzed if you give them ten. So they won't move. And bodies at rest tend to stay...

You know how it goes.

Celebrating.

And improving.

When we embrace the mindset that does both, generosity ushers in a creative flow. That mindset motivates us and stimulates our imagination. It keeps us in the game when we're tempted to tap out. It creates paths that can be sustained for the long haul. It encourages and corrects. It connects and redirects. The key to a great dish is the right amount of acid, balanced with the right amount of salt, and the right amount of heat. Go too heavy on any, and it's a failed dish.

The practice of celebrating the progress in ourselves and others is the juice we get from squeezing the lemon. The practice of improving one thing is *sprinkling* (as opposed to dumping) the salt. Hospitality is the right amount of warmth that lets all the flavors emerge.

Let's eat.

Principle One: Speak the Good

Practice One: Speak Kindly to Yourself

Practice Two: Speak Kindly About Others

Principle Three: Earn Their Respect

Practice One: Stand in Their Shoes

Practice Two: Pursue Reconciliation When Others Feel Let Down

Principle Two: Honor Those You Serve

Practice One: Mine for the Gold by Being Curious

What Do I Have in Common?

What Is Inspiring?

Practice Two: Apply What You Discovered

Proactively Respond

Customize Your Generosity

Principle Four: Celebrate and Improve

Practice One: Celebrate What's Working

Practice Two: Improve One Thing

PART FIVE

FROM HUNTING AND GATHERING TO EMERGENCE

In 1962 Michael Murphy and Richard Price opened a retreat center called Esalen in the Northern California coastal town of Big Sur. Shortly after, in the early 1980s, the cold war between Russia and America was descending into a deep freeze. Any diplomacy that could lead to peaceful resolutions for the escalating conflicts between the two world superpowers seemed unlikely. Bridges between politicians were crumbling. So in an attempt to build bridges between citizens, the US State Department commissioned a foreign service officer named Joseph Montville to establish a Soviet-American exchange program. Knowing communication is the foundation of solutions, the program brought individuals together from both countries, people who had connections to their governments but weren't working for the government in an official capacity. Watching diplomatic efforts from both sides dissolve into vicious cycles, Montville knew the high tables of foreign negotiations were failing to deliver. Possibly, a humble but strategic starting point would be to just get a conversation started among perceived foes. Knowing the inherent connection between our surroundings and our experiences, Montville set the table at Esalen, saying:

> "You could have a meeting at the Carnegie Endowment for International Peace in Washington, but it doesn't have dolphins and whales, the sounds of waves hitting against the rocks, flowers and ancient trees, and all of the natural beauty that's denied us in our centers of power...It's a stunningly beautiful place, and a lot of people would loosen up."

Montville knew first and foremost that, for the cold war to end, the opposing sides would need to start talking. And the surroundings of that conversation mattered deeply. He thought like a host. He knew what such a conversation needed urgently was *creativity*. He came up with a term he called "Track II Diplomacy." The effort to resolve conflict among the nations by appealing to a common humanity among their citizens was a completely different "track," an unconventional alternative, a different cycle.

Basic.
Kindness.
Civility.

Montville knew that the power players were too blind to the needs of the other side for any creative solutions to emerge. Entitlement blinds us to emergence. It shuts down imagination. Describing his vision of Track II Diplomacy, Montville said:[9]

> "It was an additional way to try to understand the difficulty of human relationships, particularly in avoiding violence and war. Citizens can't sit by because of the lack of imagination of Track I politicians and diplomats, who are acting out tribal roles. They can't be creative. Citizens can."

How limiting our tribal roles can be.

How much damage is multiplied beyond just our tribe when entitlement locks our feet and eyes in place, unwilling to step or look beyond where we stand.

---

9 Laskow, Sarah. "How a Famed New Age Retreat Center Helped End the Cold War". *Atlas Obscura,* December 2015.

The groundwork of the "hot tub diplomacy" started at Esalen is credited by many to have thawed the freeze and end the cold war. It was the citizens, not the politicians, who were hosted in a place of warmth and exercised the creativity and imagination that the leaders then followed.

The stakes were slightly lower, albeit still very high, nearly twenty years later when the Republican-appointed Special Counsel Ken Starr investigated Democratic President Bill Clinton, leading to his impeachment. Though mere mortals, each man became a symbol for their respective parties, as the embodiment of good or evil, depending on where you stood.

The division in the country was sadly palpable, exacerbated by a media ever at the ready to scream "fight! fight!" on the playground. And, as if on cue, nearly twenty years after that, another party appointed a special counsel to investigate the president of the opposite party. And so the vicious cycle spins.

Ironically, we hosted events for both President Bill Clinton and Ken Starr within months of each other. Starr's event was an intimate dinner among friends in Malibu; Clinton's was an intimate dinner among friends in Palm Springs. What struck me was how gracious both men were. I know public figures can sometimes work the room with skill. But both men went beyond in the graciousness they showed their guests and, all the more telling of their character, to our staff. After watching news cycle after news cycle of two archenemies, it was such an odd juxtaposition to be at the shoulders of both men, serving their plate, pouring their wine.

Seeing the warmth they were able to evoke in the people around them as hosts, the humility they both exuded, the way they weren't just interesting but had mastered the art of being *interested*, and the way that curiosity drew out the best in their guests, showed how the virtuous cycle can exist even among people under a bright light. I could not help but wonder what could happen if, like Montville did at Esalen, we set a beautiful table for the two men and let the hospitality of a virtuous cycle do its thing.

You may think it naïve to believe virtuous hospitality can change the world. It's not. For almost forty years, I've had a front-row seat as I watched literally hundreds of thousands of people be drawn into something beautiful with the people around them, just by being hosted. Something valuable emerges when people feel valued. Every. Single. Time. While my seat has been in the arena of meals and events, that's not important. All that matters is your willingness to present your offering to someone with an intention of valuing them.

I referenced those moments where the life force taps into a deeper part of ourselves, and the beauty we feel causes us to express something beautiful back, and in that moment, we've touched generativity. Something has been created by that virtuous cycle. Hospitality sets the stage for something valuable to be *created*. The table is set, the candles are lit, the music is selected, the wine is poured, the dish is served, and—as the creator in me feels hosted by the creator in you—we create something together that we couldn't have accomplished alone.

A good idea.
A peaceful solution.
A new technology.
A song.
A reconciled relationship.
A memory.
A new life.

One reason I love hospitality so much is that those moments often occur in conversation, and the shared table of hospitality is the world's best place for a conversation. In a good conversation, time stands still. Like that infinite river, there's a flow that is so natural and so captivating.

I had one of those conversations with my friend Brock; it was about everything I've just shared. Like I have in these pages, I poured my heart out.

I shared the vision of the virtuous cycle of generosity and the vicious cycle of entitlement. I spoke about the existential role hospitality plays in our society and how the virtuous cycle isn't psychology, it's ecology. It's the cosmic pattern of picking what we plant. If we want to harvest value, we need to plant it. I spoke about how it applies to everything. How, from the micro to the macro, from the relational to the existential, the personal to the professional, hospitality is urgent. I spoke about how literally every single human is a host. That hosting is bigger than a set of services. That it's a space we all hold throughout our lives. I spoke about how we're all creators, not just the ones that label themselves "a creative." I spoke about hosts setting generous intentions as a way to extend the timeless virtue of hospitality. I spoke about what thirty-five years of hosting had taught me about life and how the virtue needs to be recovered from the industry it's become. I spoke about the practices that we could actually put into place that take the concepts from the ethereal to the practical. I shared my sadness at the viciousness that is so easy to find. I shared my hope for the generosity that is there to be found if we look for it.

I shared my vulnerability that I feel utterly insignificant to effect any change. And that my offering of service would be to write down these thoughts. If for no other reason than to do right by the vision that came to a show-off like me, sitting alone and defeated on the beach. I shared that if no one else needed to walk this way, *I* needed to walk this way. And I knew that the way to move the thoughts from my head into my heart was through my hands.

Brock is one of the sages in my life. Like the true sages, he's utterly content to be underestimated or overlooked. He has no time for perception management. He doesn't need to display his trophies. He has plenty of them, but they're dusty, in the back rooms of his life. He's interested in other things. He's more curious about what can be discovered than what has been accomplished. He knows the deep magic. He's learned the secret that the best creators let their light disappear in the light of something greater than themselves. They aren't diminished by this invisibility; they're *magnified*. They become part of a greater whole and resist the lower urges of wanting to shine brighter than others. He knows the power of getting attention is playground-type power. It's child's play. Real power is generative. It's the power to create. And that true creativity is cosmically linked to relationship.

Like a good and wise friend, he listened deeply to everything I shared, and after I finished, he sat quietly for a while. In conversations I've learned to expect the unexpected from Brock. The way he sees the world, the way he hears and says words is different. I find it refreshing, and he often gives language to something my soul is trying to say, but the right words are hard to find. I'm not sure what I expected to hear after I poured the heart of my philosophy out, but I never expected his response to so profoundly capture what has taken me a lifetime of mining for words to find. This is what he said:

Humanity is in the hunter-gatherer stage of value extraction from the world:

A venture capitalist stumbles upon a founder while traveling in San Francisco.

An A&R agent stumbles upon an artist performing a show in Vancouver.

A book publisher stumbles upon an author with a hefty Twitter (X) following.

The hunters of value are not curious how the tree came to be in the forest.

They know little of seeds, germination periods, and prop-

agation.

*They know little of community building, emergence, and collective consciousness. They are pleased to be in the right place at the right time to harvest fruit—**and do not question the conditions that create value.***

The next generation of leaders will:

Nurture emergent values forming in a given community.

Weave shared passions into shared language.

Use this shared language to incite action.

Rinse and repeat.

That's the essence of the whole point. Hunting and gathering whatever we deem valuable isn't evil, it's a phase. We're taking for ourselves, and we don't see it, because we're not mal-intended, we're not bad, we're not flawed. We're just in survival mode; we're playing the game by the rules we've been taught: survival of the fittest. Deeply encoded in our programming is a philosophy that survival is based on taking, *getting*, and getting *more*, finding what is valuable and leveraging that to survive and thrive. Somewhere along the way, like the boy with the Giving Tree not realizing what he'd done, we forgot to reflect on how the tree that gave so much got there in the first place. What was initially *given*, so that the tree could emerge, flourish, and continue the cycle of giving? How might the tragic ending of the Giving Tree, that gave till there was nothing left, change, if a different boy came to the tree? A child from a different generation that thought about value creation, instead of allowing fear to drive an obsession with value extraction? What if there was a collective shift in consciousness so monumental, that when people said: "you've got to play the game" it meant something different than it does today? What if "the game" changed, and a generation of leaders knew the way to *win* was to make sure the opponents win as well? What if collectively, we understood this shift not as utopian idealism but *strategically superior* in getting what we need and want? What if there was a generational shift in mindset that knew the only thing vicious cycles of taking creates is entropy?

We need a new generation of leaders.
We need a change.
We need you.

Our families, our communities, our companies, our cities, our countries, our world, our planet *need* you. What faces us personally and collectively needs value to be *created*, not just extracted. Our program needs an update. If we're preoccupied with what we're owed or being in the right place at the right time to extract maximum value, we'll miss the moments where the magic happens. We need you to weave your thread into a shared tapestry that incites creative action. We need you to see what emerges when virtuous cycles start generating new life. We can't keep trying to relentlessly extract value, falling for the lie of scarcity. When we endlessly scan for more because we fear there's never enough, fear *we're* never enough, we take and take, until there's no life left.

Hospitality says, *I have enough.*
In fact, I have enough to share with you.
I want to share with you.
It's actually *fulfilling* to share with you.
And in feeling nourished, you delight in what's been offered…
And offer something back.
And together, we create something beautiful.

Hospitality does that. It creates the environment where we feel inspired to weave our threads together to create something new.

My all-time favorite story to read to my kids is a book called

Extra Yarn by Mac Barnett. Maybe you've read it. But if you haven't, a little girl named Annabelle finds a box of yarn, so she makes herself a sweater.

But there's still extra yarn.
So she makes a sweater for her dog.
But there's still extra yarn.
So she makes one for the bully who made fun of her sweater.
But there's still extra yarn.
So she makes one for each of her classmates.
Then her teachers.
Then everyone in her town.
But there's still extra yarn.

So she makes sweaters for the buildings and the cars in the town. A town of black and white is filled with color and becomes beautiful. As happens when we share beauty, word gets out. People come from all over the world, and she just keeps knitting and giving away what she's created. A wealthy archduke who's in the clothing industry, looking to extract value from the opportunity, comes to buy the magic box of yarn.

She won't sell it.
He raises his offer.

What I have to give isn't for sale, she says.

So he takes it.

But when he opens it, it's empty.

He didn't understand the magic.

He didn't get the cycle.

He was vicious and tried only to extract value for himself.

He throws away the box, cursing Annabelle.

But life force creates a way for the box to find its way back to Annabelle.

And she keeps on knitting.

That's the deep magic of virtuous hospitality.

When you give what you create to make other people feel valued, you never run out.

There's always extra yarn.

Rinse and repeat.

Hospitality makes the world beautiful.

It's urgent.

It's magical.

Here's to you.

AN INTENTIONAL TYPO AND A SHORTCUT

I've used a lot of words to convey the deep conviction I have that recognizing two potential cycles in our interactions can make them better. I've drawn on examples in my own life, the lives of people I know, the trajectories of companies, macro relationships like those between nations, and micro encounters like the everyday conversations that make up our lives, to demonstrate that we can apply this awareness anywhere and everywhere.

In being transparent about aspects of my own life, I've also shared from my own spiritual journey, without identifying a solidified beginning, middle, and end. If you couldn't name the specific developments, simply put, the stages would be:

1. Recognizing a deep, innate spiritual compass at a young age and cultivating that part of me through nature, music, and serving others.

2. A joining and departing from the "Evangelical Christian" tribe into the brutal and beautiful quest to find new ground and a new tribe.

3. Discovering and building something spiritually new inside that I resist the pressure to name.

4. Integrating my innate spiritual compass with a new, more mysterious container that is both familiar and foreign.

In the spirit of keeping the main point the main point, I've purposely decided not to unpack the technical definition of the word "evangelical" nor describe how my interpretation of that word manifested in my life. Suffice it to say, we all have our tribes. And whether explicit or implicit, all of our tribes have beliefs, rituals, representatives, fools, sages, ancient traditions, latest trends, blessings, and curses. The Evangelical Christian movement in America has made enough of a name for itself that I'm intentionally assuming you, the reader…get it. Many of us have experienced the destabilizing realization that for one reason or another, our tribes need to change. Those that have had that type of foundational disruption in their life know how hard, messy, and scary leaving our tribe can be, especially when you haven't yet found a new one.

Like many of us who have moved out from our formative villages, I don't disparage where I came from nor the humans who still abide there. First, I'm not qualified to pass judgment, and secondly, I can point to so many people from my early seasons who cared for me, loved me, and invested in me. And the discoveries I've shared in these pages have taught me that disparaging groups of people different than ourselves is a fast track to vicious cycles. Generalizations and stereotypes can be dangerous and blind us to wisdom of nuance. I know many people from the "evangelical" tribe who are amazing and generous humans. I just know the path I'm on now is not accurately contained by that label.

It might not surprise you then to hear that I haven't picked up a Bible in years. Years.

As the best-selling book of all time and one of the oldest texts that exists, I have a great deal of respect for the Bible.

My reading sabbatical has more to do with having spent a lifetime memorizing and extensively studying the Bible and interpreting it through a certain set of lenses. I'm finally able to confess without guilt that the way I read the Bible leaves me more confused than comforted and more lost than found.

I've found it ironic that in widening my source material, voices like Pema Chödrön, Deepak Chopra, Alan Watts, Tara Brach, Anne Lamott, Bono, Ram Dass, and countless others all reference biblical wisdom and specific passages from the text. I'm realizing my reticence toward the Bible has more to do with flaws in my lenses than flaws in the content.

I have wrestled hard to trust that whatever Divine Spiritual source is holding me, they are perfectly secure and happy for me to explore unknown spiritual territory. As I learn cosmic Truths from lived experience, as opposed to being told what I "should" believe, every once in a while, a passage from the ancient biblical text will drop into my mind from the archives of my memory and connect with laser accuracy to something new I'm discovering.

"Ah…that's what that means."
Time for my final confession.
And this is a vulnerable one.

Marriage is the hardest thing I've ever done.

By far.

Marriage has been wonderful.

And it has been sustained, deep, hard…work.

Last night, as I lay in bed, I thought about the long-awaited birth of this book that has been growing inside me for five years. As I reflected on the concepts I've discovered, developed, and honed that became the reason to write in the first place, thoughts of my marriage simultaneously came to the front of my mind. I didn't leave one chain of thoughts for another. Thoughts of the cycles and my marriage blended together like the meat and sauce at long last coming together for a complete presentation of the dish.

While thinking about all the important components of these cycles that came to my mind, I thought about Nicole and me. As the marriage and the cycles simultaneously coexisted in my mind, my thoughts went to the words at the center of the cycles.

For one final recipe refresher, here's the ingredients that make up the flavor of the cycles:

THE VICIOUS CYCLE:

- About Me
- Hosting as a Demonstration
- Economy of Taking
- Fear Is Driving

THE VIRTUOUS CYCLE:

- About Us
- Hosting as an Invitation
- Economy of Giving
- Empathy Is Driving

Most of the ingredients in the center of the cycles are opposite. But is the opposite of fear empathy? Not quite. The opposite of fear is…

Love.
Some say the opposite of love is hate.
I disagree. Like anger, hate is a secondary emotion.
We feel something else, first.

We feel attacked, diminished, dismissed, scorned, sad, abandoned, afraid, and then…we can feel hate.

It's a natural habit to compartmentalize aspects of our lives. In running a company, I often hear distinctions between the personal and professional. Understandably, we choose our words from the invisible glossary of terms society has given us to define our work life versus our home life.

Believing that these cycles apply in every interaction we have, when deciding on the words, I tried to pick what would have the broadest application possible. The reality is, for some it might feel a little awkward to use the word "love" to describe how we should treat, or want to be treated by, colleagues, clients, competitors, collaborators, employees, employers, friends, foes, and strangers. Love can feel like a concept too… syrupy for our professional lives.

But here's the thing: the animating force behind many of our generous intentions is love. Love for ourselves and love for others is what motivates us to value others, to speak kindly, to be curious, to look for the best, to honor others, to stand in others' shoes, to celebrate, to improve. Yet, even though we all know love is what every breathing human needs most, it could possibly feel too naïvely sentimental to admit we want to feel loved by our bosses or be encouraged to love our employees. So when choosing the words to describe the opposite energies inside the cycles, I picked "empathy" as the virtuous force that fights the fear of the vicious cycle.

Call it an intended or strategic "typo." Make no mistake, empathy changes everything for the better. It is critical in a virtuous cycle of generosity, but it's the fruit of a deeper planted seed. *Love* is what enables us to offer real empathy. The relationship between love and empathy is like the relationship between our heart and our hand. Love is the heart of empathy.

It's ironic that the empathy that really helps people is the kind they don't have to ask us for. We give it naturally, voluntarily. Expressing the empathy that soothes and heals is more like opening a window than lifting a weight. If the person trying to empathize feels a lack of love, they won't feel safe. And when we don't feel safe, we feel scared. And when we try to empathize with someone while we're afraid of them or afraid of what they might say or not say, they can sense the strain in our efforts to empathize.

Back to my middle-of-the-night reflection. As I sat thinking about how these cycles apply to my marriage, I realized that so many conflicts in marriage are rooted in fear.

Fear of being unseen

Fear of being seen

Fear of being hurt

Fear of hurting

Fear of not being enough

Fear of being too much

Fear of being punished

Fear of being rejected

Fear of doing it wrong

Fear of being criticized

Fear of failure

Fear of distance

Fear of conflict

Fear of being guilty

Fear of being the only guilty party

Fear of being unloved

Fear of being unlovable

As images of strife and struggle throughout the marriage scrolled through my mind, I realized that in some way, fear was at the heart of

every.
single.
fight.

I could see how many discussions, which turned into arguments, had enabled the vicious cycle in my marriage. And I could see how fear was at the foundation of every conflict. As many of us have experienced, the contents of our conflicts are never the heart of the matter. It's how we speak about the contents. The times where Nicole and I are trapped in a vicious cycle, what winds the knot tighter is that for twenty-one years, our tool to stop the cycle has been empathy. It's complicated because someone has to volunteer to do something scary, first. Deferring your turn to share big feelings, so someone else can share theirs, summoning an empathic response that leaves them feeling satisfied on a heart level, and trusting that you will get the equal, reciprocal response when it's your turn is frighteningly hard.

For the first time in over two decades, isolated dots that have long left me feeling defeated in knowing how to disrupt this particular vicious cycle around empathy began to connect. Like breathing, I began to comprehend the physics of the virtuous cycle that had been hidden in plain sight.

I'm hurt.
This person hurt me.
I need empathy from them for what I'm feeling.
It needs to be sincere if I'm going to actually feel better.

They're saying all the words, but I don't think they mean it…I can tell they're struggling.

What I need most is to *feel the love* in their empathy.

I might feel more loved by their empathy if they feel more love from me.

I don't feel like expressing love right now. I'm hurt.

Is there a way I can reassure them enough so the space between us feels at least *safe?*

The more fear they have of being punished by me, the less empathy I'll feel from them.

I need air to breathe. The only way to get more air is to give away whatever air I have.

Love from this person would really help this hurt.

Breathing has taught me, give whatever I have of what I need more of.

That's just how it works.

When Nicole and I argue, we are prone to vicious cycles of conflict in our marriage.

(I knew that.)

The vicious cycle that can erupt between me and the person I love most in the world is a cycle of fear. Both of us are deeply afraid.

(I hadn't realized that.)

Forced empathy is scary. Obligatory empathy just adds fear to the fear that caused the fight in the first place. Voluntary empathy is much more effective, but I need to feel safe before the person getting it can tell it's the real thing.

(I hadn't realized that.)

Empathy doesn't drive out fear. Love drives out fear. What did I just say?
"Love drives out fear."
(Dude. I had forgotten that. That's in the Bible. That's true.)

> *"There is no fear in love, but perfect love drives out fear, because fear involves punishment, and the one who fears is not perfected in love."*

> 1 John 4:18

Punishment. It's what we're all afraid of. Whether we deserve it or not, there is something hard coded in us that fears punishment. The fear of punishment (or consequences if you prefer) is real. And there is no fear in love. The words connected what had previously been separate streams of consciousness (my marriage and this content) into guidance a child could follow: when it gets vicious, someone is afraid. Love is what makes fear go away. Just as I was marveling at how a verse I learned as a child, from a text I haven't read in years, came to the front of my mind, wouldn't you know it, two more passages from the archives of my youth dropped into my mind.

"A soft answer turns away wrath, but a harsh word stirs up anger."

Proverbs 15:1

And then one of the greatest hits we often hear played at weddings:

"Love is patient, love is kind. It does not envy, it does not boast, it is not proud. It does not dishonor others, it is not self-seeking, it is not easily angered, it keeps no record of wrongs. Love does not delight in evil but rejoices with the truth. It always protects, always trusts, always hopes, always perseveres. Love never fails."

1 Corinthians 13:4-7

As awkward and unnatural as it feels to quote passages from the biblical text (and despite the pressure a part of me feels to manage how you label me), when I look at those ancient words, I think: *"who could argue with that?"*

I mean, sadly, in today's outrage culture, people can argue with anything, but like a flat note being tuned to perfect pitch, my soul knows those words are true. I know love is what drives out fear. I've seen it: in me, in my wife, in my kids, my friends, customers, strangers…even my Australian Labradoodle Luca, who can be a little skittish…when hearts are scared, love makes threatening situations feel safer.

There's lots of complicated and sophisticated terms that I won't belabor here at our end, that can provide the science behind the truth, but here's a fact we can now know empirically: tone matters.

So when a text written thousands of years ago basically says "how we say something affects how others feel" and "soft responses to the aggression of others lowers the temperature," it's hard not to acknowledge that truth.

It's real. No tribe owns that truth. The cosmos owns that one. Here then is the shortcut:

When you find yourself in a vicious cycle and can't remember the four principles or the eight practices, just do this:

Love.

I know, easier said than done.

Love is a mystery.

Why is it such hard work to feel something so universally necessary to our existence?

We have to be taught to do something for ourselves that we're accustomed to others doing for us. If you're reading this book, someone taught you how to read. Odds are, someone taught you the basics. They taught you how to eat, how to speak, how to ride a bike, how to brush your teeth, how to go to the bathroom. They loved you. That's why they taught you. Loving you meant teaching you how to do the basics of what every human needs, for yourself.

Did they teach you how to love yourself?

I started writing these words when I was forty-five years old. I'm four months away from turning fifty. I've learned a lot of lessons along the way. At this age, I'm pretty comfortable knowing how to brush my teeth, but learning how to love myself is a lesson I'm still learning. So you won't get any teaching from me on that one. Just a fellow student, trying to learn, with an entrepreneurial attraction to hacks that make the work easier.

So for all those like me who believe not all shortcuts are bad, when you can see that something is spinning in a less than ideal way, when you can feel it becoming vicious, can feel how heels are digging in on both sides of the line, and there is a faint desire for a shift in the energy, here's the hardest and simplest shortcut you can take:

Love.
Do I give it to others? Or find it for myself?
Yes.
Do I say it? Or just feel it?
Yes.
Love.
Those questions come from the mind.
But the mind doesn't love.
The mind asks: "how?"
But the mind can't *figure out how* to love.
Love comes from the heart.
The mind's job is apprehending.
The heart's job is comprehending.

Apprehending "how" to love is like giving a hungry person a wrench.

Love is comprehended, not apprehended.

My attempts to describe love would pale in comparison to words that have lasted thousands of years. So for a picture of what love is like, see the words above, written long ago to a tribe in the ancient city of Corinth.

When all we can see is what we're owed, things turn vicious. When we long for something more virtuous, something less entitled, more generous, an energy that creates instead of divides, an environment where beauty emerges, instead of disappears, that is about us, instead of just about me, less taking, more giving, less threatening, more safe, something a little less mean and a little more kind, a little less hostile and a little more civil…

After years of refining the words of a framework, it's new (and with all the books in the world), somewhat uncomfortable to have had a middle-of-the-night reflection distill all the words down to one word. Seeing things new when a book is about to finish is odd. But it leaves me with a deep sense that while our time together might be coming to a close, I can feel that we will talk again soon. Something new is brewing, and

I can't wait to discover it with you. For now, thank you so much for sharing this time with me and I'll let the best word be the last word.

The shortcut is:
Love.

ACKNOWLEDGMENTS

Nicole, thank you. For all of it. Watching you live, and living next to you, and living with you, is a gift. You are a gift. Everyone who meets you sees the gift you are to the world. You give me and our three so much of your gold. I am the luckiest.

Sofia, Dario, and Giovanna, you are the gold. It's hard to find words that express what I feel for you. The way each of your lives touches me and touches others in a uniquely beautiful way is one of the few things that leaves me speechless. Since words fail when trying to say what I feel toward you three, I'll just spend the rest of my life trying to show you.

Mom and Dad, thank you for loving me and giving me life. You exposed me to the love of music, the love of meals, and to making it nice. Thank you for raising me among the redwoods and the ocean and giving me a place where I can hear my soul.

Mom Michelle. Thank you. You demonstrate your support in action and gave 10 tireless years of running our finances while we built this. You love me, your daughter and your grandkids so well. I can't wait for this next season of slowing time down, playing more games, and growing epic gardens.

Stephanie and Ed, I love you guys. Stephanie, now that I have a daughter who is a big sister to a brother, I see that the love of a big sister is cellular; and like a light that's always on, younger brothers easily take it for granted. Thank you for never turning off that light.

Kelley Gott, my sister from another mister. Thank you for a lifetime of loving friendship, support, honesty, and encouragement. For minimizing the collateral damage of my rebel phase, for buying me ten thousand dinners when all I could afford was ramen, for allowing me to be part of your journey, for being part of every chapter of my journey and for the honor of officiating your marriage to a gem of a man, thank you. You're one of the good ones.

To the pride of Lions that has walked closest to me for three decades or more: Dave Matt, Josh Cummins, Colin Hewitt, and Carl Lentz. It's just starting to get good. Let's make the next forty epic.

Dave and Josh, thank you for showing me what lifelong friendship can be. Thank you for loving me when I was showing off, and kindly pointing to a better way. Thank you for being endless encouragers of me, my life, my relationships, and my work. Dave, whether it's in the line-up waiting for a set, or Josh, on course eight of a twenty-course meal, slow times with you guys feels like home.

Colin Hewitt, we aren't the same people when we started this friendship. I'm so glad that through all the changes, we're still together. Thank you for your friendship, consistency, and love of connection. The conversation has been going for almost thirty years, here's to thirty more years of good conversation.

Carl Lentz, you were my brother before all the craziness. You've been my brother through the storms, yours and mine. You'll be my brother till the wheels come off. Thank you for loving me, for letting me love you, for getting my back, and letting me get yours. I'm proud of you and proud of us.

Paul Korver, thank you for being a killer entrepreneurial sounding board, a fellow dude among brides, and most importantly, showing me the peace that comes after the shadow bout.

Brock Human, your life makes me better. You made this book better. Our paths collided at just the right time. You make me feel a lot less lonely in the world. Here we go...

Brad O'Donnell, the vulnerability you bring to our friendship gives me permission to be the most authentic version of myself with you. Thank you.

Mike McHargue, thank you. Thank you for refusing to love my performance, and showing me that without doing anything, I'm worthy of love. Thank you for opening the veil and walking me into a world that has forever changed me.

Tom Crouch-Fortunato, thank you for being part of our family. Thank you for the beautiful music, the hilarious laughs, the loyal friendship, and the British treats you bring to our family.

Paul Bolles-Beaven, there's far too few elders today. Thank you for being a guide, friend, and elder in my life. You gave me a vision of what I want to become.

Susan Reedy, thank you for your guidance, sage wisdom, and for helping me hold what I've been given. Thank you for endless boxes of Kleenex, and for being a maverick therapist.

Mostly, thank you for helping me hold the call.

Jason Parry and Savant Young, you're more than just MMA coaches. You're elders for a community that is desperate for lighthouses at sea. You've trained me, and have helped me heal a very young, very wounded part of myself. Thank you for making me get in the ring, making me stay when I'm scared, teaching me to that strength can be calm, and teaching me the difference between heroes and warriors. Thank you for helping me channel the roar.

To the Pepperdine Crew: Brian Moats, Kevin Millikan, Matt Frye, Tracy Stay, Hilary Rozinkranz (and Ragnar!), I love you guys. Our history brings so much joy to the present. Thank you.

Jim Stewart, thank you for being a big brother when I needed it most. Thank you for teaching me how to surf and promising me that I wouldn't drown. You introduced me to a part of nature that has become the metronome in my heart. You gave me a safe place when the world felt mean. Thank you.

Malcolm DuPlessis. Once again, you gave the word that changed the course of a life. What an amazing grace you have. Thank you.

Terry and Linda Fouche, your backyard will always hold a special place in our hearts. You hosted the very first roomforty event, and supported in every way you could. Thank you.

Charles Jones, thank you for showing us the relief on the other side of courageous honesty. And thank you for sharing the music in your pipe organ of a soul. Sometimes I want to sit in the water your voice rains down.

Brent Kredel, thank you for riding the plane with me and helping me see other facets of the diamond. Jeremy Vallerand, thank you for living the virtuous cycle of generosity. You get it. Don Riddell and my Vistage Community: Thank you for being lovingly honest, asking hard questions, and cheering me on through the challenges of running a business.

Sasha Strauss, Steve Schwartz, and Jeff Russell: Thank you for being champions of me and this work. Your words gave me belief when all I felt was discouraged.

Donald Miller, thank you for making the words in the framework better.

Emily Henderson, thank you for taking a risk and trusting you weren't being asked to design a night club. You put Fig

House on the map, and I'm forever grateful.

Curt Richardson, Kim Williams, Gay Harwin, Phil Boesch, Brett Twente, Annette Walker, and Richard Mooney: Thank you for being guides and supporters and coming to the aid of my business in fragile times.

To the craftsman in food and wine who have collaborated with me and our team to make some really memorable moments through the years, thank you.

To the winemakers, who partnered with us over and over before it was sexy, thank you. Especially Curt Schalchlin of Sans Liege, Anthony Yount of Denner, Neil Collins of Tablas Creek, Russell the Love Muscle of Herman Story, Kris Curran, Bruno D'Alfonso (too many wines to count), and Stephan Asseo of L'Aventure—we've shared some unforgettable nights. Thank you.

To the alchemists in food, service, and the f&b madness, only a lifer knows the feeling. Thank you especially to descendants of Patina: Govind Armstrong, Kevin Meehan, Kevin Welby, Matt Washton, Adam Rosenbaum, Brian Cousins, Aaron Toricelli, James Lopez, Al Letizia, and Grace Kim.

To the Orange County crew that opened too many doors to count and were instrumental in growing our vision, thank you. There's too many of you to list, but Curt Pringle, Adrian Foley, and Peter Buffa—a heartfelt thank you.

Libry Darusman, you were the chef that changed everything. Some of my favorite roomforty moments have been with you. I love your love of nature and hope that whatever river you're in, you're catching a big one.

Thank you to the team of professionals that worked with me on this book to make it so much better. Cathleen Falsani, Christopher Ferebee, Miles Rote and the team at KAA, Meghan McCracken and her team at Brilliant Media.

Lastly, thank you to the team at Hospitality Collaborative and roomforty. There are too many to name, but many of you have walked with me in business through the thick and very thin. Nearly twenty years ago, we set out to make people feel valued through food, beverage, service, and cool spaces. Easier said than done. Thank you for your patience, dedication, forgiveness, grit, professionalism, loyalty, belief, and for showing up day after day, year after year. None of this would have been possible without you.

ABOUT THE AUTHOR

For Steve Fortunato, hospitality has always been about an invitation—and letting the craftsmanship be about nourishing people on multiple levels. Seeing what he calls the cycle of "Virtuous Hospitality" as the way forward, he launched room-forty, a concept in catering where everything was made from scratch—even the furniture. He has since expanded with The Hospitality Collaborative, a family of companies that brings to life Steve's vision of hospitality as across all types of events from weddings, to corporate events, to high-fashion photography, to celebrity clients, to thousands of brides and a few hundred kids celebrating their first birthday. Steve believes that when people experience real hospitality, they extend that generosity and make the world a better place.

If you would like more information on ways Steve might help your group experience virtuous hospitality, feel free to email him directly at steve@hospitalitycollaborative.com.